OTHER VOLUMES EDITED BY ROBERT COWLEY

With My Face to the Enemy: Perspectives on the Civil War

No End Save Victory: Perspectives on World War II

*What If?™: The World's Foremost Military Historians
Imagine What Might Have Been*

What If?™ 2: Eminent Historians Imagine What Might Have Been

Experience of War

The Reader's Companion to Military History
(with Geoffrey Parker)

West Point: Two Centuries of Honor and Tradition
(with Thomas Guinzburg)

Fitzgerald and the Jazz Age
(with Malcolm Cowley)

*The Great War: Perspectives on
The First World War*

NEW ESSAYS BY

Antony Beevor

Caleb Carr

Robert Dallek

John Lukacs

Jay Winik

and others

❦

Edited by

ROBERT COWLEY

WHAT IFS?™

OF AMERICAN HISTORY

Eminent Historians Imagine
What Might Have Been

BERKLEY BOOKS, NEW YORK

B

A Berkely Book
Published by The Berkley Publishing Group
A division of Penguin Group (USA) Inc.
375 Hudson Street
New York, NY 10014

PRINTING HISTORY
G. P. Putnam's Sons hardcover edition / October 2003
Berkley trade paperback edition / September 2004

Berkley trade paperback ISBN: 0-425-19818-9

The Library of Congress has catalogued
the G. P. Putnam's Sons hardcover edition as follows:

What ifs? of American history / edited by Robert Cowley.
p.   cm.
ISBN 0-399-15091-9
1. United States—History—Miscellanea.   2. United States—History,
Military—Miscellanea.   3. Imaginary histories.   I. Cowley, Robert.
E179.W535   2003   2003046911
973—dc21

PRINTED IN THE UNITED STATES OF AMERICA

10   9   8   7   6   5   4   3   2   1

ACKNOWLEDGMENTS

Once again I wish to express my special thanks to Byron Hollinshead and Sabine Russ at American Historical Publications, and to David Highfill at Putnam, for their assistance in all aspects of the development of this book.

—R.C.

CONTENTS

LIST OF MAPS AND ILLUSTRATIONS

MAPS

ILLUSTRATIONS

INTRODUCTION

America is the subject of this third volume in the What If? series. It examines key moments in a history that is half a millennium old, if you count just this hemisphere's burgeoning contacts with the world at large. Counterfactual history may be the history of what didn't happen, a shadow universe, but it casts a reflective light on what did. Why did certain events (and the trends and trajectories that grew out of them) dominate, and not others? At what point did possibilities become impossibilities? Why did America develop in the way that it did when it could easily have followed other directions? Critics attack such speculations as being mere entertainment, mind games lacking in intellectual rigor or seriousness. I would maintain that they can be entertaining and educational at the same time.

A case in point is the chapter that opens this book, Theodore K. Rabb's "Might the *Mayflower* Not Have Sailed?" The entertainment lies in his speculations that the *Mayflower*, that most famous American immigrant ship, might easily never have made it out of the harbor of Plymouth in England. Here, too, the accident of weather becomes a factor. What if storm-force winds had not blown the *Mayflower* north to Cape Cod instead of to its planned landing site, the Virginia Colony?

A geographical accident would have serious repercussions. If the Pilgrims—prickly thought—had been forced to blend in with the Anglican gentry of Virginia in an easier, more forgiving climate than that of New England, something important, a special regard for community, might have been lost. In Rabb's view, "A fundamental stream in American history and culture—shaped by ideals of sobriety, godly living, and hard work on the one hand, and a focus on the individual and the struggle for religious tolerance on the other—might never have gathered the force and influence it was to achieve over the next centuries." I think of the lines of poet Archibald MacLeish:

> *America was always promises*
> *From the first voyage and the first ship there were promises . . .*

What if this particular one had been stillborn?

Again and again we can resort to alternative scenarios to understand better the direction our history has taken. Was the schism with Great Britain inevitable? Whether by choice or compulsion, could the Thirteen Colonies have remained in the British Empire? Caleb Carr argues that the American Revolution and the establishment of the United States were "eminently avoidable." One man, William Pitt the Elder, might have prevented both, had he not been undone by illness. (Perhaps there are lessons in the management of empire that we might heed today, and Carr quotes the words of Edmund Burke: "A great empire and little minds go ill together.") But once the Revolution did start, chance and luck intervened to save the American cause.

All of the essays here—with the exception of two—are original and never before published. The reprinted essays, David McCullough's and James M. McPherson's from the original *What If?*, describe the sort of vital episodes that no collection of articles on American history would be complete without. McCullough describes how George Washington's battered army, trapped on Brooklyn Heights in mid-August 1776, was able to escape because of a providential fog. It is disquieting to think that the existence of our new nation depended on the whims of weather: At that moment, the United States was hardly inevitable. The Civil War, too, provides practically limitless grist for the counterfactual mill. How close *did* we come to permanent dissolution? To McPherson, the crucial moment comes at (or just before) the Battle of Antietam. What if the famous "Lost Order" hadn't been lost and Robert E. Lee had gone on to win a victory that might have ensured the independence of the Confederacy—and, in the process, canceled Abraham Lincoln's Emancipation Proclamation?

The war was just a year and a half old when Antietam was fought. Even at the very end, though, in April 1865, there was still a chance for the Confederacy. Jay Winik constructs a scenario in which the South fights on. The Vietnamization of the South, as it were, is a plausible alternative if only because it is a course of action that people actually (and actively) contemplated. So, too, did Americans fear the outbreak of class warfare as strikes and violence spread across the country in the summer of 1877. To many, as Cecelia Holland notes, that briefly seemed as great a danger as the coming apart of the United States along sectional lines a decade and a half earlier. What has been called "the minimum rewrite rule" of counterfactual history can also apply to the threat of war between the United States and Great Britain in the early months of 1896. The cause, which seems totally unlikely today, was a boundary dispute between Venezuela and a British colony, Guiana. President Grover Cleveland invoked the Monroe Doctrine, which seemed a good deal more sacred and menacing than it does today. There was talk of war on both the American and British sides, and Andrew Roberts makes a convincing case about what might have happened. Might, but fortunately did not. Before many years had passed, the most enduring alliance of modern times, that between Great Britain and the United States, would be formed.

Jumping ahead to the twentieth century, we can tiptoe through counterfactual minefields of World War II and the Cold War. What if Eisenhower had not ordered American armies to stop at the Elbe River in April 1945? What if they had continued on to Berlin? Might Stalin, Antony Beevor asks, have started a hot war "accidentally on purpose" (as my children used to put it)? If Eisenhower, this time as president, had not allowed Francis Gary Powers's U-2 to fly in 1959, might the Cold War have lost its threatening chill years earlier? Might there have been no Cuban Missile Crisis? What was the hidden danger of those October days in 1962 that neither John F. Kennedy nor Nikita Khrushchev might have been able to control? Might there have been a rapprochement with Cuba and no Vietnam War if Kennedy had not been assassinated? And, finally, how might American life have been different if a security guard in the Watergate complex had not noticed a piece of tape where it had no reason to be?

Counterfactual history does have its limits, and we should not deny them. To quote the perceptive words of the Cambridge historian Richard J. Evans:

> Positing an alternative outcome can help us weigh the influence or importance of the various factors we put together to build a causal explanation. Every real cause implies a counterfactual. This is important in trying to see how causes influence one another and come together to bring something about. But it's wrong to claim that we have to choose between believing that anything might have happened, and thinking that everything was predetermined. In practice, the search for causes, in history as in everyday life, concentrates on the area between the two extremes.

There is danger, too, as Professor Evans points out, in straying from the "What If?" to the judgmental "If Only." The articles in this book have escaped that temptation. Wishful thinking is an unhistorical trap and one we can do without.

America is getting to be an old country, old enough to have a serious history, old enough to have made good and bad choices, old enough to have regrets. And old enough, some would say, to know better.

WHAT IFS?™
OF AMERICAN HISTORY

MIGHT THE *MAYFLOWER* NOT HAVE SAILED?

The name Mayflower evokes a mélange of associations: the Pilgrim Fathers, Plymouth Rock, the first Thanksgiving, or the faintly aristocratic cachet attached to descendants of those who, in 1620, sailed on America's most famous immigrant ship. All that begs the real importance of the Mayflower and its passengers, who were mainly humble people by birth as well as accomplishment and, for their time, radicals. The real Puritan aristocracy would arrive a decade later on a larger and better appointed ship, the Arbella; they never did get on with their Plymouth neighbors, though both would play a part in establishing a specially American sense of destiny. As the historian Daniel J. Boorstin has written, their "beacon for misguided mankind was to be neither a book nor a theory. It was to be the community itself. America had something to teach all men: not by precept but by example, not by what it said but how it lived."

This may have begun by accident, but then, the story of the Mayflower is filled with fortunate accidents. "Might the Mayflower not have sailed?" Theodore K. Rabb asks. The answer is a decided yes. What if one remarkable and influential member of the English gentry had not intervened on behalf of the Pilgrims—as their leader, William Bradford, called them? What if they had actually landed at their original destination, the recently established

Virginia Colony, whose boundaries reached as far north as the regions around the Hudson River? But when, after a voyage of fifty-four days, the Mayflower sighted land on November 9, 1620, the Pilgrims learned that storms had carried them off course and that they were beyond Virginia and the governmental authority that their original contract would have obliged them to honor. What if they had turned south? They didn't.

As the Mayflower bobbed off the great sandy spit already known as Cape Cod because of the abundance of fish, the male family heads drew up an agreement. Just 199 words long, it bound all the signers "to combine ourselves together into a Civil Body Politic." What became known as the Mayflower Compact went on "to enact, constitute and frame such just and equal Laws, Ordinances, Acts, Constitutions and Offices . . . as shall be thought most meet and convenient for the general good of the Colony, onto which we promise all due submission and obedience." This was the first written statement by English settlers in the New World that they would make their own laws. Government would be based on the consent of the governed, that keystone of the American political system.

The windswept dunes of the Cape were hardly a fit place in which to settle, and the Mayflower would cross Massachusetts Bay to a place the Pilgrims called Plymouth, after the English port from which they had departed. The seeming barrenness of that winter landscape must have been unimaginable. "[T]hey that know the winters of that cuntrie," Bradford wrote, "know them to be sharp and violent, and subjecte to cruell and fierce storms, dangerous to travill to known places, much more to serch an unknown coast. Besids, what could they see but a hideous and desolate wilderness, full of wild beasts and wild men?" By the beginning of the spring of 1621, half their number had died, mostly as a result of scurvy, but their faith remained intact. Plymouth survived. If it had not, Rabb points out, the American experience might have assumed a very different form.

THEODORE K. RABB is a professor of history at Princeton University and the author or editor of such notable works as *The New History, The*

Struggle for Stability in Early Modern Europe, Climate and History, Renaissance Lives, and *Jacobean Gentleman.* He was the principal historical adviser for the acclaimed and Emmy-nominated PBS television series *Renaissance.* Professor Rabb notes that "John Murrin gave me invaluable comments on this essay; its faults, however, remain my own."

IF ANYONE HAD BEEN RASH enough to predict, when James I ascended the throne of England in 1603, that the new king would preside over the founding of an empire in North America, he probably would have been laughed out of court. After all, even the great queen who had just died, Elizabeth I—surrounded as she was by sea dogs, propagandists of colonial expansion, and visionaries of the nation's future at sea—had presided over nothing but failure. Despite her encouragement, and even investment, the famous explorers, geographers, and captains who were her subjects—Ralegh, Gilbert, Hakluyt, Hawkins, Frobisher: the very names are a litany of overseas ambition—had labored in vain. They may have defeated the Spanish Armada in the Channel, but across the Atlantic the rivalry with Spain had accomplished nothing, the grandiose projects had all crumbled. As a pessimistic observer noted in 1599, "Neither have the Northern people ever yet for all their multitude and strength, had the honour of being founders or possessors of any great Empire."

That observer was a member of the English landed gentry, Edwin Sandys, the son of an archbishop of York and soon to be a prominent member of Parliament. Sandys, who was to be knighted in the first days of James I's reign, had wide contacts among the seafarers and businessmen of his day, and he knew full well how pitiful had been England's efforts: some desultory exploration, a few fishermen in Newfoundland and along America's east coast, a disastrous attempt at settlement in Roanoke, and a series of brief forays around the Caribbean, notably Ralegh's search for El Dorado. Given Spain's entrenched power, and the lackadaisical ventures of the English, how could this possibly change?

We know that it did, just a few years later, at Jamestown, the pioneer settlement from which an entire continent was to be conquered. But there was more than one stroke of luck that allowed the Virginia Colony to take root; a very different story could easily have unfolded.

For a start, the Spaniards, solidly entrenched in Central America, might well have spread their tentacles in order to hold on to a coastline that they claimed to own. Already in the early 1520s, a few years before the very first exploration in the area sponsored by England, two of Spain's captains, Francisco de Gordillo and Esteban Gómez, had surveyed the eastern seaboard from Florida to Nova Scotia. Nor were they the first. In 1513 Ponce de Léon had sailed to Florida, and in 1521 he had tried to found a colony, a venture that met native resistance and ended in his death. But his countrymen were not deterred: two more Spanish colonies were started during the 1520s, and although both were unsuccessful, the efforts continued for the next four decades. The most ambitious effort, an expedition of some 1,500 colonists who set out in 1559, remained in Florida for two years, but after probes into Alabama and as far north as Cape Hatteras, it was finally abandoned in 1561.

When the captains departed, however, Spain's religious orders took over. The Jesuits had a settlement as far north as Chesapeake Bay in 1570 and 1571, and in the 1590s the Franciscans were beginning to spread throughout Florida: by 1655 they had nearly forty missions, and claimed to have converted over twenty-five thousand natives.

All of this took place to the south of Jamestown, but not that far away, and one can well imagine the Spaniards moving steadily up the coast until they were close enough to have prevented the creation of England's first permanent colony in Virginia. For their ability to crush intruders was clear. They had smashed a French colony in Florida, and Elizabeth's sea dogs had experienced firsthand the hazards of trying to take on Spanish power in the New World. In 1568, three ships led by John Hawkins and Francis Drake had ignored Spain's prohibition of foreign interlopers in her empire and had been caught trading at a port in Mexico. Though Hawkins and Drake escaped, two of their ships were destroyed and most of their men landed in the Inquisition's jails. One intrepid sailor named David Ingram, left on shore, eluded capture, and, in one of the most astonishing achievements of the age, somehow made his way over the next year, probably with the help of friendly natives, to Nova Scotia, where he was picked up by friendly fishermen and brought back to Europe.

Ingram notwithstanding, the lesson was clear: head-to-head combat with Spain in the New World was a recipe for disaster. Had her colonists moved northward—as well they might if the climate had, perhaps, been more congenial—there would have been no Jamestown. Not until the mid-seventeenth century, when Oliver Cromwell started a settlement in Jamaica, might the English have felt strong enough to challenge Spain. And by then the *Mayflower*'s opportunity would long have passed.

Yet this was not the only lucky break that made the survival of Jamestown (and hence the voyage of the *Mayflower*) possible. The company that had received a charter from King James in 1606 to settle Virginia had attracted as shareholders some of the most prominent figures in English society, including the solicitor general. Thanks to clever propaganda, promising general benefit to the country as well as individual profit, the undertaking came to be seen, not just as a trading enterprise, but as a fashionable and patriotic venture. Of the fourteen members of the first governing council named by the king, all but three were members of Parliament, and all had connections with the royal court. Nevertheless, although the Virginia Company benefited from its ability to combine a sense of public service with commercial ambitions and managed to attract a regular influx of new blood—by 1609 over twenty members of the aristocracy, including the king's chief minister, plus nearly a hundred knights, had joined up, and a membership of over 650 had invested the colossal sum of more than £10,000—the hopes were vanishing that imports from Virginia might provide a return (let alone a profit) for investors. By 1616, despite various short-term attempts to raise money, such as a lottery, bankruptcy loomed. The historian of the Virginia Company has called this the "low ebb" of its fortunes, when grave doubts arose as to whether it could continue to supply the dwindling band of settlers around Jamestown (by early 1618, their numbers were to fall to four hundred, as few as they had ever been, and half of what they had been at their height).

It was at this point that Sir Edwin Sandys, who had been a member since 1607, began what he regarded as a rescue mission for a potentially moribund enterprise. Having stressed the "honour" of founding an empire, he felt he could not stand by and watch the collapse of England's first multiyear effort to enter the imperial stakes. Throughout a long parliamentary career, he repeatedly summoned up a vision of the country's "interest" that seems to have been more than rhetoric. In the House of Commons, for instance, he made the unprecedented argument that elected representatives had to consult with their constituents before making major decisions. It is in this light that one has to see his determination to try to save the Virginia Colony. So engaged with the fate of the colony did he become that eventually, in 1619, he was to take control of the enterprise away from the London merchants who had managed it from the outset: a remarkable event in an age when landed gentry kept their distance from commerce. Gravely concerned that the shrinking settlement would vanish, and that England's honor was at stake, he convinced a number of his friends to join him as he started out on what he regarded as a rescue mission. The first step came in 1616, when he joined the directorate of the company.

Here was yet another stroke of luck in the run-up to the voyage of the *Mayflower*. Sandys's takeover of the Virginia Company was an unprecedented event, accomplished despite the high odds that traditional social conventions (manifested either as gentry qualms or as merchant resentment) would have prevented it. Moreover, without the special interests and commitments Sandys brought to the enterprise, the Pilgrim Fathers would never have received the encouragement they needed.

Two interests, in particular, became crucial to the story. First was Sandys's belief that the colony's population had to increase. Putting problems of finance and supply aside, he believed that the settlement could not survive unless it expanded. Admittedly, the problems caused by his relentless dispatch of colonists (including the first transport of convicts overseas) were to wreck both the company and Sandys's own administration by 1623. Yet there is little doubt that the colony itself would not have survived into the 1620s (when at last it developed a profitable product, tobacco) if its numbers had not been maintained by the stream of people Sandys sent across the Atlantic.

His first success came in 1618, when he and his friend the earl of Southampton, Shakespeare's patron, arranged for over three hundred settlers to sail to Virginia. Under his prodding, other investors matched that number, so that by early 1619 the colony had grown from four hundred to one thousand people. This campaign to ship colonists to Jamestown is the context in which one can understand why a group of Puritans from Leyden came to sail to America.

Ever on the lookout for willing settlers, Sandys in 1617 became the essential middleman who made possible the voyage of the Pilgrim Fathers. Without his help, the group of English religious dissenters[1] who had settled in Holland to escape the threat of persecution at home would have been unable to realize their aim of starting a new life overseas. The Puritans' hope of bringing further reform to the official Anglican Church had been dashed; their disdain for its hierarchical structure and its rituals had been denounced; and they knew it was

---

[1] In what follows, the words "dissent" and "Puritan" are used generically, to indicate the beliefs of those who found it difficult to conform to the Anglican Church. It should be noted that the group from whom the Pilgrims were drawn were not like other dissenters or Puritans, but rather "separatists," because they refused even to attempt to conform, and preferred to leave England altogether. Since it is such a familiar term, however, it seems appropriate to put all these shades of dissent under the umbrella designation of "Puritan."

unlikely that they would be able to pursue their "godly" ways in England unmolested. Their new hosts, the Dutch, tended to leave them alone, but in the mid-1610s the Pilgrims began to look for a new home where they could run their own affairs. They gave some thought to Guiana, but they concluded (fortunately for them) that the climate was too forbidding and that they should aim for cooler climes. So they decided to try to find a corner of the territory granted to the Virginia Company (their plan was to head for its northern edge, along the Hudson River), where they could create a community on their own terms.

It was at this point that Sandys's mediation became crucial. Of all the leaders of the Virginia enterprise, he was the one who had the most direct personal connections with the Leyden community. His brother had contacts among their number, and their most important elder, William Brewster, had been close to a talented young man, George Cranmer, who had been Sandys's best friend at school and university, and throughout their twenties and thirties, until Cranmer was killed in Ireland in 1600. Sandys cannot have been too surprised, therefore, when he was approached by emissaries from Leyden in 1617, seeking his support for their settlement in the New World.

This was the very time when Sandys was beginning his campaign to enlarge Virginia's population—within a few months he was to send out the first group of over three hundred new colonists—and he seems to have taken up their proposal with alacrity. He wrote to Cranmer's friend William Brewster in November 1617, promising "all forwardness to set you forward," and in the reply, a month later, Brewster piously acknowledged that "under God, above all persons and things in the world, we rely on you." Fortunately for him, Sandys not only acted as the prime strategist in the negotiations that ensued, guiding the Puritans' representatives through Virginia Company meetings, but also commanded the connections at the royal court to follow through. One of his friends, Sir Robert Naunton, had just been appointed secretary of state, and his advocacy helped persuade the king and his council to allow the Puritans to settle in the Virginia Colony. Their request for toleration was turned down, but the permission to sail (with the one requirement that they keep the peace—i.e., stay out of sight) was itself a notable breakthrough for a group that regularly, and with good reason, called itself "despised."

By the time the Pilgrims set sail, Sandys had taken charge of the Virginia Company—in their eyes, the final indication of God's approval for their mission. And it was indeed an extraordinary combination of circumstances that paved their way. Not only was Sandys's enthusiasm for the shipment of settlers vital to their mission (the Virginia Company proudly included the one hundred people aboard the *Mayflower* in its official list of the voyages that enlarged the colony in 1620), but he was also, crucially, a figure of sufficient prominence to make the dreams of this unorthodox group come true. The whole sequence of events has about it an air of improbability that lends credence to the notion of divine intervention.

Nor was this the end of the lucky strokes that enabled the *Mayflower* voyage to prosper. Despite the expectations of many participants, the endless quarrels and endemic leaks that almost kept the ship from leaving England were all settled and repaired. The storms that drove her toward Cape Cod persisted and prevented her from heading to the Hudson (where they might soon have found themselves again under Dutch rule). And the potentially fatal inexperience of the weary travelers, landing on a barren shore long after the harvest season, was remedied when they discovered (miraculously, in their view) a native store of corn, bean, and seed that kept them alive during their first months in America. All these outcomes were essential to the success of the voyage. But none of the later acts of fortune could compare in importance to those that enabled the *Mayflower* to sail in the first place.

And what if one of the circumstances had not fallen into place and she had not planted a "godly" community at Plymouth? That question leads us to the crucial moment for the long-term success of the colony: the arrival from England in 1630 of John Winthrop, a Puritan lawyer,

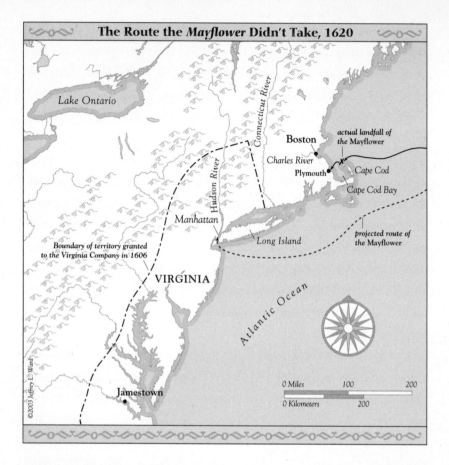

with a fleet of eleven ships carrying some seven hundred colonists. Would they have come if the *Mayflower* had not preceded them? It can be argued that they would not.

The genealogy of Winthrop's group was quite separate from that of the Pilgrims. It starts in the early 1620s with a dissenting minister from the town of Dorchester in the west of England, the Reverend John White. Aware that, in contrast to Virginia, there had been little to show for colonizing efforts farther to the north, he determined to do better. A colony at Sagadahoc in Maine had been started at the same time as Jamestown, but had failed within a few months. Thereafter, despite the plentiful cod, which seemed to offer good economic prospects, no more than a few fishing settlements had survived. Convinced that the fisheries would prosper only if there were a permanent plantation, White and a few associates began sending out settlers. They received the right to do so by creating and funding colonizing companies: first the Dorchester Company and then the New England Company, which was given legal control of an area roughly between the Merrimack and Charles rivers. Their one permanent achievement was to be the foundation of Salem in 1628, but by then a new company was already in the works, the Massachusetts Bay Company. It was at this point that Winthrop and his colleagues entered the picture, and the question arises whether they would have done so without the precedent of Plymouth to reassure them.

Five months after the Massachusetts Bay Company was founded, twelve of its leaders, all Puritans and including Winthrop, signed an agreement to emigrate with their families to New England *if* they could take the company with them. Faced with a regime ever more hostile to religious dissent, they wanted to leave only if they could avoid having the governance of the company (as in all previous cases) remain in London. The lawyers among them, possibly including Winthrop himself, had noticed that the company's royal charter did not specify where the annual meeting was to take place. Seizing on this loophole, they headed out across the Atlantic, taking the charter with them. Thus was founded the city of Boston and a cluster of nearby communities, and thus did the development of New England begin in earnest.

But would this story have unfolded if the Pilgrim Fathers had not led the way? The odds are good that it would not. Without the beacon planted at Plymouth to reassure them, these staid, comfortable, and conservative creators of a "Bible Commonwealth" would scarcely have risked their families and their possessions on so hazardous an enterprise. Again one must say that without the *Mayflower*, there could have been no Massachusetts Bay.

Nor was there a long window of opportunity for this kind of follow-up. Only a decade after Winthrop sailed, the beginnings of revolution in England gave the "godly" such a new burst of hope that all idea of emigration ceased. Indeed, many who had left now returned, and their New England experience was to prove important when a highly influential Congregationalist structure of church organization was created during the 1650s. Moreover, the returnees remained, because after the collapse of Oliver Cromwell's brave new world in 1660, the restored monarchy extended enough tolerance to religious minorities to keep all but a few dissenters at home. The only major exception, the Quakers, were to found a colony that had none of the influence on the religious outlook of America that one associates with Massachusetts.

As for those Puritans who might still have managed to emigrate during the 1620s and 1630s, they would probably have had to make their peace with the Anglican, gentry world of Virginia and give up hopes of an errand into the wilderness or setting a light upon a hill. A fundamental stream in American history and culture—shaped by ideals of sobriety, godly living, and hard work on the one hand, and a focus on the individual and the struggle for religious tolerance on the other—might never have gathered the force and influence it was to achieve over the next three centuries.

Given the history that brought the Pilgrims to New England, it is perhaps not surprising that their descendants should have been the first to sound what became two persistent American themes. In some respects, they were already embodied by two very different figures from the early years of the seventeenth-century colony, Cotton Mather and Roger Williams, both of whom, in their own ways, were reacting against the world of state-organized religion and strict social hierarchy that they had left behind. For the Pilgrims were to be unique among the early settlers in their commitment to religious ends. The small sprinkling of Catholics who went to Maryland aside, no other group was so single-minded in the motivation that drew it across the Atlantic. Elsewhere we find land hunger, dreams of wealth, imperial ambition, political dissent, or simple wanderlust, but here all the talk was of religion.

The result, given the harsh climate and terrain the adventurers inherited, abundant only in fish, was a society very different from its neighbors to the south. To some extent, of course, it was the Puritans' Calvinism that had long emphasized thrift, sobriety, and hard work as especially godly virtues. But there is no question that their insistence on discipline and honest labor (to be rewarded by God both in this world and the next, they hoped) was reinforced, and to some extent inspired, by the land that they inhabited. These qualities also fed into the preference for autonomous communities, responsible only to themselves for success or failure, which was encouraged by their congregational system of religious organization.

It was thus a combination of belief and circumstances that enabled the Puritans to inject into American culture an expectation of religious faith, a commitment to self-reliance and daily toil as morally worthy, and a stern regard for the virtuous life that have given their country a quite distinctive coloration among the modern nations of the West. That these qualities were reinforced by the experience of the frontier, and took very different forms as they resurfaced in such guises as the antislavery or Prohibition movements, does not lessen the importance of their origins in Puritan Massachusetts. And it is almost impossible to imagine such commitments taking so firm a hold on the American imagination had the New Englanders been absorbed by the colonists of the Middle Atlantic and the South.

For religion itself their heritage was more ambiguous. As the sociologist Richard Sennett has noted, Americans' "deep-seated religiosity" supports "faith-based hospitals, schools, and charity," and in this way "religion cements civil society, as government does not." The result is an "inseparable faith in God and Country" that makes the United States distinctive among Western nations. To the extent that this has been an essential thread through 250 years of history, its origins lie in the Puritans' conviction that faith is the foundation on which a person's life is built and thus the foundation of society itself.

From the outset, however, this commitment has been riven by an irresolvable tension. As with Luther and Calvin themselves, it was one thing to demand respect for the private conscience when facing persecution by a majority; it was quite another to permit what one reformer called "private paths to hell"—that is, dissent—when those who were certain of the road to salvation were in a position to require conformity. Hence the intolerance and retribution that punished Thomas Morton, Mary Dyer, Anne Hutchinson, and the Salem witches, products of a blinkered and aggressive rectitude that was captured by Hawthorne in *The Scarlet Letter* and retains its force even in the twenty-first century.

Yet the response to narrow-mindedness has had an influence no less profound. When Roger Williams left a Massachusetts that would not accept him and created in Rhode Island a community that took respect for individual belief seriously, establishing an open and tolerant community without parallel or precedent in Western history, he struck the first blow for the separation of church and state that was to become an American hallmark. It may have been the Virginians who, a century later, enshrined the principle in legislation, but it was the dissenters among the Puritans who first fought for the inviolability of individual conscience and the right of each congregation to decide its own beliefs. The outcome did not merely set the United States apart; it made the nation a model for the civilized treatment of religion thereafter.

We may now take for granted the role of these traditions—the force of religion, the equation of work with virtue, the focus on the individual, and the insistent devoutness alongside the tolerance—in determining the course of American history. But there is little doubt that they might well have died in infancy if the *Mayflower* had not set sail.

CALEB CARR

WILLIAM PITT THE ELDER AND THE AVOIDANCE OF THE AMERICAN REVOLUTION

The American Revolution, Caleb Carr maintains, was "eminently avoid-able" and the establishment of a United States of America cannot be regarded as a foregone conclusion. One man, William Pitt the Elder, had it in his grasp to prevent the British Empire in North America from fragmenting. It was Pitt, whom many regard as the greatest British statesman of the eighteenth century, who guided his country through the Seven Years' War (1756–1763)—what Americans call the French and Indian War—and who trans-formed Great Britain into an imperial power. That power was founded on the twin colonial pillars of North America and India. But within twelve years, the American pillar had begun to crumble. Too late Britain learned the lessons that would save the rest of its empire. What if illness, both physical and men-tal, had not curtailed Pitt's influence and ability to lead in the crucial years after the war's end? Lexington and Concord did not have to be an inevitable confrontation.

Individuals do matter—and more specifically, individual decisions. The presence (or the absence) of a single leading actor in history can make all the difference. "If the most publicly beloved political figure of his age," Carr asks, "and the only man who could hold the power of the reactionaries, the plunderers, the American Radicals, and the crown in check had retained the strength to do all of those things—how might the next two centuries have played out?"

We would do well to heed the practical wisdom of "the Great Commoner."

CALEB CARR may be best known for his novels, *The Alienist, Killing Time,* and *The Angel of Darkness.* But he has also written three books of history, *America Invulnerable* (with James Chace), *The Devil Soldier,* and *The Lessons of Terror.*

IT HAS BECOME COMMONPLACE to refer to the contemporary United States as a "global hegemon"; what is less generally recognized is that America is the first nation in history that can truly lay claim to such a title. In describing not only American power but the reach of that power, no qualifying words or phrases are necessary: Rome, for instance, is said to have commanded "the *civilized* world," while at its height the British Empire predominated over "the *known* world"; but only America can project its physical might into *any* part of the world, known, civilized, or otherwise, and only America possesses a culture (crass as many may find it) that is either dominant or vying for dominance on every continent. In truth, all the empires of old, impressive as they may have been, only fantasized about and pretended to such universal reach and sway: the United States of the twenty-first century is, simply, an unprecedented phenomenon.

What, then, would the last two and a quarter centuries have been like had the comparatively insignificant nation that would become that phenomenon never been conceived?

It is most common, when speculating along these lines, to imagine the possibility not of contracepted United States but rather of an aborted one: to posit, in other words, the failure of the rebellious colonies on the defeat of colonial arms at any one of the remarkably numerous "decisive moments" of the American Revolution. But in fact it is more unrealistic than speculative to suppose that so fundamental a change in the course of world civilization as was embodied in the American colonies' struggle for freedom, as well as in their subsequent and explosive geographic, economic, and military expansion, could have been forever ruled out if, say, Gentleman Johnny Burgoyne had not been let down by those British units that were supposed to support him at Saratoga, or if Lord Cornwallis had planned the movements that led up to the battle of Yorktown with greater care. The evolution of sociopolitical ideas that took place in America during the years leading up to the Revolution, as well as during its denouement, was something much more than just a struggle to determine who would control the purse strings of colonial trade, as cynics have so often portrayed it; and had the military attempt to separate from Britain failed in 1777 or even 1781, that evolution would (assuming that British administrative systems and abuses remained unchanged) almost certainly have continued, causing another violent outbreak as soon as the colonists had replenished their resources and their caches of arms and found new leaders capable of reigniting their cause.

The only thing that might actually have quelled the American revolutionary movement was the thing that eventually became the war's greatest side effect: British imperial reform. Because the crown and Parliament came to understand within some six or seven decades of their defeat at the hands of the colonists exactly what mistakes they had made with respect to those rebellious subjects, as well as how to put things right, Britain became the uncontestedly supreme empire of the late nineteenth century and, prior to modern-day America, the most powerful national force in world history. And the tragedy (for Britain, obviously, but also, I would argue, for the rebellious colonies) was and remains that more than a few enlightened British statesmen were aware of just what the empire was doing wrong in North America long before the revolution started. Had their calls for reform been heeded prior to Lexington and Concord, not only would the American Revolution have been rendered unnecessary, but some of the greatest tragedies to befall the world as a whole during the generations that witnessed America's rise might also have been avoided. America would have remained within a reformed British Empire, the less fortunate of its colonists' tendencies controlled and its strength devoted to Britain's future struggles;

the power of progressive constitutional thought would have been doubled, rather than dissipated; and humanity would have been far the better for it.

What was Great Britain in 1763, the year of its international victories in what was called the French and Indian War in North America and the Seven Years' War everywhere else? Certainly, it was the most benign of the global European empires that had risen up since the Renaissance: it had never attempted campaigns of outright genocide such as the Spanish had prosecuted in Central and South America, nor did it exhibit the onerous Catholic evangelism and systematic amorality of the French imperial system. This is not to say that the British were not capable of enormous chauvinism and periodic brutality, or that British Protestant ministers could not be just as obnoxious to indigenous peoples as were French Jesuits; but *trade* was the greatest animating force behind British imperial expansion, and trade was a language (as America has discovered in the years since the Second World War) that much of the rest of the world was only too anxious to speak, some of them so badly that they were willing to relinquish national sovereignty without a fight in exchange for the opportunity.

But along with trade, Great Britain offered the world something else, too, something that was arguably even more vital: exposure to their tradition of constitutional government. True, the British, in the middle of the eighteenth century, still had not managed to specifically elucidate just what their constitution *was* (as indeed they never would), and their society was still afflicted by enormous stratification and inequality, the great political and land reform movements of the nineteenth century still lying ahead. Nevertheless, Britain's government in 1763 was, comparatively, the most progressive and enlightened in the world: London, and specifically the houses of Parliament, were (and since the Middle Ages had been) places in which reform aimed at the steady amelioration of the lot of all men could at least be talked about and in fact had, to an appreciable degree, been effected. The slow battle to control the power of the English crown by asserting first that of the nobility and later that of Parliament, and even more the active and unending struggle to eradicate what was consistently condemned with the rubrical indictment of "oppression" of English citizens, had filled the centuries between King John's reluctant signing of the Magna Carta in 1215 and the execution of Charles I for tyranny in 1649 with turmoil—and advances. No other country had prosecuted anything even approaching this campaign to make constitutional progressiveness the driving force of national life, and it was this campaign, ironically, that would create a situation in America that allowed colonists to think of freedom in even broader (if much more defined) terms.

Its long constitutional struggle had made the British Empire a place in which law was not civil but common: that is, a place where the legal (and by extension the political) system was designed not simply to serve the interests of the stewards of the status quo but to guarantee the rights of the ruled to a unique and unprecedented extent. Emigration to overseas colonies was an important part of the British constitution's continued development and appeal along these lines: for while many rights of average citizens were indeed protected under British common law, the rights of the ruling and commercial classes still held most-favored status, creating a situation in which positions of wealth and privilege within the mother country tended to be limited and—whether based on aristocratic titles or less glorified personal fortunes—hereditary. In the absence of the sorts of socioeconomic and political reforms that would arrive in the following century, opportunities to join the privileged class were severely limited at home, and the possibility of making good in the ever-expanding empire became essential to maintaining the promise of escape from the oppressions of poverty, class stratification, and religious intolerance—a promise that was, in turn, vital to the onward march of common law.

The economic system that grew up around these and other legal and philosophical principles was called mercantilism, a dry and dispassionate name for what was, in Britain's case, a dynamic set of relationships and arrangements, one ultimately more enlightened than it was destructive.

From the colonies, London took such raw materials as were to be had or cultivated; in exchange, the colonies received goods manufactured in Britain's proto-industrial cities. There were blemishes on the system, without doubt, the most obvious and obscene being the import of African slaves into the colonies to perform the sorts of manual and service labor that whites and natives either could not or would not do. But unlike her European imperial competitors, most of whom were even more slave-dependent than she was, Britain once again had the advantage of her rich constitutional history: from the beginning slavery sat very uncomfortably with an empire steeped in common law, particularly in the mother country, where regulations were passed that confined slavery to the colonies. Complete abolition would come comparatively quickly throughout the empire (more quickly than it would in the young United States), and in the meantime abolitionist sentiments remained widespread throughout British society.

But in 1763 London had more immediate and mortal problems with which to reckon. The war that had lately made them the greatest of the colonial powers had cost a great deal of money; so much, in fact, that they were faced with the ugly reality of needing to tinker with what had been a comparatively advanced and profitable imperial system in order to pay for its expanded operation. (This lesson, that the financial costs of hegemony may prompt self-sabotaging changes in the fundamental principles of the system that facilitates such hegemony, holds apparent and chilling lessons for the United States in the present age of "globalized" commitments.) To a felicitous extent, many British colonies had, prior to 1763, been allowed economic and political autonomy within the empire, which inclined them generally toward loyalty to their imperial masters. But that autonomy had been, like the British constitution itself, informal, and it was therefore quite open to abuse by avaricious ministers, as well as by members of Parliament anxious to see the government repaid for its expenditures—both of which types became increasingly easy to find in the Houses of Lords and Commons in the years before the American Revolution.

William Pitt the Elder, known as the "Great Commoner," was regarded by many as the foremost English statesman of the eighteenth century. Would there have been an American Revolution if his influence had not been diminished by debilitating illness?
© Bettmann/CORBIS

Fortunately, however, stewardship of the empire during the imperial war (or wars) of the 1750s and '60s was primarily entrusted to William Pitt the Elder, who was called "the Great Commoner" because of his distinctly yeoman roots, his antielitist attitude, and his independent behavior in Parliament. In return for his exhausting and successful efforts to establish his country's predominance, Pitt was eventually allowed the earldom of Chatham by a jealous and grudging George III, although he was plagued by intermittent bouts of severe mental illness and painful gout by an obscure providence; but at heart he remained, though highly educated and ferociously brilliant, a man of the people—and the people knew it. Although he made too many enemies among the self-serving aristocratic and commercial classes to see the war through to its end (King George dispensed with his services in 1761), Pitt did manage to orchestrate an array of commercial and diplomatic policies, as well as military appointments, that mortally weakened French imperial power in much of the world and destroyed it altogether in North America. Underlying those policies and appointments was a consistent appreciation of the contribution of colonists to Britain's ultimate victory, as well as of their sensibilities with regard to their proper place within the empire. Both of these crucial factors were underestimated by Pitt's political enemies, however, and even many of his colleagues, a misreading that would lead to crisis soon after Pitt's departure.

When ominous debt seized Britain's economy following the conclusion of the war, many British ministers and representatives, along with a sizable number of British citizens, began to view drastically increased tax revenue from the colonies as an appropriate way out of their economic fix. The multitheatered conflict had, after all, been an "imperial" endeavor, fought to defend and expand Britain's overseas possessions; surely the occupants of those possessions could not object to shouldering the greater part of the cost of the undertakings. This line of thinking, although seductively simple, ignored several important realities. First, the collection of increased taxes in the colonies would mean tightened imperial administration of those far-off places, and that would mean effective repeal of the unofficial policy of "salutary neglect," in which such colonies as those of North America had existed prior to the war. Yet this practice, to the colonists, had become something very much more than simply a loose political and economic bond—it had become one of the principal reasons that they were loyal to their home country, which allowed them to form their own assemblies, elect their own leaders, and even determine many of their intercolony tariff systems. To ask them to surrender such privileges in the name of imperial considerations—to ask North America to surrender money and freedoms so that London could bail out the East India Company, as the thinking in the thirteen Atlantic coastal colonies went at the time— was to remove much of what made the British Empire distinct from its openly and ruthlessly exploitative rivals. Furthermore, such a position avoided one central point: the world war that Britain had successfully conducted had not been fought for the interests of the colonies alone, but for those of manufacturing towns and firms at home, as well, which needed new markets for their goods and greater supplies of raw materials with which to make them. The empire was an integrated system, not a series of component parts—or at least, London had always been wise enough to operate it as such, quietly aware of and perturbed by the fact that the colonies had a much greater chance of achieving true self-sufficiency than did the mother country.

But perhaps most galling to colonists who were suddenly asked to pay a greater portion of the costs of empire was the fact that it was never once hinted that they would in return be granted political representation in the central British government, and with it the kind of power and voice that might allow them to defend their own interests within the system. The empire, said George III and the ministers that replaced Pitt's government, was run by the king and Parliament; colonies might conduct some of their internal affairs on their own, but such imperial questions as rates of taxation would be settled by London and by its appointed agents. And from 1763 on, the word from London, delivered by those generally arrogant messengers, was that the days of salutary neglect, low taxes, and free protection against Indian tribes and lingering French troublemakers by British troops were over.

William Pitt, though out of power, immediately recognized where this policy would take the empire that he had done so much to not only defend but expand; indeed, there were those that said it was this realization that drove him into periodic states of mental imbalance and ultimately to utter and terminal nervous exhaustion. Such would not have been surprising: for the truth was so plain, and all attempts to contradict such thinly veiled avarice, that the situation would have been enough to send a less highly strung spirit over the edge. Britain's rich American colonies had never agitated for greater political power and had remained loyal to the crown precisely because no onerous military, political, or tax obligations had been required of them: industry and trade had been the mutually profitable bond that had connected the colonies and mother country, and the arrangement had been for the most part entirely equitable. If taxes were now to be raised and colonial administration to be tightened—to the point that regular army troops would be stationed in the colonies and billeted among civilians to ensure compliance—then the colonies would resemble less what they had until then been, and more Britain itself: all of which would have been acceptable, if the colonists had been given the voting rights and the representation in Parliament that British citizens enjoyed. But George III (for it was George who believed most sincerely in an extremist policy, though many colonists refused to believe as much) was adamant: the colonists would have the responsibilities of Englishmen, but not the privileges. They had been protected by the crown, just as indentured servants or slaves might be protected by their masters, and they should, indeed must, offer services for that protection in return, without giving any more voice to ideas about "rights" than a slave would do.

The long battles over various taxation programs that were to fill the years between 1763 and 1775 in the thirteen colonies (and, to a lesser extent, in other, poorer colonies such as Canada) never strayed very far from this simple disagreement. The now trite phrase "No taxation without representation," which seems somehow inadequate to explain all the troubles of the pre-Revolutionary and Revolutionary eras, was in fact concise rather than simplistic: the Revolution was not simply an argument over who controlled colonial profits, but also—indeed, much more—a battle over whether various accidents of birth made the worth of one man's labor and opinions greater than another's, and his place under common law more or less advantageous. It was, effectively, a dress rehearsal for the nascent crises over slavery, and it was eminently avoidable.

Not only avoidable, but avoidable by way of the very reforms that Britain would institute after the Revolution, in part to avoid losing any more of her possessions. In pre-Revolutionary Britain, these reforms were most eloquently promoted by William Pitt, in a series of near-frenzied yet wondrous speeches that sometimes even succeeded in swaying decisive numbers of votes. Such was the case when he appeared several times—often seriously ill and on crutches—to argue against the infamous Stamp Act. The American colonists, Pitt declared in 1766, "are the subjects of this kingdom, equally entitled with yourselves to all the natural rights of mankind and the peculiar privileges of Englishmen." No illness could keep his rhetoric from becoming lofty, scathing invective: "When in this House we give and grant, we give and grant what is our own. But in an American tax, what do we do? We give and grant our own property? No—we give and grant to Your Majesty the property of Your Majesty's commons of America. It is an absurdity in terms."

Thanks in large part to Pitt's desperate efforts, the Stamp Act was repealed, and in that same year, the ailing oratorical giant became the earl of Chatham and returned to lead the government as lord privy seal. His administration was at first successful at rooting out corruption and supporting justice for the colonies, but soon Pitt had exhausted himself, and he became too sick to effectively control his chancellor of the exchequer, Charles Townshend, a political appointee who came up with a new batch of ideas for robbing the American colonists. Pitt's influence was felt less and less in the Commons as well as among the people, not only because he was ill, but because he was serving in the remove of the far more arcane House of Lords, which undercut or at least mitigated his credibility as the Great Commoner, and the tide began to run increasingly against his reforms. For every tax repealed, a new slate seemed to appear, and war between Britain and the thirteen colonies seemed to become inevitable.

Just before it broke out, one of the younger generation of great British statesmen in favor of conciliation with the colonies, Edmund Burke, warned the Commons that "an Englishman is the unfittest person on earth to argue another Englishman into slavery. . . . Magnanimity in politics is not seldom the truest wisdom; and a great Empire and little minds go ill together." A few weeks later, musket fire was echoing through eastern Massachusetts—but suppose it never did? Suppose the exhortations of one of history's truly pivotal leaders and orators, Pitt the Elder, and his followers had been heeded, and the House of Commons had first decided for conciliation, then dragged the House of Lords with it, and finally either forced or persuaded George III to see that not only was his cause wrong, but that it was of uncertain outcome?

Such a result is by no means more improbable than the notion that some one of Britain's military commanders in North America could have permanently exterminated the sentiments of outrage, rebellion, and patriotism in the thirteen rebellious colonies with even a significant victory; indeed, it is far more plausible.

War is, of course, as much affected by the vagaries of human nature as are diplomacy and statesmanship. The mere and deceptive fact that military affairs encompass such sciences as engineering and ballistics does not alter the fact that, at their moment of execution, military plans depend above all on the relative ability of opposing commanders to manage themselves, their officers, and their men, as well as to anticipate the thoughts of their counterparts and the mood and condition of enemy troops—all of which has little to do with any set of quantifiable laws. Why, then, do we speak of "military science" at all? For the same reason that the bastard discipline of political science was created: out of hope. Hope that man's most capricious and terrible activities actually obey knowable, suprahuman rules, and therefore can be rationally controlled. This attitude bleeds over into speculative military history perhaps even more than it does into counterfactual political exercises, precisely because of war's more mortal costs. When we declare, for instance, that, "if the British had won at Saratoga, the fledgling United States would have lost the American Revolution," we are not so much stating a certainty as we are indulging this comforting tendency to believe that war is governed by the law of cause and effect, and is somehow, though vicious and tragic, free of the maddeningly capricious behavior that dominates all other realms of human intercourse.

But an alternative result to the Battle of Saratoga would have been less a matter of changed military outcomes than of transformed human personalities: a victory for Burgoyne would have required a sudden and fundamental shift in his remarkable and well-defined character, from vanity and recklessness (although he did evidence rather charming forms of each quality) toward humility and prudence. It would also have demanded an equally unlikely shift in the psychology of Major General William Howe, the man who was supposed to provide the southern anvil to Burgoyne's northern hammer during the campaign, but who delayed his movements out of caution, a disinclination to play second fiddle to Burgoyne, and finally (if subtly and perhaps even unconsciously) because his family had always opposed the policy of coercing the rebellious colonies to obey the Townshend duties and the other taxation measures that had eventually followed the repeal of the Stamp Act. But again, even if Burgoyne and Howe had gotten hold of their personal idiosyncrasies long enough to understand the full importance of their every action during the Saratoga campaign, can we really believe that the spirit of independence in America would have been destroyed by a single military defeat, however devastating? Postponed it might have been, but the two sides in the conflict had by 1777 grown so far apart that reconciliation under the terms of the status quo antebellum was likely impossible.

Thus we return to the notion that altering those terms was the most feasible and indeed the only alternative historical course that could have pacified colonial restlessness. In imagining such alteration, we wander back into the realm of psychology and human interactions—and the first question we ought to ask ourselves is: When were the complex interactions of the various members of the British government, both among themselves and with the representatives of the colonies, closest to producing a genuine resolution? The answer, without question, is during the period immediately following the repeal of the Stamp Act in 1766. William Pitt, as has been said, rode a wave of proconciliation sentiment back into power, the Stamp Act having been repealed by a strong majority; George III, while a generally loved and respected king, nonetheless continued to be the subject of rumors concerning a mysterious months-long illness that had stricken him at the time of the

Stamp Act's passage (in fact it was the first bout of the metabolic disorder porphyria, which over the next thirty years assaulted various of George's bodily functions and drove him to nervous distraction before actually attacking his brain per se); and much of Britain's influential aristocracy had taken up the colonists' cause and made of it high fashion, while making the most famous of the colonists' agents in London, Benjamin Franklin, the focus of much romance and intrigue, and thus providing him with additional tactical leverage. Circumstances had never been and would never be better for effecting a peaceful reconciliation between Britain and America.

But mistakes were made, some of them tragic, some merely stupid. The greatest of the former was the ailing Pitt's decision to lead his party not as prime minister in the House of Commons but as lord privy seal in the House of Lords, along with his determination not to impugn the judgment or the authority of King George. As the Great Commoner, Pitt was (like most common Britons, as well as, for that matter, most colonists) a true servant of the king, violently committed to the integrity and importance of the monarchy. It would never have occurred to him to publicly question either King George's physical or mental health or his fitness to rule, no matter how much the king insulted him privately. In addition, Pitt's position in the remove of the Lords meant that his ear was not sufficiently to the ground in the Commons to allow him to quickly and easily exterminate those corrupt elements that spread word of the great financial rewards to be had from propagating and exploiting the image of the North American colonies as disobedient and ungrateful servants: for the opening weeks of his administration he would keep these elements in check, but the effort to do so—particularly from an unfamiliar remove—would cost him precious physical and psychological resources.

As for Benjamin Franklin, although he desperately wished for reconciliation in 1766, his pro-empire feelings were eroded by repeated offers by corrupt ministers of money and imperial postings in return for cooperation in the new schemes of taxation without representation. Nor did his constituency at home do much to help the cause of reconciliation: those colonists who rightly saw all the various taxation schemes as unjust and exploitative not only talked loudly, insultingly, and increasingly of separation from the mother country and of the unacceptable evils of parliamentary and cabinet ministers, but they took to agitating publicly, periodically destroying crown-owned and -protected property while all the time remaining ironically steadfast in their belief that George III was their ill-advised best friend—when in fact no man alive held them in greater contempt.

Yet it is Pitt who remains the central figure of both the pre-Revolutionary era and any imagined alternative course for Britain and her colonies during that period. And, unlike the various cases of Britain's military leaders during the war, we do not have to imagine for Pitt a different character in order to cast him as the author of a plausibly different outcome to the long chain of deteriorating events. In fact, we only have to imagine for a moment that, far from doing anything *out* of character, Pitt determined to be even *more* faithful to the principles that had set him up so high. Had he abandoned (or at least postponed) the idea of becoming the earl of Chatham and led his party and his cause in the Commons rather than the Lords, his strong hand would have prevented Charles Townshend from giving in to the temptations of corruption and greed, and the infamous Townshend duties would never have seen the light of day. Furthermore, the power of Pitt's oratory in the "popular" house, as well as among the people it was supposed to represent, cannot be overestimated, and his gift for exposing graft and self-interest (particularly when such exposure served his purposes) was considerable: such corruption would have found the ground of the Commons far less fertile had Pitt been present.

It is highly unlikely, as said, that Pitt would ever have impugned King George's judgment, but the king's private animosity toward Pitt would likely have made conflict between the two men far more frequent, had Pitt been conducting daily business from the lower house. Given such circumstances, other members of Pitt's faction might well have been inspired to speculate not so privately about the soundness of George's judgment. Pitt was also enormously popular in the colonies (when the Stamp Act was repealed, South Carolinians erected a statue not of the king but of Pitt), and he might well have been able to soothe colonial tempers once it was clear that no new program of onerous duties was going to be imposed.

The certainty that all such programs would have been out of the question rests only in part on the assumption that Charles Townshend would have been denied the power to suggest, much less implement, them; it follows even more from Pitt's recognition that the government's best hope of deficit recovery lay not in America but in India. There, the corruption of the East India Company's directors and officers had brought that august firm into a state of near bankruptcy. Had London assumed its debts and cleaned its ethical house, the government would have stood to make an eventual profit that would have been more than enough to bring its war debt woes into the realm of manageability, while concurrently offering a way out of the large-scale conflict that Pitt was certain the Americans intended to offer the mother country if new taxation programs were pressed on them. Finally, Benjamin Franklin's affection and enormous admiration for Pitt would likely have induced him to stay the course of conciliation despite his indignation over being repeatedly offered bribes to betray Pennsylvania's interests, as well as those of the other colonies. In combination with the absence of further new programs of taxation, this would almost certainly have prevented Franklin's journey home in 1774 and his subsequent somber pronouncement to his countrymen that reconciliation was impossible—which, of course, it would not have been.

But if Pitt's retention of tight personal control over the House of Commons could have changed the course of imperial history, why did he decide to go to the Lords? And once in that noble house, why did he eventually abandon even this more indirect method of controlling affairs, when for two months that method gave enough signs of being successful as to make one hope that it could keep doing so? The answer lies with one of those factors that the British diplomat and author Harold Nicholson—a participant in the Versailles conference at the conclusion of World War I and author of the definitive study of the Congress of Vienna that concluded the Napoleonic Wars—described as being among the most underrated yet powerful influences on statecraft: the physical health of key players.

Pitt's body and mind were heading into irreversible decline in 1766, despite his being just fifty-eight years old, and he suspected as much. He believed that his decision to become lord privy seal would spare him some of the more trivial yet punishing day-to-day stresses that lay ahead: as it happened, the reverse was almost certainly true. Despite this unhappy result, he was nonetheless able to summon the additional strength needed to make sure that the first two months of his ministry saw the wheels of both policy reform and his own personal dominance over foreign, fiscal, and military affairs set upon their paths: he denounced and exposed corruption among those who wished to go on looting not only America but the East India Company as well, proposed new military and naval measures with which to meet the possibility of revived French power, and finally, while indeed pursuing a policy of conciliation with America, made it quite clear that he did not intend to appease the colonists if they followed the advice of their most radical (or simply greedy) leaders and tried to take advantage of his good nature. It was an ambitious program, but it represented Britain's only hope of escaping her crucial predicament without a severe loss of imperial power at any point along the chain of her global holdings. The strain of holding a government laced with profiteers and reactionaries on such a course would have been enough to tax a far younger and more robust man: viewed this way, it is not only small wonder that Pitt's nerves and physical health gave way after eight weeks—it is a testament to his will that they lasted so long.

Forced to retreat to Bath to recuperate, Pitt lost touch with much of the business of government altogether. In the vacuum created by his absence, not only Charles Townshend but seemingly every corrupt official in the government made quick plays for profit. Townshend's yearly budget was such a betrayal of Pitt's goals that the ailing political master—after only a few months of what should have been several years' recuperation—made a hurried and immensely painful journey back to London. But the weeks of absence had been enough to do irreparable damage: with the fruits of corruption now tantalizingly close, even former supporters abandoned Pitt, and when he fired Townshend he was unable to find a competent—or indeed so much as a willing—replacement. Refused even by Lord North, that mediocre man who would later, as prime minister, become the nemesis of America, and increasingly aware that war with the colonies and all it implied was becoming daily more inevitable, Pitt spiraled into a full-fledged nervous breakdown, one that this time would last two years.

Would the breakdown have come if, again, Pitt had realized that the supposed relief offered by retirement to the House of Lords was a trap? Quite possibly not: the collapse was the last tragic ripple of that terrible, that so very uncharacteristic, mistake. And precisely because it *was* so uncharacteristic, we are on firm speculative ground when we imagine all that might have happened had he never made it. If the Great Commoner had waited to become the earl of Chatham—if the most publicly beloved political figure of his age and the only man who could hold the power of the reactionaries, the plunderers, the American radicals, and the crown in check had retained the strength to do all of those things— how might the next two centuries have played out?

We begin, of course, with the obvious: knowing how important it is for the American colonies to be allowed continued autonomy so that they can develop commercially and industrially at the same rapid rate they have already established, and thereby offer Britain the fruits of increased trade, Pitt fights off those who favor plundering America for short-term gains by using not only the water of moral castigations but the fire of increased revenue: he shows them how much wealthier they will become, and for how many more generations that increased income will last, if they will simply accept lower projections and incomes in the short term. Supported by the growing power of younger members such as Edmund Burke, as well as by Benjamin Franklin and ever-increasing numbers of eminent colonial representatives whom Pitt summons to highly publicized councils of conciliation in London, the prime minister passes laws that confirm the special relationship between America and the mother country. "No taxation without representation" becomes, for the moment, an irrelevant slogan: the colonies will keep their own legislatures and decide almost all of their own internal economic and political issues. In short, the arrangement with Canada that Britain will work out in the mid-nineteenth century is anticipated in the thirteen colonies, and the bones of the commonwealth system come into being.

Freed from international political distractions and their own internal political machinations and jockeying, the thirteen colonies prosper at an accelerated pace. This process is also facilitated by general freedom from the depredations of Indian tribes: official policy toward those tribes is determined in London and is heavily influenced by those colonial subjects—most notably the enormously powerful Johnson family in New York's Mohawk Valley—who live among and in peace with the Native Americans. As they are in Canada, colonists are forbidden from widespread, self-serving violence against the Indians, and although the tribes cannot help but resent much of the settlement movement, the pace of the movement is regulated: there are no "land rushes," and no large-scale exterminations of Indians along the Spanish model. The revenue lost by sharing land with the tribes rather than stealing it from them is made up for by the lack of large-scale Indian wars: genocide is not, after all, a necessary component of the modernization of North America.

The slavery question is a somewhat more complicated issue and will not be resolved before William Pitt the Elder's death in 1788. The slave trade is outlawed throughout the empire in 1807, although the possession of slaves remains legal. The British antislavery movement has real teeth, however, and in 1833 the institution of slavery is abolished altogether. In areas of the empire such as the American South, the moment is an uncertain one, with the local economy dependent on slave-based agrarianism. Some in the South begin once again to agitate for independence from Britain, but the combined might of the empire and the industrial northern colonies makes any such move unthinkable, and the southern states are forced to adapt by changing the basis of their economy. This process will take a great deal of time, but will actually be assisted by the availability of large numbers of freed African Americans to work in the new southern factories.

The elimination of the slave trade and the steady march of voting franchise reform in Great Britain proper and, in variously altered forms, throughout the empire establish Britain as the empire to whom peoples staggering under the yoke of less enlightened governmental systems look for inspiration and assistance; but this does not include Britain's ancient nemesis, the French, who begin to show domestic signs of revolution toward the end of the eighteenth century. With no specific, written model of a constitution or a bill of rights on which to base any similar documents of their own, however, the leaders of France's revolution become lost in confusion and bickering long before their movement gains any real steam. The Bourbon family retains control of France, but Louis XVI's ministers and successors take the warnings of the aborted revolution seriously, and by the early nineteenth century the French have developed into a "bourgeois empire," the royal family peacefully relinquishing effective governmental authority to an elected assembly, which severely curtails the authority of the Catholic Church. The British watch all this with cautious optimism, but since 1763 the French have never been in a position to challenge London's imperial supremacy, and the lack of serious conflict between the two nations only augments the momentum of the juggernaut that is British imperial power. And, of course, the abortion of the French Revolution and absence of any generalized war during the same period means that Napoléon Bonaparte never becomes more than a capable artillery officer, and the millions of lives that he eventually squandered and ruined are allowed to unfold free of his monomaniacal influence.

In Latin America, meanwhile, as in a great many other restive colonies around the world, "native" citizens of the Spanish empire begin to envy the enlightenment of the British system, and to curse the medieval inequality of their own. In the 1820s, Britain's prime minister George Canning recognizes this not-so-subtle Anglophile sentiment among Spanish Americans and offers sponsorship to all those revolutionary movements that are working to break free of Madrid, provided, of course, that they are willing to become incorporated into the British commonwealth. One after another the former Spanish colonies respond, agreeing to abolish slavery within their borders as a second principal precondition of absorption into the empire.

Like the French, the former Spanish holdings lack a successful model of a revolutionary movement on which to base their actions and give remarkably little thought to any idea of becoming "free"—nor do they have any great reason to, for all their desires for effective autonomy can be happily accommodated by their new arrangements with Britain. As this remarkable process of the entire New World becoming part of the British system continues, Prime Minister Canning delightedly declares, "The deed is done—the nail is driven. We have managed our affairs well, and Spanish America is British!" In Madrid, some bitter thought is given to declaring war against Britain in protest, but advisers to the child-queen Isabella tell her that the cause is hopeless. Like France, Spain drifts without complaint toward shrinking her possessions and accepting constitutional monarchy as the only method of survival.

In those parts of the world where British rule is seen as less admirable and less benign—where the traditions associated with common law and constitutionalism mean comparatively little—London is forced to back its expansion up with military action at regular intervals during the early and mid-nineteenth century. But with the industrial might of America still squarely behind them (North and South America are often referred to as the "arsenals of imperial democracy"), a succession of expansionist British prime ministers have little trouble subduing indigenous resistance in Africa, India, and other parts of Asia, such as Afghanistan. With Africa thus firmly under control, and with British antislavery feeling running as high as ever, many African tribes are forced to abandon their long tradition of enslaving one another, while native tribal governments are forced at gunpoint—as are similar local authorities in India—to adopt some effective form of the British constitutional system, often down to the smallest details of a civil service. This eradication of tribal law is violently condemned by many indigenous leaders as cultural chauvinism, but the peoples who have been ruled by such leaders are in the main happy to give quiet assent to the new way of doing things. Rebellions, particularly those inspired by religion, are not unknown, but they generally fail to gather real force, and even when they do, they are crushed by the overwhelming technological superiority of the British army.

The new rivalries and dangers that arise on the European continent in the later nineteenth century amid the pressures of the Industrial Revolution cause momentary friction between Britain and the predominant continental power, Germany, which has unified under Prussia after that nation's defeat of Austria in 1866, and then gone on to wage successful campaigns for continental supremacy against France in 1870–71 and Russia in 1875. But a series of diplomatic summits between England's prime minister Benjamin Disraeli and Germany's chancellor Otto von Bismarck produce agreement that Britain's interests are not continental, while Germany's are not imperial: the situation is rapidly defused. When Bismarck is dismissed by Germany's kaiser Wilhelm II, who is known to be mentally unreliable, the young monarch is said to give serious thought to fighting Britain for a share of her imperial holdings, but not even Wilhelm is mad enough to take on the greatest imperial power the world has known since Rome at its height—not when it can bring the entire power of the industrialized New World to bear against its enemies. German-British friendship lasts well into the twentieth century, and the two nations even unite for a common purpose when revolution strikes imperial Russia. Throwing their weight behind the representative government headed by Aleksandr Kerensky, and dispatching an expeditionary force to destroy a small Bolshevik-led army that tries to undo Kerensky's experiment, the British and Germans ensure that Russia's experiment with British-inspired democracy succeeds—though only after much of western Russia (what was once called Poland) has been ceded to Germany.

The later twentieth century passes uneventfully enough, until the largest and oldest parts of the British empire begin to request greater autonomy within the commonwealth system. Some even advocate independence, a request that at first sends shock waves through the London Parliament. But cool heads prevail: many members of Parliament recall an earlier time when British colonies asked for similarly increased autonomy as a reward for their steadfast loyalty. At that time, too, there were reactionary forces in Parliament that were unwilling to modify the imperial system; but, then as now, there were other, wiser leaders who pointed out that the most important aspect of the entire imperial system was the transplantation of the British constitutional tradition and British common law. This process has now taken place throughout almost the entire world, with the notable exceptions of isolationist China and Germany (which has its own constitutional tradition, one that, although not as old as Britain's, nonetheless has proved almost as vital). Remembering those days two hundred years earlier and the mistakes that were very nearly made, the British Parliament votes to loosen the commonwealth system, feeling safe in the knowledge that the effective export of their constitution and legal system has indeed ensured the triumph of representative democracy as the most common form of government on earth—a triumph achieved less by force (though force has sometimes been used) than by example.

Can one really posit such a drastically altered history of the last two centuries (one that, admittedly, has received a rosy gloss in this brief treatment) on the altered political strategy, level of personal participation, and physical and mental health of one man? If it seems an impossible exaggeration, remember that we in the United States have learned only too well what the untimely removal of a key leader can do to the development not just of a nation but of that nation's role in the world. And in our own inimitable way, we have learned that lesson less through the effects of natural death or mental deterioration than by way of assassins' bullets—yet the lesson's essential elements remain the same. . . .

What would the domestic history of the modern United States have been like, for example, had Abraham Lincoln lived to do what only he could have done, impose an enlightened and charitable version of Reconstruction on the defeated Confederacy, while simultaneously demanding that they never waver in their march toward progress in racial laws and policies? How much would the survival of John F. Kennedy have meant to the preservation rather than the deterioration of America's international prestige during the 1960s, as well as the prevention of the Vietnam War? How would America's race relations, indeed the very fabric of its society (most especially black culture and political participation), have developed if both Martin Luther King and Malcolm X had survived their assassins? Or, turning to natural deaths for a refreshing moment, would there indeed have been so dangerous a Cold War had Franklin Roosevelt rather than the bellicose Winston Churchill been the man to set the tone of the competition with Soviet Russia?

Speculative, counterfactual history teaches us one thing above all: that the lives and minds of individual men and women count far beyond what most people find believable, beyond even what many historians (particularly those of the Marxist economic school) are willing to accept. And William Pitt the Elder is among the most tragic of history's pivotal figures because he could see so clearly where failure to implement his enlightened policies (though that failure was not entirely his own) must eventually lead: not just to the loss of the American colonies, but eventually to the loss of the empire itself. This clear knowledge first drove him mad, and then destroyed him, and the world was much the worse for the loss. It may seem rather treasonous for an American historian to wish for a better fate for Pitt, or to maintain that the avoidance of the American Revolution could have been the starting point of two far more beneficent centuries of human experience than those the world has actually suffered through. But try, if nothing else, taking a quick glance at the map of the world some time, and mark off all the truly successful, well-established democracies you can find: how many were not once British colonies? Was a period of colonialism really such a terrible price to pay for that future stability and egalitarianism?

America at the dawn of the twenty-first century finds itself in a position very similar to that of Great Britain on the eve of America's bid for independence, and as one observes the problem of mounting tension with countries that we have for decades exploited economically, that we have overloaded with misused foreign aid, or that we have made pawns in our attempts to secure that indefinable and finally unattainable thing we call "national security"—generally without offering any greater education about or indoctrination into the community of democratic nations than token exposure to two scraps of paper (was America really so wise to write its constitution down?)—this author, at least, cannot help but hope for the appearance of a statesman of Pitt's stature in our own country, or to be haunted by those timeless words of Edmund Burke:

"A great empire and little minds go ill together . . ."

42

DAVID McCULLOUGH

WHAT THE FOG WROUGHT:
The Revolution's Dunkirk, August 29, 1776

For all that can be said for a deterministic view of history—for the inevitability of what T. S. Eliot called "vast impersonal forces"—chance and luck (two related but altogether different phenomena) also play a part. How else to explain the events of mid-August 1776, when, badly beaten at the Battle of Long Island (Brooklyn, actually), George Washington and his small army faced what seemed to be certain annihilation by a larger British army, one of the world's best. As David McCullough points out, nothing less than the independence of the United States was at stake. But the whims of weather were beyond prediction then, as they often still are. Perhaps in this case the most you can say about inevitability is that Washington almost always had the knack of seizing the right moment.

DAVID McCULLOUGH is one of the most deservedly popular historians of our time. His *Truman* won the National Book Award and Pulitzer Prize for biography; *The Path Between the Seas*, his account of the building of the Panama Canal, also won the National Book Award for history. His other books include *The Johnstown Flood*, *The Great Bridge*, and *Mornings on Horseback*, and, most recently, *John Adams*, winner of the 2002 Pulitzer Prize for biography. Millions know him as the host, and often the narrator, of television shows like *The American Experience*. The past president of the Society of American Historians, McCullough has also won the Francis Parkman Prize and the *Los Angeles Times* Book Award.

"THE DAY OF THE TRIAL, which will in some measure decide the fate of America, is near at hand," wrote General George Washington in mid-August 1776 from his headquarters in New York.

The Declaration of Independence had been signed in Philadelphia only days before, on August 8—not July 4, as commonly believed—and for six weeks an enormous British expeditionary force, the largest ever sent to dispense with a distant foe, had been arriving in lower New York Harbor.

The first British sails had been sighted at the end of June, a great fleet looking, as one man said, like "all London afloat." It was a spectacle such as had never been seen in American waters. And the ships had kept coming all summer. On August 13, Washington reported an "augmentation" of ninety-six ships on a single day. The day after, another twenty dropped anchor, making a total of more than four hundred, counting ten ships-of-the-time, twenty frigates, and several hundred transports. Fully thirty-two thousand well-equipped British and hired German troops, some of the best in the world, had landed without opposition on Staten Island—an enemy force, that is, greater than the whole population of Philadelphia, the largest city in the newly proclaimed United States of America.

The defense of New York was considered essential by Congress, largely for political reasons, but also by General Washington, who welcomed the chance for a climactic battle—a "day of trial," as he said. Yet he had scarcely twenty thousand troops and no naval force, not one fighting ship or proper transport. His was an army of volunteers, raw recruits, poorly armed, poorly supplied. The men had no tents—to cite one glaring deficiency—and few were equipped with bayonets, the weapon employed by the British with such terrifying effectiveness. As a surgeon with Washington's army wrote, "In point of numbers, or discipline, experience in war . . . the enemy possessed the most decided advantage; beside the importance of assistance afforded by a powerful fleet."

Among the considerable number of men who were too sick to fight was Washington's ablest field commander, Nathanael Greene. Few American officers were experienced in large-scale warfare. Washington himself until now had never led an army in the field. The battle to come was to be his first as a commander.

With no way of knowing where the British might strike, Washington had chosen to split his troops, keeping half on the island of Manhattan, while the rest crossed the East River to Long Island, to dig in along the river on the high bluffs known as Brooklyn Heights—all this carried out in disregard of the old cardinal rule of never dividing an army in the face of a superior foe. When, on August 22, the British began ferrying troops across the Narrows to land farther south on Long Island, about eight miles from the little village of Brooklyn, Washington responded by sending still more of his army across the East River, which, it should be noted, is not really a river at all, but a tidal strait, a mile-wide arm of the sea with especially strong currents.

"I have no doubt but a little time will produce some important events," Washington wrote in classic understatement to the president of Congress, John Hancock.

In fact, it was a situation made for an American catastrophe. With at most twelve thousand troops on Long Island, Washington faced an army of perhaps twenty thousand. Should there be no stopping such a force, he and his amateur soldiers would have to retreat with the river to their backs. Which is just what happened.

The furious battle of Long Island was fought several miles inland from Brooklyn Heights on Tuesday, August 27, 1776. The British, under General William Howe, outflanked, outfought, and routed the Americans in little time. The British officers under Howe included James Grant,

Henry Clinton, and Lords Cornwallis and Percy, and all performed expertly. As John Adams was to conclude succinctly, "In general, our generals were outgeneralled."

Astride a big gray horse, watching from a hillside, Washington is supposed to have said in anguish, "Good God! What brave fellows I must this day lose!" By later estimates, his losses were higher than he knew; more than 1,400 killed, wounded, or captured. Two of his generals had been taken captive. Many of his best officers were killed or missing. British use of the bayonet had been savage and on men who had surrendered as well, as one British officer proudly recorded, explaining, "You know all stratagems are lawful in war, especially against such vile enemies of the King and country." Washington and his exhausted men fell back to the fortifications on the Heights, waiting as night fell for a final British assault, the river to the rear.

And right then and there the American cause hung in the balance. The British, as Washington seems not to have realized—or allowed himself to think—had him in a perfect trap. They had only to move a few warships into the East River and all escape would be sealed. Indeed, but for the caprices of weather, the outcome would have been altogether different.

What actually happened was extraordinary. What so obviously could have happened, and with the most far-reaching consequences, is not hard to picture.

To be sure, the individual makeup of the two commanders played a part. On the day following the battle, influenced no doubt by his experience of the year before at Bunker Hill, General Howe chose not to follow up his victory by storming the American lines on Brooklyn Heights. He saw no reason to lose any more of his army than absolutely necessary, nor any cause to hurry. William Howe almost never saw cause for hurry, but in this case with reason—he had, after all, Washington right where he wanted him.

For his part, Washington appears to have given no thought to a withdrawal, the only sensible recourse. All his instincts were to fight. On

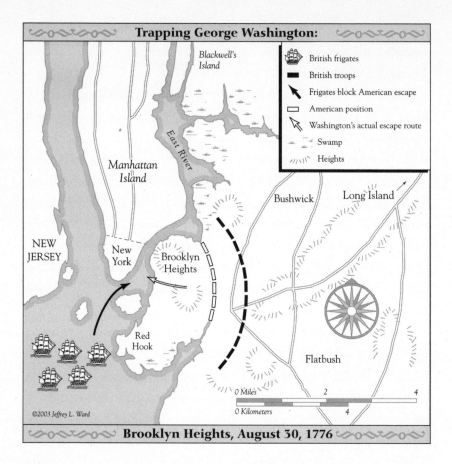

Trapping George Washington:

- 🚢 British frigates
- ▬ British troops
- ↖ Frigates block American escape
- ▭ American position
- ⇖ Washington's actual escape route
- Swamp
- Heights

Blackwell's Island

East River

Manhattan Island

NEW JERSEY

New York

Brooklyn Heights

Red Hook

Bushwick

Long Island

Flatbush

0 Miles 2 4

0 Kilometers 4

©2003 Jeffrey L. Ward

Brooklyn Heights, August 30, 1776

Wednesday, August 28, and again on Thursday, August 29, his food supplies nearly gone, his time clearly running out, he ordered that still more reinforcements be rowed over from New York, a decision that seems almost incomprehensible.

His men, for all their bravery and devotion to him, were worn out, hungry, and dispirited. And it had begun to rain. On August 29, the temperature dropped sharply and the rain came in torrents on the unsheltered army. During the afternoon, according to a diary kept by a local Brooklyn pastor, "Such heavy rain fell again as can hardly be remembered." Muskets and powder were soaked. In some places men stood in flooded trenches in water up to their waists. Expecting the enemy to attack at any moment, they had to keep a constant watch.

Many had not slept for days. A New York man who saw them after it was all over said he never in his life saw such wretched, exhausted-looking human beings.

Washington's presence along the lines and his concern for the men were felt day and night. Seldom was he out of the saddle. On both August 28 and August 29, he appears to have had no rest at all.

But in their misery was their salvation. The driving rain and cold were part of a fitful, at times violent, nor'easter that had been blowing off and on for better than a week, and for all the punishment it inflicted, the wind had kept the British ships from coming upriver with the tide. For the new nation, it was an ill wind that blew great good, so long as it held.

Meantime, as the British historian Sir George Otto Trevelyan would write, "Nine thousand [or more] disheartened soldiers, the last hope of their country, were penned up, with the sea behind them and a triumphant enemy in front, shelterless and famished on a square mile of open ground swept by fierce and cold northeasterly gale . . ."

In a letter to John Hancock written at four o'clock in the morning, August 29, the crucial day, Washington reported only on the severity of the weather and the lack of tents that Congress had failed to supply, but said nothing of a retreat. He had seen five British ships attempt to come up the river and fail; and so he appears to have been banking on no change in the wind. Possibly he believed, too, that obstructions in the harbor— hulks sunk as hazards—had truly blocked the passage of all but small craft, a notion that was to prove quite wrong. In any event, having been outflanked on land, he stood perilously close to being outflanked by water.

The decision that so obviously had to be made came only later in the day, after it was learned that the British, under the cover of dark, were advancing by "regular approaches"—working through the night, throwing up entrenchments near and nearer the American lines—and after Washington at last accepted the likelihood of the British fleet at his back. Importantly, as he himself was to emphasize, the decision came on "the advice of my general officers."

According to one firsthand observer, it was General Thomas Mifflin, a self-assured thirty-two-year-old "fighting Quaker" from Philadelphia, who was the most emphatic. Mifflin, who had come over from New York with the last reinforcements only the day before, had been the one who, on his night rounds, discovered that the British were digging their way forward. Immediate retreat was imperative, the only remaining choice, he told Washington. Lest anyone question his character for making such a proposal, Mifflin asked that he be put in command of the rear guard, by far the most dangerous of assignments in a retreat.

With the rain still pounding down, Washington and his generals gathered for a council of war in the Brooklyn Heights summer home of Philip Livingston, a signer of the Declaration of Independence, who was in Philadelphia attending Congress. The time was early afternoon. The purpose of the meeting, as stated in the official minutes, was "whether under all circumstances it would not be eligible to leave Long Island." Two of the reasons given for an affirmative resolution were that the northeast wind might shift and that the consoling thought of obstructions in the harbor was now considered erroneous.

So it was decided. Preparations were set immediately in motion. An order from Washington went over to New York to collect every boat "from Hellgate on the [Long Island] Sound to Spuyten Duyvil Creek [on the Hudson] that could be kept afloat and that had either sails or oars, and have them all in the east harbor of the city by dark."

It was said the boats were needed to transport the sick and bring still greater reinforcements over to Brooklyn. Officers on the Heights, meanwhile, were to be ready to "parade their men with their arms, accoutrements and knapsacks at 7 o'clock at the head of their encampments and there wait for orders."

In all, it was a straightaway lie by Washington, intended to keep the truth from the men until the last moment—and thereby reduce the chance of panic—and hopefully to deceive the British—and the innumerable British spies in New York—once the roundup of boats was under way.

Most of the troops took the order to mean they were to go on the attack. A young captain of Pennsylvania volunteers, Alexander Graydon, would recall men taking time to write their wills. He, however, sensed something else was afoot. "It suddenly flashed upon my mind that a retreat was the object, and that the order . . . was but a cover to the real design." Yet, who was to say? None of the other officers who listened to his theory dared believe it. Never in years to come could he recall the long wait without thinking of the chorus in Shakespeare's *Henry V*, describing the "weary and all-watched night" before Agincourt.

The first boats began crossing as soon as it turned dark. How it was all managed is almost beyond imagination. Every conceivable kind of small craft was employed, manned by Massachusetts men—soldiers from the ranks but sailors and fishermen by trade—from Marblehead and Salem, under the command of General John Glover and Colonel Israel Hutchinson. It can be said that the fate of the American army was in their hands. How readily the night could turn disastrous on the water, no less than on land, was more apparent to them than to anyone.

Everything was to be carried across—men, stores, horses, cannon. Every possible precaution had to be taken to keep silent—oars and wagon wheels were muffled with rags; orders were passed on in whispers. Every boat that pushed off, every crossing, was a race against time, and in black night and rain.

At one point, all seemed lost. Sometime near nine, the northeast wind picked up at ebb tide. The wind and current were more than sail could cope with, even in expert hands, and there were too few rowboats to carry everyone across before daylight. But in another hour or so, the wind mercifully fell off and shifted southwest, becoming the most favorable wind possible; and so the exodus resumed, all boats in service.

It went on hour after hour almost without a hitch. If ever fortune favored the brave, it was that night on the East River. Washington, who had proven considerably less than impressive in his first battle command, handled this, his first great retreat, with a steadiness and dispatch that were masterful. As untrained and inexperienced as his men may have been, however wet and miserable, they more than rose to the occasion. They stood for hours waiting their turns; then, when told, they moved off as silent ghosts, heading down the slopes to the river in pitch darkness, to the Brooklyn ferry landing, which was about where the Brooklyn Bridge now stands.

As the night progressed, and one regiment after another was withdrawn, the front lines grew perilously thin, to the point where there was almost no one left to stop an attack, should the enemy discover what was happening. It was the rear guard under Mifflin that had to stay to the last, keeping campfires burning and making sufficient noise to maintain the illusion of the full army in position.

The one hitch happened about two in the morning, when somehow Mifflin received orders to withdraw, only to learn on the way to the landing that it had been a dreadful mistake and that he and his men must return at once to their posts. "This was a trying business to young soldiers," one of them later wrote. "It was nevertheless complied with." They were back on the line before their absence was detected.

Another officer, Colonel Benjamin Tallmadge, would recall, "As the dawn of the next day approached, those of us who remained in the trenches became very anxious for our own safety . . ."

Troops in substantial numbers had still to be evacuated and at the rate things were going, it appeared day would dawn before everyone was safely removed. But again "the elements" interceded, this time in the form of pea-soup fog.

It was called "a peculiar providential occurrence," "manifestly providential," "very favorable to the design," "an unusual fog," "a friendly fog," "an American fog." "So very dense was the atmosphere," remembered Benjamin Tallmadge, "that I could scarcely discern a man at six yards' distance." And as daylight came, the fog held, covering the entire operation no less than had the night.

Tallmadge would recall that when the rear guard at last received word to pull out, and "we very joyfully bid those trenches adieu," the fog was still "as dense as ever."

When we reached Brooklyn ferry, the boats had not returned from their last trip, but they very soon appeared and took the whole regiment over to New York; and I think [I] saw General Washington on the ferry stairs when I stepped into one of the last boats . . .

When the fog lifted at about seven o'clock, the British saw to their astonishment that the Americans had vanished.

Amazingly, the entire force, at least nine thousand troops, possibly more, plus baggage, provisions, horses, field guns, everything but five heavy cannon that were too deep in the mud to budge, had been transported over the river in a single night with a makeshift emergency armada assembled in a matter of hours. Not a life was lost. It is not even known that anyone was injured. And as Tallmadge remembered, Washington, risking capture, had stayed until the last boat pushed off. As it was, the only Americans captured by the British were three who stayed behind to plunder.

The "day of trial" that Washington had foreseen deciding the fate of America had turned out to be a night of trial, and one that did truly decide the fate of America as much as any battle.

It was the Dunkirk of the American Revolution—by daring amphibious rescue a beleaguered army had been saved to fight another day—and tributes to Washington would come from all quarters, from those in the ranks, from officers, delegates in Congress, and from military observers and historians then and later. A British officer of the time called the retreat "particularly glorious." A latter-day scholar would write that "a more skillful operation of this kind was never conducted."

But what a very close call it had been. How readily it could have all gone wrong—had there been no northeast wind to hold the British fleet in check through the day of the Battle of Long Island was fought, not to say the days immediately afterward. Or had the wind not turned southwest the night of August 29. Or had there been no fortuitous fog as a final safeguard when day broke.

What the effect would have been had British naval forces come into play off Brooklyn Heights was to be vividly demonstrated just weeks later, when, with favorable wind and tide, five warships, including the *Renown* with fifty guns, sailed up the East River as far as Kips Bay and, from two hundred yards offshore, commenced a thunderous point-blank bombardment of American defenses on Manhattan. "So terrible and so incessant a roar of guns few even in the army and navy had ever heard before," wrote a British naval officer. Earthworks and entrenchments were destroyed in an instant, blasted to dust, while American troops fled in terror.

Had such overwhelming power been brought to bear at Brooklyn, the trap would have been closed tight. Washington and half the Continental Army would have been in the bag, captured, and the American Revolution all but finished. Without Washington there almost certainly would have been no revolution, as events were to show time and again. As the historian Trevelyan would write, "When once the wind changed and leading British frigates had . . . taken Brooklyn in the rear, the independence of the United States would have been indefinitely postponed."

Significantly, the same circumstances as at Brooklyn were to pertain again five years later, in 1783, except that the sides were switched, when American and French armies under Washington and Rochambeau had the British trapped at Yorktown, a French fleet at their back, sealing off any possible escape and leaving the British commander, Cornwallis, and more than seven thousand men no choice but to surrender.

"Oh God! It is all over!" Lord North, the British prime minister, is said to have exclaimed on hearing the news from Yorktown. It is what might well have been heard in the halls of Congress or any number of places the summer of 1776 had there been no fateful wind and fog at Brooklyn.

TOM WICKER

"HIS ACCIDENCY" JOHN TYLER

There is an argument to be made (as it has been) that John Tyler was one of the most important presidents of the nineteenth century: not because of what he accomplished but because of what he set in motion. His was a presidential career compounded of what ifs, ones that, as Tom Wicker points out, would have prodigious implications for the future, both near and remote. That he became president at all has to be the first of many twists. If only William Henry Harrison hadn't caught a cold at his inauguration in 1841.

John Tyler became the first vice president to move up to the presidency when an elected president died. A Virginian—the last to occupy the White House—he had started his political life as a states' rights Democrat, but had switched to the Whig Party. But before he had been in office very long, the Whigs in Congress, outraged by vetoes of pet projects by this actively negative chief executive, tried to impeach him (another first), and then simply disassociated themselves from Tyler—who proceeded to load his cabinet with Southern Democrats. A month before he left office, Tyler presided over a grand ball in the East Room of the White House. "They cannot say now that I am a president without a party," he later remarked.

Even so, Wicker reminds us, he presided over a congressional manipulation that would be his monument: the annexation of Texas. There was a widespread sentiment against it, especially in the North, because Texas would obviously come into the Union as a slave state. "To Northern Whigs," Samuel Eliot Morison has written, "there seemed to be no more danger to the United States in leaving Texas independent than in Canada remaining British; the only things threatened were slavery, and the dominance of the Democratic party."

To the what ifs that Wicker enumerates, another might be added, one of those random calamities that can have a profound effect on history. On February 28, 1844, Tyler led a gala excursion on board the newly commissioned USS Princeton, a 950-ton ancillary screw frigate, designed by John Ericsson (more famous for a later invention, the Monitor). A highlight of the celebratory voyage was the firing of the ship's main battery. One of the guns blew up, killing Tyler's secretaries of state and the Navy, as well as a New York state senator, whose daughter swooned into the arms of the widower president (he later married her). Tyler replaced the dead secretary of state with John C. Calhoun of South Carolina, the South's foremost spokesman for slavery. Calhoun made the Texas annexation his chief mission. Would it have happened without his intervention? Would a delay have tempered its consequences— which were nothing less than war with Mexico and a decade and a half of sectional turmoil? John Tyler, the accidental president, the historian William W. Freehling writes, "not-at-all-accidentally helped precipitate the near-destruction of a nation."

TOM WICKER is a former *New York Times* Washington bureau chief and a columnist for the newspaper. He is the author of numerous books, the most recent of which is *Dwight D. Eisenhower,* in the American Presidents series.

W HAT IF WILLIAM HENRY HARRISON, the ninth president of
the United States, had not died in 1841, after serving just one
month of his term?

In that non-event, Texas probably would not have been brought into
the Union as soon as it actually was, in 1845. Its accession might not
have been accomplished before gold was discovered in California in
1849—in which case Mexico might not have been willing to give up
what would have become her richest territory. As it was, she yielded
California (along with Nevada, Utah, most of New Mexico and Arizona, and parts of Colorado and Wyoming) only after being defeated in
the Mexican War—but that conflict might not have happened at all,
had not Texas been annexed to the Union when and how it was. And
that might not have happened as it did, had William Henry Harrison
served out his term, rather than dying on April 4, 1841.

Had Harrison—in 1840, at sixty-seven, the oldest president ever
inaugurated, a record exceeded only by Ronald Reagan—survived the
pneumonia that killed him, it's likely that the nation's expansion to the
West Coast would have been long delayed or even somehow thwarted.
Perhaps more important, the three most important vice presidents in
American history—Theodore Roosevelt, Harry S Truman, and Lyndon
B. Johnson—might well have been unable to make their remarkable
presidential achievements (to cite one for each: the Panama Canal, the
Marshall Plan to rebuild Europe after World War II, and the historic
Voting Rights Act of 1965).

That's a mighty string of "ifs" to dangle from the nearly forgotten death
of an almost forgotten president. Harrison is recalled today primarily as

In February 1844, during a gala cruise led by President John Tyler (the lanky figure at the far left), a gun blew up, killing the secretaries of state and the Navy. Would the annexation of a slave state, Texas, within the year and the sectional turmoil that resulted have occurred without the intervention of the new secretary of state, John C. Calhoun of South Carolina? © PictureHistory

the first half of "Tippecanoe and Tyler Too"—though, owing much to that immortal slogan, he was also the first president elected in anything like a "modern" campaign similar to those of the twentieth century. The other half of the slogan[1]—John Tyler of Virginia—became the first vice president to move up to the presidency when an elected president died, since William Henry Harrison was the first chief executive to expire in office. The precedent Tyler set, bitterly resisted at the time, stood for more than a century until finally validated in 1967 by its inclusion in the Twenty-fifth Amendment to the Constitution.

The Tyler precedent, moreover, was largely responsible, in the nineteenth century, for the accession of Texas and all those other Western

---

[1] In two centuries of presidential campaigns, perhaps only "I Like Ike" in 1952 was equally catchy and memorable.

states and areas that extended the United States to the West Coast. In the twentieth century, that same Tyler precedent made possible those landmark presidential achievements, cited above, by three later vice presidents who, following Tyler's example, moved into the Oval Office when death took their predecessors.

By 1840, William Henry Harrison—the son of a signer of the Declaration of Independence, the grandfather of the later twenty-third president of the United States—had compiled a notable political career, including twelve years as governor of the Indiana Territory; he also had been U.S. minister to Colombia and was a Whig candidate (among several) for president in 1836, narrowly losing to Martin Van Buren. Harrison earned his half of the later slogan in 1811 by nearly losing, then recovering to win, the Battle of Tippecanoe Creek, a tributary of the Wabash River, when his force was surprised and attacked by Indians led by the great Tecumseh. But Harrison became a national figure only after pursuing Tecumseh's band into Canada and killing the renowned chief at the Battle of Thames River in 1813.

Nearly three decades after that fight, "Tippecanoe and Tyler Too" were nominated for president and vice president by the Whigs, a rising but divided party hardly able in 1840 even to agree on a platform—as in 1836 Whigs had not been able to unite on Harrison as their single presidential candidate. In 1840, however, in a continuing economic recession, they faced an unpopular Democratic incumbent (Van Buren again, who was called "Van Ruin" by his critics), used their splendid slogan to great advantage, and nominated as Harrison's running mate a Virginian and a former Democrat, John Tyler, who was expected to "balance" the ticket by attracting Southern votes. Harrison and Tyler— "Tippecanoe and Tyler Too"—won going away, tallying 234 electoral votes to a mere 60 for Van Buren.

Harrison took office on March 4, 1841, with Daniel Webster as his secretary of state and Henry Clay in control of the Whig congressional majority. These two giants of the day chose the rest of Harrison's cabinet and nudged him into quickly calling Congress into session to consider Clay's "American System" of internal improvements (mostly roads and canals).

All looked rosy for Tippecanoe and the Whigs too, but in politics as in most of life, "the best-laid plans of mice and men," etc. Harrison was anxious to show he was an educated man, not an uncouth backwoodsman, so he produced an inaugural address,[2] the longest on record, that took an hour and forty minutes to deliver even after Webster edited it ("I've just killed seventeen Roman proconsuls," he quipped after completing the task). Unfortunately, Harrison also chose to demonstrate his stamina and wore no hat or overcoat for his inauguration and his long speech. A month later, he was dead—having caught a cold, which turned to pneumonia, when a chilly March rain fell on the lengthy ceremony.

That quickly, John Tyler—not even a Whig—was president. Or was he? A "strict constructionist" of the relatively new Constitution, Tyler while a Democrat had served two terms in the House of Representatives—until he found he could no longer stomach what he considered the ruthless regime of Andrew Jackson. In 1832, therefore, Tyler became an independent and was subsequently elected governor of Virginia and U.S. senator from that state. In 1840, the Whigs had given Tyler second place on their national ticket (a less important balance, it seems today, than the alliterative "Tippecanoe and Tyler Too": substituting, say, "Tippecanoe and Webster Too" wouldn't quite have cut it).

In 1841, when Harrison died, the Constitution was silent on the matter of succession; no precedent had been established since all earlier presidents had served full terms. Perhaps because Tyler, a proud and stubborn man, already had been a governor and senator, the Virginian was determined to be president-in-full—not a mere "acting president," as many political and other leaders of the day believed proper and con-

---

[2] Harrison's speech requires six pages of small type, compared to three for James K. Polk, Tyler's successor, and one for John F. Kennedy, in *To the Best of My Ability* (New York: Dorling Kindersley, 2000), pp. 342–353, 431.

stitutional. In their view, another election should be held and a new president elected. (If that wisdom had prevailed, TR and Truman almost certainly never would have been elected, and a victory for LBJ in 1963 or 1964 would have been far from ordained).

Tyler stood his ground, though he was ridiculed in the press as "His Accidency." In effect, he seized the presidency by taking the prescribed presidential oath on April 6, 1841, as soon as he could get to Washington after Harrison's death. Defiantly, he delivered his own inaugural address, shorter than that of the unfortunate Harrison and deceptively concilia-tory to the Whigs. Tyler moved into the White House, too, and began to be president-in-fact—the first for whom bands played "Hail to the Chief."

Congress had not yet achieved the dominance it would exercise in the latter half of the nineteenth century, and possession, as usual, proved to be nine-tenths of the law. Both House and Senate soon passed resolutions recognizing John Tyler as the tenth president. Though a for-mer Democrat elected on an official Whig ticket, he remains the first and only practicing independent to hold that office.

No vice president since Tyler, moreover, has been seriously chal-lenged on his right to succeed to the office after the death of the presi-dent. One can only imagine the commotion Theodore Roosevelt would have created had someone—perhaps the Republican boss, Mark Hanna—tried to break the Tyler precedent by blocking TR from taking the presidency after the assassination of William McKinley in 1901.

"Tyler Too" soon showed that he was a genuine independent and that he would not be a front man for big players like Webster and Clay. He appointed numerous Democrats, and later in 1841 vetoed as unconsti-tutional two bills in which Congress had tried to revive the second Bank of the United States.[3] Clay fumed that His Accidency ought to resign, as he had contradicted the views of his Whig Cabinet and the

---

[3] Andrew Jackson had vetoed the bank in 1832, believing it provided unfair advantages to the wealthy and improperly involved itself in politics.

Whig majority in Congress. Tyler was having none of that—so, instead, his entire Whig cabinet resigned (save Webster, who was busy negotiating a Canadian border treaty with Great Britain). Unmoved, Tyler used recess appointments to dodge Senate confirmation proceedings and replaced all cabinet members within two days (again save Webster, who clung to the State Department until 1843).

Tyler went on to wield the veto so often and so vigorously that a resolution to impeach him was introduced in the House of Representatives—another first in American history. The resolution was backed by former president John Quincy Adams but nevertheless failed, leaving to Andrew Johnson—another former vice president who would rise to the White House owing to the Tyler precedent—the dubious honor of being the first president actually to be impeached (though he was acquitted by the Senate).

Texas, meanwhile, had been an independent republic since the Battle of San Jacinto in 1836. Tyler, a Southerner who was anxious to welcome another slave state, first negotiated a treaty of annexation; the Senate rejected it in June 1844 because Northern states, opposed to the admission of another slave state, blocked the constitutional requirement that a two-thirds majority approve a treaty. Apparently thwarted, Tyler resorted to the kind of political tactic that would not have been pursued by the Northern Whig Harrison: he proposed annexation by a congressional joint resolution requiring only a simple majority in each house.

The annexation resolution became a major issue in the presidential election of 1844—but in that campaign, the parties Tyler had disowned spurned *him*, neither nominating him for reelection. Tyler toyed with running as an independent but gave up the idea when the Democrats—still under the dominance of Andrew Jackson—nominated James K. Polk and included annexation in their platform. Late in the Tyler administration, Congress passed the annexation resolution, offering statehood to Texas.

In October 1845, with Polk in the White House, the Lone Star Republic voted to accept and became the twenty-eighth state (and the fifteenth with legal slavery). The new state, granted no right to secede, later seceded anyway—in 1861, to join the Confederacy. Secession was fiercely opposed by Governor Sam Houston, who for his defiance was promptly removed from office (even though the old hero of San Jacinto had been the first president of the Lone Star Republic).

After leaving the White House in March 1845, John Tyler went home to Virginia. Sixteen years later, he served in the Confederate Congress. His monuments in Washington are at least two: the right of a vice president automatically to become president of the United States after the death of an elected president; and the Texas annexation resolution, conceived and passed on his watch, resulting in the twenty-eighth state. But it might also be noted that this underrated[4] president settled the Maine boundary dispute; extended the Monroe Doctrine, forbidding European colonization, to the Hawaiian islands; and sent the first U.S. trade mission to China.

Texas and the new president, Polk, had a major problem in 1845: Mexico had proposed a treaty to grant Texas its independence and to end the state of war still persisting (bloodily, on occasion) between the two governments—but the offer was good *only if Texas remained independent.* When Texas, instead, accepted American statehood, the proposed treaty became a dead letter and the undeclared Texas war with Mexico continued.

Polk—the most expansionist of American presidents—avidly pursued what he considered his nation's "manifest destiny," and was not satisfied with its tenuous hold on Texas. He offered Mexico $30 million

---

[4] In more ways than one: Tyler also was the first president to marry in the White House; and by two wives he fathered fifteen children, the youngest of whom lived until 1947.

for what is now California, New Mexico, and Arizona. Unwilling to hand over so much of its territory to a bumptious and threatening neighbor, Mexico refused to sell. Then, on May 9, 1846, word reached Polk in Washington of a reported Mexican attack on U.S. forces on April 25. A sort of nineteenth-century Tonkin Gulf incident, the "attack" took place, if it did, on land claimed by both nations (the new state of Texas regarded its border with Mexico as the Rio Grande; Mexico insisted on the Nueces River farther north) and it's no longer clear, if it ever was, who attacked—or at least provoked—whom, or why.

Polk nevertheless asked Congress for a declaration of war, and got it—though U. S. Grant later said the war with Mexico was the least justified the nation ever fought.[5] The South, anxious for more slave states, generally backed the war; for the opposite reason, the North mostly opposed it (including an unknown Illinois congressman named Abraham Lincoln). As it turned out, the United States scored a famous victory—but at the cost of 13,700 dead (mostly from disease) and many wounded, as well as expenditures of at least $97.5 million. Mexican casualties are officially unknown but may well have reached 25,000.

The Treaty of Guadeloupe Hidalgo, signed by the United States and Mexico on February 2, 1848, not only ended this war of conquest but recognized Texas as part of the United States and granted the future "Colossus of the North" all or most of the modern West.[6] For all this, Polk's administration paid $15 million plus the assumption of U.S. citizens' claims against Mexico amounting to another $3.25 million.

Some haul! And all because of a war that might not even have been fought had not John Tyler first insisted on becoming president, then cal-

---

[5] He, Robert E. Lee, Stonewall Jackson, George B. McClellan, and numerous other Civil War luminaries got their first combat experience in Mexico. Jefferson Davis also fought there and carried away a fatally inflated notion of his military expertise.

[6] The Gadsden Purchase of 1853 completed the acquisition, for $10 million, of territory making up much of New Mexico and Arizona today.

culated that Texas could be annexed by majority vote of Congress rather than by a treaty that one-third plus one of the states could block. What if he had dropped the idea of Texas as a state after that proposed treaty failed? What if he had agreed to being only "acting president" for a while, until someone else had been elected to take over? Was it really "manifest destiny" that all of North America between Canada and Mexico sooner or later was to be U.S. territory, no matter who was in the White House?

After that same John Tyler had set his vital precedent, *eight* vice presidents in just over a century succeeded to the presidency upon the death of an elected president: Millard Fillmore following Zachary Taylor; Andrew Johnson after the martyred Lincoln; Chester Arthur upon the assassination of James Garfield ("Chet Arthur President! Good God!" headlined a New York newspaper when the shady old pol took office); TR more than replacing McKinley; Calvin Coolidge taking over for Warren Harding; Truman succeeding FDR; LBJ being sworn in within hours of John F. Kennedy's murder; and Gerald Ford (appointed vice president by Richard Nixon to replace the disgraced Spiro T. Agnew) moving into the White House after Nixon's resignation under threat of impeachment.

Anyone can do the math—nine out of forty-three presidents, up to and including George W. Bush, were vice presidents who succeeded to the office rather than being elected. That's just over a fifth of the total. Most of these "accidental presidents" are more or less forgettable, but the first Roosevelt, Truman, and Lyndon Johnson are among the most significant presidents we have had. What if they had had to win party nominations, then defeat the other party's nominee in a national election? Could any of them have done it?

To these three extraordinary presidents, it may be that we should add Tyler Too—at least for his stout insistence on first taking the path those others later were to tread with such distinction. What if he had not been courageous (or perhaps arrogant) enough to stand up for what he, but few others, considered his rights?

VICTOR DAVIS HANSON

LEW WALLACE AND THE
GHOSTS OF THE SHUNPIKE

Two Roads diverged in a wood, and I—
I took the road less traveled by,
And that has made all the difference.

— ROBERT FROST

You can think of this book as an American Baedeker of roads that could have been, or almost were, taken. But only one career discussed in these pages actually turned on a choice of roads, and ones that did diverge in a wood. The man was Lew Wallace of Indiana, handsome, flashy, self-assured, a showboat, and at thirty-five, the youngest general in the Union Army. The roads led to the battlefield of Shiloh, Tennessee, and the date was April 6, 1862, the first day of what was the most costly battle in American history until that time. By its end, 3,400 Americans on both sides would be dead, out of a total of 22,000 casualties. The battle, which first promised a Union rout, ended a day later as a Union victory, though not the devastating one that it could have been. It came close to destroying the military career of U. S. Grant, who was caught off guard by a massive Confederate attack; Grant survived. But it did effectively end that of Lew Wallace, who was forced to choose between two roads, and chose the wrong one.

Wallace did go on to achieve distinction, though that day in 1862 would haunt him for the rest of his life. He is, of course, most famous as the author of Ben-Hur, the best-selling American novel of the nineteenth century, a book *that would set a cultural trend. In that sense, it may be one of the most important books in our history. "Wallace's apotheosis," Hanson writes, "presaged the twentieth century in its transmogrification of the acclaimed writer to popular icon, a literary celebrity whose fame rested not with book reviews in literary journals, but entirely as a result of popular readership and sales figures—and mostly oblivious to the opinion of intellectuals, academics, and other novelists." He was the first American writer to preach (as someone has written) "from the bully pulpit of best-sellerdom." But if Wallace had taken the right road at Shiloh, would Ben-Hur have been written? Would he have been too busy wrestling with military and political glory? Did the ghosts of the Shunpike and his obsessive sense of injustice in the aftermath of the battle spur him to confront his demons through literature?*

VICTOR DAVIS HANSON is a professor of classics at California State University, Fresno, and the author of fourteen books on subjects ranging from Greek military and rural history to the history of warfare and contemporary agriculture. His most recent books are *The Land Was Everything*, *The Soul of Battle*, *Carnage and Culture*, and the about-to-be published *Ripples of Battle* and *Mexifornia*.

BEN-HUR TURNED OUT to be the most popular work of fiction written in nineteenth-century America. Its aggregate sales were not surpassed until the success of *Gone with the Wind* in the late 1930s. By 1883 it was selling 750 copies a month, by 1886, 4,500. The American publishing industry had never seen anything like it. In a mere nine years the novel had sold 400,000 copies in thirty-six editions and surpassed the phenomenal totals of *Uncle Tom's Cabin*. It was also by far the most requested book in America's public libraries.

A mere ten years after the appearance of *Ben-Hur*, its author, Lew Wallace, was the most successful novelist in the history of America. But the novel would turn out to sell even more rapidly in the next half-century of its publication. A million copies were published by 1911; the next year alone, Sears, Roebuck printed another million copies to sell at thirty-nine cents each in the largest single-year print edition in American history. The last official recorded sales figures in the 1940s put the total copies purchased at somewhere between two and three million; in fact, the true total was probably millions higher. By 1936, *Ben-Hur* had earned the greatest financial returns of any single novel in American history.

Americans were fascinated by Wallace's exotic descriptions of the Holy Land, the singular mission of Ben-Hur to exact revenge, the multicultural milieu of ancient Rome and Jerusalem, and, of course, the message of divine salvation through faith. Even as the Boston Brahmins of the literary elite—James Russell Lowell, Oliver Wendell Holmes, Thomas Bailey Aldrich, and William Dean Howells—snubbed Wallace and scoffed at the amateur's clumsy efforts at fiction, the American public bought the book in droves. For many, it became the first—and only—novel they ever read.

In that regard, *Ben-Hur* marked a radical change in American letters, as millions of Americans for the first time felt that reading fiction was neither sacrilegious nor the sole esoteric pursuit of intellectuals, but was rightly intended for the secular enjoyment and edification of common people. Lew Wallace, as it turned out, introduced more Americans to reading than any other author of the nineteenth century.

The plays and movie versions to follow reached millions more. The stage production alone—requiring thirty tons of machinery with horses and chariots on a treadmill—was performed six thousand times before twenty million Americans, touring almost every major city in the United States during the first two decades of the twentieth century. To this day, *Ben-Hur* has drawn a greater aggregate audience than any dramatic presentation of an American author.

Thousands of derivative books, songs, toys, and ads followed, the popular avalanche only to be surpassed by the (four) motion picture versions to come. Hollywood had seen nothing like the December 1925 release of the long-awaited film starring Ramon Navarro as Ben-Hur, with gigantic sets for the galley battle and chariot race that cost hundreds of thousands of dollars. And while the silent movie set a record of expenditures at over $4 million, it also proved the most lucrative moneymaker in Hollywood's then brief history—earning over $9 million in its first two years.

William Wyler's 1959 monumental remake with Charlton Heston as Ben-Hur (and another 365 speaking roles) was even more successful—nominated for eleven Academy Awards, winning seven (including Best Picture and Best Actor). The panoramic film grossed over $40 million its first year alone; its prime-time television debut in February 1971 (shown over four nights) achieved the highest rating of any movie presented on television up to that time. The Hollywood extravaganzas in turn reignited book sales nearly sixty years after Wallace's death. By

1960, *Ben-Hur* had appeared in over sixty English-language editions—and is selling well in its third century of publication.

Everything from bicycles and cigars to toys and drinks—and even towns—were named Ben-Hur. Chariot racing became an American folk spectacle at rodeos and fairs. The modern idea that historical epics—*Quo Vadis?*, *Spartacus*, or *Gone With the Wind*—can appeal widely to supposedly ahistorical Americans we owe largely to the popularizer Lew Wallace. But more importantly, Wallace's novel began the strange nexus in American life, for good or ill, between literature, motion pictures, advertising, and popular culture. The novel led to the stage and then to the movies, but in the process it spun out entire ancillary industries of songs, skits, ads, clothes, and fan clubs, ensuring that within fifty years of its publication, nearly every American had heard the word "Ben-Hur" without necessarily ever reading the book.

In that sense, *Ben-Hur* prefigures the world of *The Ten Commandments* to *Gladiator* (the latter's movie script is hauntingly similar to Wallace's own play *Commodus*) and established the now predictable evolution of successful novel to movie blockbuster to advertising gold mine to permanent place in the popular folk tradition of America. Wallace's brilliant adventure tale accounts for most of the larger *Ben-Hur*'s mystique—but not quite all. At least some of the novel's inexplicable popularity was due to the tireless plugging of the author himself, who for two decades made it a point to tour, appear in public, give lectures and signings, oversee dramatic adaptations, answer fan letters, and promote his book with influential Americans (like the Shiloh veterans Garfield, Grant, and Sherman) in a frenzied effort to become known, rich—and so perhaps at last taken seriously in wiping away the stain of Shiloh.

While America had long honored its gifted men of letters like Longfellow or Twain, the Wallace phenomenom was something entirely different. Wallace's apotheosis presaged the twentieth century in its transmogrification of the acclaimed writer to popular icon, a literary celebrity whose fame rested not with book reviews in literary journals, but entirely as a result of popular readership and sales figures—and mostly oblivious to the opinion of intellectuals, academics, and other novelists. At his death, Wallace had became a national folk hero, one mobbed by the American public, called on tour for an endless series of *Ben-Hur* lectures, hounded by devoted fan clubs, and canonized by politicians (his likeness sits in Statuary Hall in the Capitol building in Washington). Yet, it had all started four decades earlier in a chance, innocent miscommunication that put Lew Wallace in the wrong place at the wrong time when the eyes of his nation were upon him.

On that long-ago morning, Ulysses S. Grant, on his way up the Tennessee River to the Shiloh battlefield, had stopped to warn General Lew Wallace to be prepared to support a dazed Union Army that had just suffered a brutal surprise dawn attack from some forty thousand Confederates under Albert Sidney Johnston. And when Grant himself finally arrived at Shiloh and saw the state of his crumbling armies, he sent a second, stronger message back to Wallace's reserves at Crump's Landing some time around midmorning: Wallace was now immediately to march his division the six miles south to Shiloh and join the rest of the Union Army of the Tennessee. Grant's orders were not written but transcribed by an aide from his oral communications—a minor lapse for the normally meticulous Grant that would change the course of the battle and American culture for a century to come.

That hurried summons must have reached Wallace sometime around 11:30 in the morning—several hours after his restless men had first heard the firing. Had Wallace departed at once, Grant later surmised, he should have been on line and pouring in critical reinforcements by 2:00 P.M.—at precisely the time that the Northern center and left came under the most intense attack by Johnston. But when Wallace failed to show up on the battlefield in the early afternoon, Grant sent another desperate message, to no avail. He finally dispatched his most trusted subordinates, Colonel McPherson and Captain Rawlins, to ride over and personally escort Wallace along the river road to the killing fields.

But when the two messengers made it back to Grant, they brought back incredible tales of wrong roads, time-consuming countermarching, and cumbersome wagons and caissons. Wallace was no nearer Shiloh than when he had started and thus Grant's battle was about to be lost without the help that was only a few miles distant. It was now near dark, indeed well past 7:00 P.M.; Grant's army was nearly annihilated—and thousands of his critical reserves mysteriously had disappeared a mere few miles from the battlefield. Where exactly had Lew Wallace taken his men?

Grant had reason to be worried. He had been caught unaware at Shiloh. On the morning of April 6 he was miles downstream at his headquarters to the north in Savannah, Tennessee—and without a clue that Johnston's enormous Confederate army had surprised his unprepared divisions. Now his forces had been retreating all day. Nearly half his regiments were no longer in existence. Hundreds of his men were dying. Many were shot down while running away. Rumors circulated that Union soldiers had been bayoneted in their sleep. Without reinforcements he was likely to lose the first great pitched battle of the war in the West—and with it his own future in the Union Army.

Although he had sent word to General Buell on the other side of the Tennessee River to march immediately with his supporting 20,000-man Army of the Ohio, Grant was not convinced that those critical divisions could cover the five miles to the river, be ferried across, and fall in line before his own army collapsed. And an earlier midafternoon advance meeting with a grumpy General Buell had not given him confidence about any salvation from that quarter.

If Buell were to be late with his 20,000 men, Grant would be finished both at Shiloh and for good. So now Grant desperately turned to Lew Wallace, his own division commander, to march the six miles from Crump's Landing and save the tottering Army of the Tennessee.

Yet, Grant had problems with Lew Wallace as well. At thirty-five he was the youngest general in the Union Army. Wallace was a political appointee without much military experience and no formal training at West Point, who nevertheless was enjoying a meteoric career of his own, beginning with proven gallantry at Bull Run. As a major general, in theory he had no real superiors in rank. The dashing Wallace also had a tendency to be theatrical. At Fort Donelson he had magnified his role to reporters and claimed key responsibility for much of Grant's victory. He bragged to his wife, "I saved the whole army from rout." Among the West Point generals, the amateur but cocky Wallace was hardly popular due to his innate talent as well as his self-serving dispatches to reporters, his airs of intellectual superiority—he was said to write and paint—and his hypersensitivity to any perceived slight.

In fact, April 6 would turn out to be the worst day in Lew Wallace's long life. Wallace's Third Division had heard gunfire at daybreak and had been ready to march in that direction for at least two hours prior to Grant's brief appearance. Now it would wait in readiness for *another critical three hours* for further orders—while a mere six miles away, William Tecumseh Sherman's men were being slaughtered. At 11:30, a Captain Baxter, Grant's quartermaster, finally arrived with the anticipated command to move. But for some reason the commands were not signed. Stranger yet, the orders had simply been poorly copied in pencil on lined paper. After asking Baxter a few more details about the murky, unsigned, and transcribed orders, Wallace was wrongly told that the Union forces were "repulsing the enemy"—when, in fact, the entire Union army was in retreat.

It was now nearly noon. Wallace was forced to make a quick decision about these strange ad hoc mandates from his commander. Did his superiors realize that there were not one but *two* roads to Shiloh? True, the one course along the Tennessee River was the quickest to Grant's base at Pittsburg Landing. But it did *not* end up at the "right" of the Union army, where Wallace thought he had been ordered to deploy his reserves. And in many places, that river path was swampy, nearly impassable for wagons and caissons, and indeed sometimes underwater altogether. In contrast, the inland route—the so-called Shunpike—led directly to Sherman's right wing. It was also at least two miles shorter to that destination and a much better road. Wallace himself had previously repaired and reconnoitered it in the weeks before the battle just for the purpose of reinforcing the Union right wing should a crisis arise.

So now Wallace wondered about this vague order that was scrawled on ordinary ruled paper: was he to take the shortest route to Grant's camp or the most direct way to the right wing of Grant's army? Was he to march thousands of men and their guns along a partly submerged road or over a route he had previously corduroyed and knew to be passable? Was he to arrive to join a victorious army in pursuit, as Baxter had (wrongly) implied, or to save a defeated force from annihilation? Which leg of the triangle was he to follow to its base of the Union battle line?

Wallace gave his men a mere half hour to eat. At noon he ordered them to set out to Shiloh along the inland route to join Sherman's right wing: "So, to save the two and three-quarter miles," Wallace wrote of his fatal choice, "and because it was nearer the right and in better condition, I decided to go by the Shunpike." That decision in and of itself changed the life of General Wallace, ensuring that the Union Army could not win the battle outright on the first day—and ultimately that we would have *Ben-Hur*. Had Grant's orders been written, signed, and precise—or had Wallace on his own chosen to take the river route that Grant preferred—Wallace would either have been lauded as a heroic deliverer or relatively ignored as a dutiful subordinate who did what he was told; but either way, he would never have emerged as Shiloh's scapegoat that so changed the latter half of his life.

Be that as it may, in a mere hour and half, the Third Division had covered some five miles, and its advance guard was at last set to cross Owl Creek, a few thousand yards from Sherman's last reported position. In terms of ground covered, he had made much better time than any of General Buell's generals, who were still on the wrong side of the Tennessee River. By 2:00 P.M. Wallace was at last about to send at least five thousand of his men to the Union right, when a dispatch rider galloped up from his rear and said, "General Grant sends his compliments. He would like you to hurry up."

Wallace was dumbfounded. Instead of coming to the rescue of the Union right wing, Wallace was now on the verge of arriving behind the Confederate army. "Fortunately for me," Wallace later recalled of his stunned surprise, "the eclipse of my faculties did not last long, and I was able presently to comprehend that, with my division, *I was actually in rear of the whole Confederate army!*"

Wallace, taken aback, now wondered what to do. In sight of the battlefield, he was without warning ordered to retrace his steps to his original camp miles away and then turn back again to follow a marshy and nearly submerged road. Thousands of Union soldiers were wounded and dying, and Lew Wallace's relief division was no closer to the battlefield than when it had first left hours earlier. Grant's panicky messengers demanded that Wallace now abandon his batteries and march his division the rest of the way on the double to Pittsburg Landing. He refused, insisting that his division must arrive fully armed, in close order, and ready for battle. The panicked envoys McPherson and Rawlins rode back in disgust—and with wild tales of Wallace's incompetence and insubordination. His army was marching in circles.

Wallace finally arrived at the landing in the rain after dark and groped his way through the mess of Union fugitives, wounded, and dead. No one from Grant's staff even met him; he spent most of the night getting his division to the right of Sherman on the Union's last-ditch circumference. His poor men had been forced to march in a near-circle, *over fourteen miles* in a wild-goose chase to arrive late at a battlefield a mere five miles away. His army arrived wet, cold, and in the dark—an object of derision rather than celebration.

At 6:30 A.M. the next morning Wallace's Third Division counterattacked with the rest of the Union Army—his reserve 7,000 soldiers and General Buell's 20,000-man Army of the Ohio meant that Grant's army had suddenly doubled in size. Indeed, it now outnumbered the tired and decimated Confederates by two to one. Wallace performed adequately on the second day, although his exhausted troops, not pitted against the main resistance, suffered only 41 killed and 251 wounded in the steady Union counterattack.

On the evening of the seventh, with the retreat of the Confederate Army, Wallace, as he had at Fort Donelson, once more proclaimed himself a near-hero. After all, he and Buell had purportedly turned the tide, lost few men, and chased the rebels off the battlefield. The mix-up on the day before was quickly forgotten: the now victorious Union Army no doubt would now chase General Beauregard's defeated army back to Corinth and then storm the city, opening all of Mississippi to the advance of a huge force of nearly 100,000 troops. Two days after battle, he was near ecstatic and wrote his wife, "My whole command behaved like heroes, never yielding an inch."

Wallace made no efforts to hide his pride, predicting a quick pursuit, and with the destruction of the fleeing Confederates an early end to the Civil War itself. Yet four days after the battle ended, a strange sequence of events began to unfold that would destroy Wallace's career—and create the conditions for the writing and remarkable sales of *Ben-Hur*. Indeed, within weeks of Shiloh the purported hero would find himself in disgrace and removed of command. The once small ripples of the missed road were suddenly crashing as storm waves upon an outraged nation—and poor Lew Wallace was now in the center of the hurricane.

Wallace's disaster perhaps began on April 12, with the arrival of punctilious General Halleck. The latter relegated Grant from active control of the Army of the Tennessee, apparently on grounds that Grant had been negligently surprised at Shiloh. As the new commanding officer of all Western forces, the bookish Halleck was at last ready to lead from the field.

At first, the plodding Halleck disingenuously boasted that he had been the mastermind of the entire western campaign and tried to take credit for the strategic victory of Shiloh. Then he faulted Grant for the high casualties of April 6, only to waste nearly seven weeks in moving his ponderous army a mere thirty miles to Corinth—to find the Confederate Army long gone and the city largely deserted. What was won at Shiloh by Grant was thrown away by Halleck in the days that followed. Someone or something would now be needed to explain to a nation how a victory that had cost thousands in casualties had not led to the destruction of a beaten and retreating Confederate army.

Demanding that his generals erect breastworks and fortifications each night, the jittery Halleck often made less than a mile's progress a day—a slow-moving Albert Sidney Johnston had covered the same distance from Corinth to Shiloh in the April rains in little more than three days. The dawdling Union pursuit, the escape of the defeated Confederate army, the inexplicable removal of a popular Grant, the mounting criticism of the dilatory Halleck, the final tallying of the horrific Union losses at Shiloh—12,217 casualties with over 1,700 killed—all set the stage for months of controversy and mutual recriminations as Shiloh was reexamined as no American battle before. The press and the war department in Washington seemed to forget that Shiloh was a tactical victory and a strategic bonanza; instead both demanded heads for the appalling losses and the escape of the defeated Confederates.

Shiloh would have been seen as nothing novel by summer 1864, but in spring 1862 the very idea of well over ten thousand casualties in a single engagement was appalling to the Northern populace and demanded punitive measures. Had Halleck destroyed the vulnerable retreating Confederates, the mistakes of April 6 would have been forgotten; instead, the Northern public gradually was told that its youth had been butchered without a sure victory or indeed much change in the strategic picture in the west at large. The dominos that would lead to *Ben Hur* were now lined up and began falling in earnest.

The mounting tension between Halleck and Grant would soon make Wallace's own position nearly untenable. After Halleck's laggard generalship eventually led to his transfer back east in midsummer, Grant was returned to command of the western theater—with the endorsement of Lincoln ("I can't spare this man, he fights"). Although Grant had survived Halleck's efforts to sabotage his career, he was nevertheless still shocked by the fury of public criticism of his conduct at Shiloh among the Northern press and politicians. Especially galling were the often wild charges that he had been absent from the battlefield when the shooting started, may well have been drunk, was completely surprised, had ordered no entrenchments, and thus was responsible for the first day's shocking casualties.

In reaction, Grant slowly directed his wrath onto Wallace and subtly began to suggest a scenario that might account for the near fiasco of the first day: had his orders only been followed by Wallace, the Union losses were entirely avoidable. Seven thousand reinforcements should have arrived by 2:00 to 3:00 P.M. at the latest. Their surprise appearance would have stopped the Confederate onslaught cold. General Buell's help would not have been all that necessary. If any general was responsible for the shocking butchery, perhaps it was the young, amateur, flamboyant—and completely lost—Lew Wallace, not himself.

Contradicting his first official report written on April 9 that had praised Generals McClernand and Wallace—both "had maintained their places with credit to themselves and the cause"—most of Grant's numerous later accounts of the battle painted a damning portrait of Wallace's earlier incompetence. In fact, Grant claimed that he had ordered Wallace to move at 11 A.M., not 11:30—and not once but three times. While his official orders were not written but copied by a messenger, his own staff could "vouch" that he had expressly commanded the use of the river route. Furthermore, common sense should have convinced anyone that a Union general in earshot of the fighting should not have marched in circles for seven hours to cover a mere five miles. Grant's final account of the battle, reiterated with some slight qualification in his memoirs two decades later, would add to Wallace's undoing.

General Lew Wallace never recovered from the ignominy of Shiloh nor did he regain Grant's confidence. Although Wallace would later play a key role in the defense of Cincinnati, assume the influential military command of Maryland, help defend Washington from Jubal Early's raid of July 1864 at the critical Battle of Monocacy, and serve on commissions investigating everything from Lincoln's assassination to the Confederate prison wardens at Andersonville, he could not and would not let go of Shiloh. Before April 6, he had been a rising star and a savior of Union lives; after the battle he was unfairly discredited and blamed for thousands of dead Americans.

Take away Shiloh and Lew Wallace would have ended the war as one of two dozen or so revered Union war generals with political and business offers aplenty that would have ensured a comfortable and probably nondescript life. But receive an ambiguous order, take a different road, arrive hours late, get on the wrong side of Halleck and Grant—add that up and the combined ingredients equal a ruined career and the frantic lifelong effort to rectify what should not have ever happened and yet could never be changed.

We shall never know exactly what transpired on the first day at Shiloh. But the preponderance of evidence, both written records and drawn from later interviews, in fact, favors much of Wallace's account. Most likely, Grant sent an unclear order through an aide, without specifying the exact route of advance. He was also probably both ignorant of the Shunpike route and then became so immersed in the chaos of the Union disaster that he felt no need—and had no time—for specifics. The more reflective and occasionally fussy Wallace at the rear logically assumed that he was to take the shorter inland road to arrive at Sherman's right. Perhaps he also entertained private hopes that his sudden appearance on his "secret" road might surprise the Confederates and gain him renown. In any case, Grant should have ordered Wallace to march much earlier in the day and should have given him precise written orders about the direction and purpose of his mission. Failing that, his aides should have allowed Wallace's veteran division in transit to enter the battlefield from the Shunpike and hit the Confederates from the rear. Any of those scenarios would have saved Wallace's career.

Lew Wallace would live for another forty-three years after Shiloh. He became heavily involved in Mexican politics, served as a territorial governor of New Mexico, and was appointed by President Garfield, another Shiloh veteran, as United States minister to the Ottoman court at Constantinople—good, though minor, appointments for someone young like Wallace whose pre-Shiloh ascendancy had been dazzling. Yet throughout his long and near storybook career—he dealt on numerous occasions with Billy the Kid, the Apache renegade Victorio, and Abdulhamid Khan II, the sultan of the Ottoman Empire—Wallace continued his obsession with Shiloh, all the more desperately so as his chief nemesis, Ulysses S. Grant, grew in stature from general of the Army to president of the United States. In some sense, Lew Wallace's entire life between 1862 and 1905 is a chronicle of his efforts to exorcise the ghost of the Shunpike.

Wallace himself visited the battlefield almost every year. In 1903, just two years before his death, he made a final journey to inspect the official commemoration and monuments, urging changes in the manner in which his march was presented in the official guide and tourist literature. Earlier he had vehemently lobbied the Shiloh National Military Park Commission to adopt all his own maps and reports as the basis for the park guide sold to visitors. But for all Wallace's frantic efforts in his last years to set the record straight to generations of Americans, his diplomatic and government posts in themselves never allowed him either the power, much less the money, to regain his good name.

Instead, it would be his writing career, not high government service or political patronage, that would restore his reputation to the American public in a way that all his impassioned briefs and pamphlets, his obsequious letters and visits to Grant, and his continual tours of Shiloh could not. His disaster at Shiloh had spurred the disconsolate Wallace to vent through writing. And he was not just to write but to publish what he had written—and to publish with the intent that thousands of Americans would read what he wrote and at last know who he really was.

Wallace turned out to be quite prolific, publishing dozens of poems, articles, plays, and novels, among them two moderately successful epics, *The Fair God* (1873), which retold the historian William Prescott's story of the Spanish conquest of Mexico, and *The Prince of India* (1893), a swashbuckling account surrounding the conquest of Constantinople. But Lew Wallace is not associated with either novel, which are now rarely read, or even with his ambiguous role at Shiloh. Rather he is known solely as the author of *Ben-Hur*—and thus the creator of the entire *Ben-Hur* popular phenomenon that has swept America since the novel's first appearance in 1880.

What was the exact connection between Shiloh and *Ben-Hur?* There were, of course, the superficial influences of the battle upon the novelist Wallace. The fighting experiences of Shiloh's second day proved critical in the writing of Ben-Hur's martial and equestrian excellence. Many characters in the novel mirror Wallace's own interests in battle tactics, the intricacies and jealousies of military command, and the thrill of leading men into combat.

Wallace may have written of the leper colonies endured by Ben-Hur's mother and sister out of his own horror of briefly running a detainee center after his removal from command, and then serving on the board of inquiry over the horrendous conditions in the Confederate prison at Andersonville. And by his own admission, Wallace claimed that a debate with an old Shiloh acquaintance, the agnostic Colonel Robert G. Ingersoll, prompted him to explore the idea of presenting through *Ben-Hur* a counterdefense of Christianity. President Garfield, another veteran of Shiloh, wrote Wallace an ecstatic fan letter of thanks, which had the effect of markedly increasing sales: "With this beautiful and reverent book you have lightened the burden of my daily life—and renewed our acquaintance which began at Shiloh." A facsimile of that letter was wisely used as a frontispiece to the famous 1891 "Garfield" edition of *Ben-Hur,* which became the most successful and expensive two-volume set of any novel in nineteenth-century America.

Far more importantly, in some sense the entire plot of *Ben-Hur: A Tale of the Christ* eerily resembles much of Wallace's own sad odyssey following that disaster of April 6, 1862. For all its subplots revolving around Christ, *Ben-Hur* is mostly the saga of a young, brilliant Jewish hero whose entire life is devoted to seeking revenge for an injustice done him and his family—by a friend who knew better and would benefit from this duplicity.

Judah Ben-Hur, a prosperous Jewish aristocrat, while watching from his veranda a triumphal procession below, accidentally loosens a roof tile that nearly kills Gratus—the ancient Grant?—the Roman procurator of Judea. In response, the evil Roman official Messala conspires to turn the misfortune into an "assassination" attempt, thereby condemning Judah Ben-Hur to the galleys, and his mother and sister to the dungeons. At one low point, Ben-Hur philosophizes, "Death was preferable to shame; and believe me, I pray, it is so yet." Before his final acceptance of Christ, Ben-Hur is presented as a volatile and crestfallen hero, desperate at any cost to regain his lost reputation: "The face gave back nothing to mar its youthful comeliness—nothing of accusation or sullenness or menace, only the signs that a great sorrow long borne imprints as time mellows the surface of pictures."

Because of this blow of fate (the loose roof tile turns out every bit as disastrous to Ben-Hur as the missed road was to Wallace, and the ancient Gratus, like the contemporary Grant, was nearly ruined by the innocent accident of a young protagonist), the hero suffers a series of horrors and indignities, until he proves his mettle in a sea battle and so regains his freedom. Wealth—he becomes one of the richest men in the Roman Empire—and fame follow. And at last he triumphs over all his enemies and gets his revenge on his rival Messala—only at the climax of his ordeal to accept the power of Christ through witnessing the Crucifixion. The novel ends with Ben-Hur's determination to devote his life and treasure to Christianity, by rejecting the power and authority of Rome and its grasping and amoral politicos. Throughout the narrative,

Rome's ruling elite appear arrogant, predatory, conniving, and imperialistic—in many ways analogous to Wallace's own experience with high American officials in the aftermath of Shiloh.

Far more importantly, however, *Ben-Hur* was not just an allegory of Shiloh and its principal characters; Wallace's own sense of injustice following the battle may well also have been the larger catalyst for his writing career. Even after the conclusion of Wallace's successful tenure as minister to the Ottoman Empire and when sales of *Ben-Hur* were reaching unbelievable levels, Wallace could still write in 1885 that his wildly successful fiction had almost eclipsed the setback of Shiloh: "I have letters from publishers on both sides of the sea, and so, may the end of life be swift or slow, I may be found at this work. Into such pleasant life but one hurt—the old wound at Shiloh."

An exasperated Wallace also wrote his wife in 1885 that the fame of *Ben-Hur* had almost trumped the ignominy of Shiloh: "Shiloh and its slanders! Will the world ever acquit me of them? If I were guilty I would not feel them so keenly. Ending by finding solace in *Ben Hur*, I can bear it." He added, "I have a reputation in another sphere sufficient to keep me afloat." Even in 1900, thirty-eight years after the battle, Wallace could still lament, "That awful mystery known as the Battle of Pittsburg Landing comes home more directly than to most of those engaged in it. O, the lies, the lies that were told to make me the scapegoat to bear off the criminal mistakes of others . . . Think of what I suffered."

By intent, Wallace constantly used his fame as the author of *Ben-Hur* to reopen the old wounds of Shiloh. Well into his seventies he requested that the Society of the Army of the Tennessee reexamine the forty-year-old controversy of the Shunpike march; he sought to obtain a military commission during the Spanish-American War that might bring him final military renown to absolve the old charges; and he persisted in sending copies of his acclaimed fiction to aged officers like Generals Garfield, Grant, Howard, Hayes, and Sherman, so that they might in turn finish their memoirs with favorable assessments of Wallace's march at Shiloh.

The eerie connection between the road not taken and the creation of a cultural icon raises a number of counterfactual questions. If Lew Wallace had taken Grant's river road and arrived in Grant's midst at 2:00 P.M., the arrival of his 7,000 fresh troops might have stanched the Union wound and saved hundreds of Union lives. Such a timely arrival—Wallace had only about a third the number of reserves as Buell's much larger army across the river—would not have won the battle outright, but it would have ensured a stalemate rather than a near rout, letting Grant off the hook and dispelling the image that only the later midnight arrival of the Army of the Ohio had saved the Union.

While a prompt Wallace would not have been the hero of Shiloh, he at least would not have been condemned as the scapegoat of the battle. And without the disgrace of Shiloh—nothing was more injurious to Wallace's sizable ego than the charge that he was not only timid but incompetent—much of his restlessness, desperate energy, and self-promotion that were essential to the writing, publication, and sales of *Ben-Hur* would have been absent. Wallace's own personal tragedy and his obsessive sense of personal injury were the catalysts for the dramatic fall and rise of Judah Ben-Hur—a gripping autobiographical drama absent not only in Wallace's other rather mediocre and now forgotten novels but also in most fiction written during the era.

So the ordeal of the horrific battle and the mere insinuation that such a proud and talented man like Wallace might have been responsible for needless casualties were the continual nightmares of Wallace's subsequent life—and these demons finally found their way in their entirety into one of his novels and through it the hearts of millions of Americans for the next century. The road not taken not only accounts for why a disgraced Wallace wrote fiction, rather than enjoying later acclaim in politics and an easy retirement won through a spotless service record as major general—but also why today we read or view the passionate *Ben-Hur*, and not the wooden *The Fair God* and *The Prince of India*. So, had Grant written his orders down, and had they arrived promptly to Wallace's headquarters, then Wallace would have led a happier but little-known life—and we would all be the poorer for it.

Such were the strange wages of the missed road on April 6, 1862. If today most Americans are ignorant of Lew Wallace, it is equally true—and perhaps just as regrettable—that they are far more likely to know something of his *Ben-Hur* than anything at all of the battle of Shiloh. "My God!" Wallace remarked in 1899 when first examining the stage sets to *Ben-Hur*, "Did I set all this in motion?" He did—but Shiloh had as well.

JAMES M. McPHERSON

IF THE LOST ORDER HADN'T BEEN LOST:

Robert E. Lee Humbles the Union, 1862

One of the focal moments of the American Civil War, as well as a deserved staple of counterfactual history, is the finding of Robert E. Lee's Special Orders No. 191—the legendary "Lost Order." In September 1862, Lee's Confederate Army of Northern Virginia was in the process of crossing into Maryland, on their way to Pennsylvania. He had just battered Union forces at the Second Manassas; one more big victory might bring the Confederacy official British and French recognition. The Special Order, which he dispatched to his various commanders, was his operational plan for the fall campaign. On the morning of September 13, an Indiana corporal named Barton W. Mitchell discovered in a cloverfield a bulky envelope containing three cigars and a copy of Lee's orders. The "Lost Order" was bucked up to Lee's Union opposite, General George B. McClellan. (Somewhere along the way, the cigars disappeared.) McClellan was offered a golden opportunity to divide and conquer the widely spread Confederate forces. But he frittered it away. The result was the bloodiest day of the Civil War: the Battle of Antietam—a narrow win on points for the Union but not the war-ending victory it might have been.

So much for the facts. Now for the speculation. Let us assume, as James M. McPherson does here, that the Lost Order was not lost. Lee very likely would have continued north, all but unchallenged, and military logic tells us that in the Cumberland Valley of Pennsylvania a vast battle would have taken place. Where would it have been fought? McPherson has an answer equally logical—but hardly promising for the continued existence of the United States as one nation.

JAMES M. McPHERSON is not just an expert on the Civil War but one of the finest historians writing today. He is professor of American history at Princeton University and the author of more than ten books, including *Battle Cry of Freedom*, which won the Pulitzer Prize in History, and his latest, *Crossroads of Freedom: Antietam*.

GREAT POSSIBILITIES RODE with the Army of Northern Virginia as it began to cross the Potomac at a ford thirty-five miles upriver from Washington on September 4, 1862. Since taking command of this army three months earlier, General Robert E. Lee had halted the momentum of Union victory that had seemed imminent in May. At that time, the Army of the Potomac had stood only five miles from Richmond, poised to capture the Confederate capital. Coming on top of a series of Northern military successes during the previous four months, which had gained control of one hundred thousand square miles of Confederate territory in western Virginia, Tennessee, the Mississippi Valley, and elsewhere, the fall of Richmond might well have toppled the Confederacy. But Lee launched a series of counteroffensives that turned the war around. His troops drove Union forces back from Richmond in the Seven Days' Battles (June 25–July 1) and then shifted the action to northern Virginia, where they won the battles of Cedar Mountain (August 9), Second Manassas (August 29–30), and Chantilly (September 1). Dispirited Union troops retreated to the defenses of Washington to lick their wounds.

This startling reversal caused Northern morale to plummet. "The feeling of despondency is very great," wrote a prominent New York Democrat after the Seven Days' Battles. His words were echoed by a New York Republican, who recorded in his diary "the darkest day we have seen since [First] Bull Run . . . Things look disastrous . . . I find it hard to maintain my lively faith in the triumph of the nation and the law." Reacting to this decline in Northern spirits, President Abraham Lincoln lamented privately: "It seems unreasonable that a series of successes, extending through half a year, and clearing more than a hundred thousand square miles of country, should help us so little, while a single half-defeat [the Seven Days' Battles] should hurt us so much."

Unreasonable or not, it was a fact. The peace wing of the Democratic party stepped up its attacks on Lincoln's policy of trying to restore the Union by war. Branded by Republicans as disloyal "Copperheads," the Peace Democrats insisted that Northern armies could never conquer the South and that the government should seek an armistice and peace negotiations. Confederate military success in the summer of 1862 boosted the credibility of such arguments. And worse was yet to come for the Lincoln administration. Western Confederate armies, which had been defeated in every campaign and battle from January to June 1862, regrouped during July and carried out a series of cavalry raids and infantry offensives in August and September that produced a stunning reversal of momentum in that theater as well. As the Army of Northern Virginia splashed across the Potomac into Maryland, Confederate armies in Tennessee launched a two-pronged counteroffensive that not only reconquered the eastern half of that state but also moved into Kentucky, captured the capital at Frankfort, and prepared to inaugurate a Confederate governor there.

Rather than give up and negotiate a peace, however, Lincoln and the Republican Congress acted dramatically to intensify the war. Lincoln called for three hundred thousand more three-year volunteers. Congress passed a militia act that required the states to produce a specified number of nine-month militia and impose a draft to make up any deficiency in a state's quota. The same day (July 17), Lincoln signed a confiscation act that provided for the freeing of slaves owned by disloyal (i.e., Confederate) masters.

Southern states had seceded and gone to war to defend slavery. Slaves constituted the principal labor force in the Southern economy. Thousands of slaves built fortifications, hauled supplies, and performed fatigue labor for Confederate armies. From the outset, radical Republicans had urged a policy of emancipation to strike a blow at the heart of the rebellion and to convert the slaves' labor power and military manpower from a Confederate to a Union asset.

By the summer of 1862, Lincoln had come to agree with this position. But so far as possible, the president wanted to keep the emancipation issue under his own control. On July 22, he informed the cabinet that he had decided to use his war powers as commander in chief to seize enemy property to issue an emancipation proclamation. Emancipation, said Lincoln, had become "a military necessity, absolutely essential to the preservation of the Union. We must free the slaves or be ourselves subdued. . . . Decisive and extensive measures must be adopted. . . . The slaves [are] undoubtedly an element of strength to those who [have] their service, and we must decide whether that element should be with us or against us." Most of the cabinet agreed, but Secretary of State William H. Seward advised postponement of the proclamation "until you can give it to the country supported by military success." Otherwise the world might view it "as the last measure of an exhausted government, a cry for help . . . our last *shriek*, on the retreat."

This advice persuaded Lincoln to put the proclamation in a drawer to await a more favorable military situation. Unfortunately, it deteriorated further as enemy armies began their invasions of Maryland and Kentucky, two border states that seemed ripe for Confederate plucking. Northern morale continued to fall. "The nation is rapidly sinking just now," wrote a New York diarist. "Stonewall Jackson (our national bugaboo) about to invade Maryland, 40,000 strong. General advance of the rebel line threatening our hold on Missouri and Kentucky. . . . Disgust with our present government is certainly universal."

Democrats hoped to capitalize on this disgust in the upcoming congressional elections. Republicans feared the prospect. "After a year and a half of trial," wrote one, "and a pouring out of blood and treasure, and the maiming and death of thousands, we have made no sensible progress in putting down the rebellion . . . and the people are desirous of some change." The Republican majority in the House was vulnerable. Even the normal loss of seats in off-year elections might eliminate this majority.

And 1862 was scarcely a normal year. With Confederate invaders in the border states, the Democrats seemed sure of gaining control of the House on their platform of an armistice and peace negotiations.

Robert E. Lee was well aware of this possibility. It was one of the factors that prompted his decision to invade Maryland despite the poor physical and logistical condition of his army after ten weeks of constant marching and fighting that had produced thirty-five thousand Confederate casualties and thousands of stragglers. "The present posture of affairs," Lee wrote to Jefferson Davis on September 8 from his headquarters near Frederick, Maryland, "places it in [our] power . . . to propose [to the U.S. government] the recognition of our independence." Such a "proposal of peace," Lee pointed out, "would enable the people of the United States to determine at their coming elections whether they will support those who favor a prolongation of the war, or those who wish to bring it to a termination."

Lee did not mention in this letter the foreign-policy implications of his invasion. But he and Davis were aware of those as well. The much-anticipated "cotton famine" had finally begun to have a serious impact on the British and French textile industries. An end to the war would reopen foreign trade and bring a renewed flow of cotton from the South. Powerful leaders and a large part of the public in both countries sympathized with the Confederacy. The French emperor, Napoléon III, flirted with diplomatic recognition of the Confederacy but was unwilling to take the initiative without British cooperation.

When the war had seemed to be going in the North's favor during the first half of 1862, foreign governments backed off from any overt dealings with the Confederacy. When news of the Seven Days' Battles reached Paris, however, Napoléon instructed his foreign minister to *"Demandez au gouvernement anglais s'il ne croît pas le moment venu de reconnaître le Sud."* ("Ask the English government if it does not believe the time has come to recognize the South.")

British sentiment seemed to be moving in this direction. The United States consul in Liverpool reported that "we are in more danger of intervention than we have been at any previous period . . . They are all against us and would rejoice at our downfall." The Confederate envoy in London, James Mason, anticipated "intervention speedily in some form." The news of Second Manassas and the invasions of Maryland and Kentucky gave added impetus to the Confederate cause abroad. Britain's chancellor of the exchequer, in a speech at Newcastle in October, declared, "Jefferson Davis and other leaders of the South have made an army; they are making, it appears, a navy; and they have made what is more than either; they have made a nation."

More cautious, Prime Minister Viscount Palmerston and Foreign Minister Lord John Russell nevertheless discussed a concrete proposal for Britain and France to offer to mediate an end to the war on the basis of Confederate independence—if Lee's invasion of Maryland brought another Confederate victory. Union forces "got a complete smashing" at Second Manassas, wrote Palmerston to Russell on September 14, "and it seems not all together unlikely that still greater disasters await them, and that even Washington or Baltimore may fall into the hands of the Confederates. If this should happen, would it not be time for us to consider whether in such a state of things England and France might not address the contending parties and recommend an arrangement on the basis of separation?" Russell responded three days later, concurring in the proposal for mediation "with a view to the recognition of the Independence of the Confederates." If the North refused, then "we ought ourselves to recognize the Southern States as an independent State."

The Lincoln administration was acutely sensitive to the political and diplomatic dangers posed by Lee's invasion. But the military crisis had to be dealt with first. The Union army that fought and lost Second Manassas (Second Bull Run) was an ill-matched amalgam of troops from Major General John Pope's Army of Virginia, Major General Ambrose Burnside's IX Corps transferred from North Carolina, and parts of Major General George B. McClellan's Army of the Potomac transferred from the Virginia Peninsula. There was no love lost between Pope and McClellan, who was sulking because of the withdrawal from the peninsula and who considered himself unjustly persecuted by the administration. McClellan dragged his feet about sending troops to Pope's aid, and two of his strongest corps, within hearing of the guns along Bull Run, never made it to the battlefield.

Lincoln considered McClellan's behavior "unpardonable"; a majority of the cabinet wanted to cashier the general. But Lincoln also recognized McClellan's organizational skills and the extraordinary hold he had on the affections of his soldiers. Lincoln therefore gave McClellan command of all the Union troops in this theater, with instructions to meld them into the Army of the Potomac and go after the rebels. To cabinet members who protested, Lincoln conceded that McClellan had "acted badly in this matter," but "he has the Army with him . . . We must use what tools we have. There is no man in the Army who can lick these troops of ours into shape half as well as he . . . If he can't fight himself, he excels in making others ready to fight."

McClellan confirmed both Lincoln's confidence and his lack of confidence. A junior officer wrote that when the men in the ranks learned of McClellan's restoration to command, "from extreme sadness we passed in a twinkling to a delirium of delight . . . Men threw their caps in the air, and danced and frolicked like schoolboys . . . The effect of this man's presence upon the Army of the Potomac . . . was electrical, and too wonderful to make it worthwhile attempting to give a reason for it." McClellan did reorganize the army and "lick it into shape" in a remarkably short time, making it "ready to fight." But then he reverted to his wonted caution, estimating enemy strength in Maryland at two or three times Lee's actual numbers and moving north at a snail's pace of six miles a day as if he were afraid of finding rebels.

McClellan clamored for reinforcements, particularly the 12,000-man garrison at Harpers Ferry. But General in Chief Henry W. Halleck refused to release these troops. That refusal created both a problem and an opportunity for Lee. The garrison threatened his line of supply through the Shenandoah Valley. So on September 9, Lee drafted Special Orders No. 191 for the dispatch of almost two-thirds of his army in three widely separated columns under the overall command of Jackson to converge on Harpers Ferry and capture it. The opportunity: a large supply of artillery, rifles, ammunition, provisions, shoes, and clothing for his ragged, shoeless, hungry troops. The problem: McClellan might get between the separated parts of his army during the three to six days it would take to carry out the operation and destroy the fragments of the Army of Northern Virginia in detail.

But two of Lee's hallmarks as a commander were his uncanny ability to judge an opponent's qualities and his willingness to take great risks. To Brigadier General John G. Walker, commander of one of the columns to converge on Harpers Ferry, Lee explained the purpose and plan of his campaign. After capturing the garrison and its supplies, the army would reconcentrate near Hagerstown. "A few days' rest will be of great service to our men," Lee said. "I hope to get shoes and clothing for the most needy. But the best of it will be that the short delay will enable us to get up our stragglers," who from exhaustion, hunger, and lack of shoes had not been able to keep up with the army. Lee believed that there were "not less than eight to ten thousand of them between here and Rapidan Station"—a fairly accurate estimate. When they rejoined the army and were resupplied, Lee intended to tear up the Baltimore and Ohio Railroad and then move to Harrisburg and destroy the Pennsylvania Railroad bridge over the Susquehanna, thus severing the Union's two eastwest rail links. "After that," Lee concluded, "I can turn my attention to Philadelphia, Baltimore, or Washington, as may seem best for our interests."

Walker expressed astonishment at the breathtaking boldness of this plan, which would leave the Union army at his rear. "Are you acquainted with General McClellan?" Lee responded. "He is an able general but a very cautious one . . . His army is in a very demoralized and chaotic condition and will not be prepared for offensive operations—or he will not think it so—for three or four weeks. Before that time I hope to be on the Susquehanna."

Even as Lee was offering these observations, however, his adversary had an extraordinary stroke of luck. On September 13, two Union soldiers resting in a field near Frederick, where the Confederates had camped a few days earlier, found a copy of Lee's Special Orders No. 191 wrapped around three cigars where they had been lost by a careless Southern officer. Recognizing their importance, the Yankee soldiers took them to their captain, who forwarded them up the chain of command until they reached McClellan. A Union staff officer vouched for the genuineness of the document, for he had known Lee's adjutant, Robert H. Chilton, in the prewar army and recognized his handwriting.

The orders gave McClellan a picture of the division of Lee's army into five parts, each at least eight or ten miles from any other while the most widely separated units were thirty miles apart with the Potomac River between them. No Civil War general ever had a better chance to destroy an enemy army in detail before it could reunite. To one of his subordinates, a jubilant McClellan declared: "Here is a paper with which if I cannot whip 'Bobbie Lee,' I will be willing to go home."

As usual, however, McClellan moved cautiously. He did drive Confederate defenders away from the South Mountain passes on September 14. But Harpers Ferry fell to Jackson on the fifteenth and Lee was able to concentrate most of the Army of Northern Virginia near Sharpsburg before McClellan was ready to attack on September 17. After an all-day battle along the ridges above Antietam Creek, Lee was compelled to retreat across the Potomac on the night of September 18. Without the discovery of the lost orders, perhaps even this limited Union victory would not have occurred.

The odds against the sequence of events that led to the loss and finding and verification of these orders must have been a million to one. Much more in line with the laws of probability is something like the following scenario. Knowing that most residents of western Maryland were Unionists, Lee imposed tighter security on the army than when in friendly Virginia, to prevent penetration of his camps by any local civilians who hung around the edge and undoubtedly included several spies among their number. Lee instructed his adjutant to deliver Special

Orders No. 191 directly to the relevant corps and division commanders. They were to read them in Chilton's presence and commit them to memory, after which all copies of the orders were burned except one, which Lee kept in his possession. In this way there could be no leaks.

Because of an inept defense of Harpers Ferry by its Union commander, Dixon Miles, and because of McClellan's failure to advance rapidly, the garrison surrendered 12,000 men and mountains of supplies to Jackson on September 15. Meanwhile, Jeb Stuart's cavalry performed outstanding service, bringing up stragglers and guarding the passes through the South Mountain range against the ineffectual probes of Union horsemen trying to discover the whereabouts of Lee's main force. On September 16, McClellan arrived at Frederick, which the rebels had vacated a week earlier. By then Lee had reconcentrated his army at Hagerstown. Thousands of stragglers had rejoined the ranks, and thanks to the captures at Harpers Ferry, the Army of Northern Virginia was well equipped for the first time in two months.

After a further pause for rest, while McClellan remained in the dark about Lee's location and intentions, the rebels moved north into Pennsylvania. They brushed aside local militia and the outriders of Union cavalry who finally located them. Spreading through the rich farmland of Pennsylvania's Cumberland Valley like locusts, Lee's army—now 55,000 strong—was able to feed itself better than it had in Virginia. On October 1, the van reached Carlisle. Lee sent a strong detachment of cavalry and part of Jackson's swift-marching infantry twenty miles farther to the railroad bridge at Harrisburg, which they burned on October 3. The Confederate commander also sent his Maryland scouts back into their home state to locate the Army of the Potomac. They found it near Emmitsburg, just south of the Pennsylvania border, marching northward with a determined speed that suggested McClellan finally meant to find Lee and fight him.

Those scouts also reported to Lee that they had discovered a series of hills and ridges around a town named Gettysburg where numerous roads converged, enabling an army to concentrate there quickly and fortify

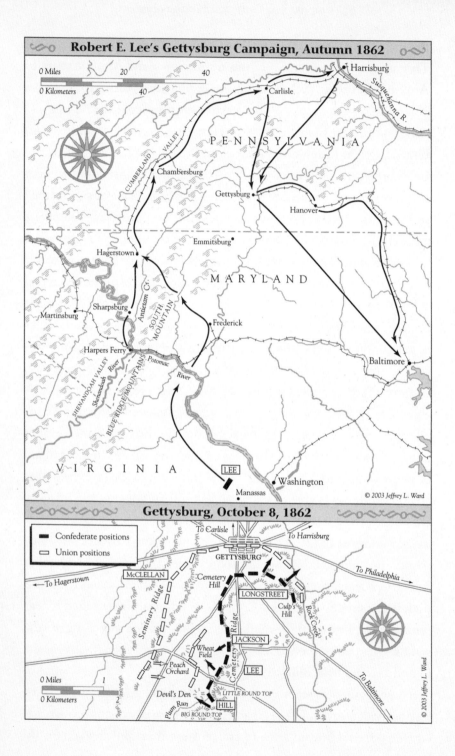

Robert E. Lee's Gettysburg Campaign, Autumn 1862

0 Miles 20 40
0 Kilometers 40

Harrisburg

Susquehanna R.

Carlisle

P E N N S Y L V A N I A

CUMBERLAND VALLEY

Chambersburg

Gettysburg

Hanover

Hagerstown

Emmitsburg

M A R Y L A N D

Martinsburg

Sharpsburg

Antietam Cr.

SOUTH MOUNTAIN

Frederick

Harpers Ferry

Potomac River

River

Baltimore

SHENANDOAH VALLEY

Shenandoah River

BLUE RIDGE MOUNTAINS

V I R G I N I A

LEE

Washington

Manassas

© 2003 Jeffrey L. Ward

Gettysburg, October 8, 1862

■ Confederate positions
□ Union positions

To Carlisle

To Harrisburg

GETTYSBURG

To Philadelphia

To Hagerstown

McCLELLAN

Cemetery Hill

Seminary Ridge

LONGSTREET

Culp's Hill

Rock Creek

JACKSON

Wheat Field

Cemetery Ridge

LEE

Peach Orchard

To Baltimore

0 Miles 1
0 Kilometers 2

Devil's Den

Plum Run

LITTLE ROUND TOP

HILL

BIG ROUND TOP

© 2003 Jeffrey L. Ward

the high ground. On October 4 Lee ordered his army to Gettysburg. They arrived there only hours before the enemy, and by October 6 the Army of Northern Virginia was dug in on the hills south of town.

McClellan came under enormous pressure from Washington to attack the invaders. "Destroy the rebel army," Lincoln wired him. From the Union position on Seminary Ridge, a reluctant McClellan surveyed the Confederate defenses from the Round Tops on the south along Cemetery Ridge northward to Cemetery and Culps hills. McClellan evolved a tactical plan for a diversionary attack on the morning of October 8 against General James Longstreet's corps on the Confederate right. When Lee shifted reinforcements to that sector, the Yankees would launch their main assault through the peach orchard and wheatfield against the Confederate left center on low ground just north of Little Round Top, held by Jackson's corps. If successful, this attack would pierce a hole in the Confederate line, giving Union cavalry massed behind the center a chance to exploit the breakthrough. Napoleonic in conception, this plan had a crucial defect: it left Union flanks denuded of cavalry.

At dawn, the Union I and IX Corps carried out the diversionary attack on Cemetery and Culps hills. Lee saw through the feint, however, and refused to shift his reserves, A. P. Hill's light division, to that sector. Longstreet held firm, so when the Union II, VI, and XII Corps attacked through the peach orchard and wheatfield, they found Jackson ready for them. Fierce fighting produced a harvest of carnage unprecedented even in this bloody war, with neither side gaining any advantage.

About 3:00 P.M., Stuart reported to Lee that the Union right was uncovered. Lee immediately ordered Hill to take his division south around Round Top and attack the Union flank in the wheatfield. Undetected by the Union cavalry, which was massed more than a mile to the north, Hill's 6,000 men burst from the woods and boulders of Devil's Den screaming the rebel yell. Many of them wore blue uniforms captured at Harpers Ferry, which increased the surprise and confusion among Union troops of the XII Corps. Like a row of falling dominoes, the exhausted and decimated Union brigades collapsed. With perfect timing the rest of Jackson's corps counterattacked, smashing the fragments of Union regiments that had rallied to resist Hill. As the fighting rolled in echelon toward the North, Longstreet's corps joined the counterattack at 4:30 P.M.

McClellan had kept his favorite V Corps in reserve. Steadied by Brigadier General George Sykes's division of regulars, they held back the yelling rebels for a brief time. But as the sun dipped below the South Mountain range, the V Corps also broke. In a desperate attempt to rally them, McClellan rode to the front. "Soldiers!" he shouted. "Stand fast! I will lead you!" As he drew his sword, a minié ball smashed into his skull and toppled him dead from his horse. Word of McClellan's death spread like lightning through the thinned and scattered ranks of Yankee units that were still fighting. The last remnants of resistance winked out. Thousands of dejected bluecoats surrendered; thousands more melted away into the dusk, every man for himself. The Army of the Potomac ceased to exist as a fighting force.

News of the Battle of Gettysburg resounded through the land and across the Atlantic. "My God! My God" exclaimed Lincoln in the White House. "What will the country say?" It said plenty, all of it bad. Peace Democrats redoubled their denunciations of the war as a wicked failure. "All are tired of this damnable tragedy," they cried. "Each hour is but sinking us deeper into bankruptcy and desolation." Even staunch patriots and Lincoln supporters like Joseph Medill, editor of the *Chicago Tribune*, gave up hope of winning the war. "An armistice is bound to come during the year '63," he wrote. "The rebs can't be conquered by the present machinery." Captain Oliver Wendell Holmes Jr. of the 20th Massachusetts, which had suffered 75 percent casualties at Gettysburg, wrote in November that "the army is tired with its hard and terrible experience. I've pretty much made up my mind that the South have achieved their independence."

In Kentucky, Union and Confederate forces had clashed in the indecisive Battle of Perryville on the same day (October 8) as the Battle of

Gettysburg. Encouraged by the news from Pennsylvania, Confederate commanders Braxton Bragg and Edmund Kirby-Smith decided to continue their Kentucky campaign. Having already occupied Lexington and Frankfort, they began a drive toward the prize of Louisville as the Union army under Major General Don Carlos Buell, discouraged by the reports of McClellan's defeat and death, fell back listlessly. In Pennsylvania, after a pause for consolidation of his supply lines, Lee began an advance toward Baltimore. Newly emboldened pro-Confederate Marylanders openly affirmed their allegiance. Although reserve troops manning the formidable defenses ringing Washington dissuaded Lee from attacking the capital, there was no Union field army capable of resisting Lee's movements.

Hesitant to goad last-ditch resistance by attacking a major city, however, Lee paused to await the outcome of Northern congressional elections on November 4. The voters sent a loud and clear message that they wished to end the war, even on terms of Confederate independence. Democrats won control of the next House of Representatives and the peace wing established firm control of the party.

At almost the moment the election results became known, the British minister to the United States, Lord Lyons, presented Secretary of State Seward with an offer signed by the governments of Great Britain, France, Russia, and Austria-Hungary to mediate an end to the war on the basis of separation. "We will not admit the division of the Union at any price," Seward responded. "There is no possible compromise." Very well, responded Lyons. In that case Her Majesty's Government will recognize the independence of the Confederate States of America. Other European governments will do the same. "This is not a matter of principle or preferences," Lyons told Seward, "but of fact."

Despite Seward's bluster, he was a practical statesman. He was also a student of history. He knew that American victory at the Battle of Saratoga in 1777 had brought French diplomatic recognition of the fledgling United States, followed by French assistance and intervention that proved crucial to the achievement of American independence.

Would history repeat itself? Would British and French recognition of the Confederacy be followed by military assistance and intervention—against the blockade, for example? As they pondered these questions and absorbed the results of the congressional elections, while Confederate armies stood poised for attack outside Baltimore and Louisville, Lincoln and Seward concluded that they had no choice.

On a gloomy New Year's Day 1863, a melancholy Lincoln called Republican congressional leaders and state governors to the White House. "This is not the duty I had hoped to discharge today," he told them. "Last July I decided to issue a proclamation freeing the slaves in rebel states, to take effect today," he continued sadly. "There is no chance of that now. Would *my word* free the slaves, when I cannot even enforce the Constitution in the rebel States?" Instead, "We are faced with a situation in which the whole world seems to be against us. Last summer, after McClellan was driven back from Richmond, I said that in spite of that setback, 'I expect to maintain this contest until successful, or till I die, or am conquered, or my term expires, or Congress or the country forsakes me.' Gentlemen, the people expressed their opinion in the last election. The country has forsaken us, and the next Congress will be against us. Whether or not we admit we are conquered, we must admit that we have failed to conquer the rebellion. Today I will issue a proclamation accepting the insurgents' offer of an armistice. Secretary Seward will accept the good offices of foreign powers for mediation." The president's voice choked as he concluded: "Gentleman, the United States no longer exists as one nation, indivisible."

THOMAS FLEMING

THE NORTHWEST CONSPIRACY

One of the strangest chapters of the Civil War is that of the Northwest Conspiracy. It is a tale that reads like pages torn from a counterfactual history of the war—if it weren't for real. Key states were involved—Ohio, Indiana, Illinois, and Kentucky—all of which had once belonged to the area known as the Northwest Territory, a name that still resonated in the 1860s. In no place was the North more vulnerable, especially in the tier of counties along the Ohio River, which were, as the cultural historian Howard Mumford Jones has put it, "tinctured with southern values." The states of the former Northwest harbored large numbers of antiwar Democrats and Confederate sympathizers. The Copperheads (as they were called, after the copper pennies some wore in their lapels as identifying badges) presented a lingering threat to the Union war effort.

Historians still argue about the potential of the movement. Thomas Fleming maintains that the threat was genuine and was only forestalled by the quirkiness and unreliability of the people who led it. At the same time, the Copperhead cause was fueled by the antidemocratic strong-arm tactics of local Republican officials and the Lincoln administration, both of whom manifested an open disdain for civil liberties and the protections of the Constitution. A civil war within the Civil War was conceivable, with the states of the Old

Northwest breaking away to form a separate confederacy, and in the process forcing the Union into a truce with the South. Uprisings in cities like Chicago and Indianapolis in the summer of 1864 might have resembled the New York draft riots a year earlier. Even if federal troops had put them down, the Union as we know it might not have survived. Would Abraham Lincoln be remembered today not as the Great Emancipator but as the man who ripped up the Constitution?

THOMAS FLEMING is the author of more than forty books of history and fiction, including, most recently, *Liberty! The American Revolution, Duel: Alexander Hamilton, Aaron Burr and the Future of America,* and *The New Dealers' War.*

IN THE SUMMER OF 1864, war weariness seeped into the minds and hearts of millions of Americans. General William Tecumseh Sherman's army was stalled before Atlanta. General Ulysses S. Grant was piling up bodies against General Robert E. Lee's fortifications around Richmond. The soaring hopes of an early peace after the simultaneous Union victories at Vicksburg and Gettysburg in July of 1863 had plummeted into the dust.

Nobody, including Lincoln himself, thought he could be reelected. Divided and discouraged Republicans began talking about finding another candidate—perhaps the man who had lost in 1856, John Frémont, who had great appeal to the radicals in the party. Others talked of Salmon P. Chase, whom Lincoln had fired as secretary of the treasury and tried to mollify by making him chief justice of the Supreme Court. There was a near certainty that the Democrats were going to nominate General George C. McClellan, the man Lincoln had dismissed as general in chief. If he won, "Little Mac" made it clear that his first act would be a call for a negotiated peace with an independent South.

The possibility that the Union would collapse in such a disheartening way filled many minds with demoralizing gloom. They predicted that the peace would be little more than an armistice before the two sections resumed hostilities to decide whether border states such as Maryland, Delaware, Kentucky, Tennessee, and Missouri would unite with the North or the South. The disgruntled abolitionists of New England might have joined their antislavery cousins in the northern tier of the Midwest and revived an idea that they considered in 1804, in the wake of the Louisiana Purchase—a union with British Canada. Lincoln's bedraggled federal government would have been reduced to a pathetic remnant of its former power.

Ironically, the Confederacy was having similar fits of gloom. A mood of desperation was daily growing darker, thanks to the Union blockade and a growing manpower shortage caused by battle casualties and desertion. There was no longer any prospect of an irresistible Robert E. Lee–led offensive that would force the Yankees to ask for terms. Hope of victory now depended on striking the federal war machine a blow where it was most vulnerable—in the disgruntled states of Kentucky, Indiana, Illinois, and Ohio.

Thus was the Northwest Conspiracy born. Geographically the Midwest today, these states were still known in the 1860s by the earlier term because they had all emerged from the old Northwest Territory. Their conspiracy is one of the least known and most misunderstood episodes of the Civil War. There are a half dozen versions of it drifting around in the history books. The plotters proposed to take these crucial states out of the Union and set up a third nation—the Northwest Confederacy—in the nation's heartland.

The plan called for an uprising by 100,000 angry Democrats in these states during the summer or fall of 1864. If it had succeeded, and this third nation achieved a political voice, its first order of business would have been a call for an immediate cease-fire between the warring sections. Although General McClellan was not a part of the conspiracy, it is hard to believe he would not have applauded this demand for instant peace.

This visionary scheme grew out of the frustrations of the Copperhead movement, in particular anger over the fate of the first leader of the antiwar forces in the Midwest, Ohio congressman Clement Vallandigham. He was arrested by General Ambrose Burnside in 1863 for making supposedly treasonous speeches and tried before a military commission. The trial was a farce. The federal judge advocate general had judicial as well as prosecutorial powers. He could and did bare witnesses favorable to the defendant, rule testimony out of order, and otherwise function as a judge.

Congressman Vallandigham was sentenced to imprisonment for treason. But Lincoln shrewdly deported him to the Confederacy. From there, he soon made his way to Canada, where he continued to exert considerable influence on his angry adherents in the heartland. In February 1864, he told one follower: "Matches are cheap. If fanatics and fools seek mob law and anarchy, by all means let them have it. Burn down or destroy theirs as they have or may destroy yours."

Beneath the heartland, Democrats' hostility to the war was something deeper and less recognized—the extralegal tactics of the Lincoln administration, especially in Indiana and Kentucky, where the Republicans created something very close to military dictatorships that manipulated elections and used terror tactics to retain political control. By 1864, the Democrats of Kentucky and Indiana were a seething mass of rage in search of a target.

The experience of these two states is seldom discussed in histories of the Civil War. Kentucky declared herself neutral shortly after the South seceded. It was a gesture that made immediate political sense—but not long-range sense. Both sides vowed to respect the declaration—and soon violated it. Armies from North and South surged into the state and in 1862–63 they fought crucial battles at Perryville and Stones River, on the Tennessee-Kentucky border.

In both these clashes, the Confederate commander was Braxton Bragg, whom not a few historians consider the nemesis of the Southern cause in the West. A cold, remote man, he had no ability to inspire his troops or work harmoniously with his subordinate generals. He constantly wavered between overconfidence and premature discouragement.

A more aggressive general would have avoided the battle of Perryville by winning the race to seize Louisville, one of the great supply bases of the Union Army in the West. Instead, Bragg wasted precious days installing a Confederate governor at Frankfort—a ceremony disrupted by artillery fire from federal troops. He failed to concentrate his army at Perryville but attacked anyway, although he was outnumbered almost three to one. Unable to dislodge the blue-clad enemy, Bragg ingloriously retreated.

At Stones River, sometimes called Murfeesboro, Bragg repeated this performance on a larger scale, losing almost 12,000 men, more than a third of his army. If the Confederacy had made a general with the driving energy of James Longstreet or A. P. Hill commander in the West, Kentucky would have become a Confederate state—along with Tennessee.

In some ways it came down to who wanted Kentucky the most. For the North, retaining control was crucial. Early in the war, Lincoln remarked that to lose Kentucky was very nearly the same as to lose the whole game. A Confederate Kentucky would have blocked Union armies and supplies from access to Tennessee and ultimately to Georgia and Mississippi, nullifying the basic Union strategy of the war—the vast flank attack that culminated in the conquest of Tennessee and Sherman's invasion of Georgia.

Once in control of Kentucky, Republicans armed the people of Appalachia, the Cumberland "knobs," as they were called. These hill folk had a long history of hatred for the pro-Southern aristocrats of the Bluegrass. Indiana and Ohio sent numerous thirty- and sixty-day home guard regiments into Kentucky to back them. Tens of thousands of resentful Kentucky Democrats vowed to get even at the polls.

The Republicans responded with brute force. On July 21, 1862, Union general Jerry T. Boyle threatened to arrest any Democrat who had the temerity to run for office against the administration's slate. This was par for the course in Kentucky politics at that point in the Civil War. The Republicans carried the state in the 1862 midterm elections by stationing troops around polling places. When a Democrat showed up to cast his ballot, he was often told by the officer in command that he would not be responsible for his safety if he voted.

Remember, these confrontations took place decades before the secret ballot. Everyone voted in public and there was no way of disguising your political allegiance. A great many Democrats went home without voting—or did not bother to show up at all. These tactics carried Kentucky for the Republicans and helped give Lincoln his narrow margin of control in the House of Representatives in 1862.

When the state Democratic convention met in Frankfort in February 1863, Colonel E. A. Gilbert marched the 44th Ohio into the meeting hall and dispersed the assembly at bayonet point. Another variety of intimidation was the job Republicans did on Democratic editors in Kentucky. No less than seventeen newspapers were smashed up by mobs, often with soldiers in uniform helping out or watching with warm approval.

When leading politicians such as former governor and federal congressman John Morehead protested these tactics, they were arrested and held in various federal prisons, where they endured verbal abuse and semistarvation until they pledged allegiance to the federal government.

In Indiana, the Democrats won control of the state legislature in the 1862 elections. They immediately prepared to cripple the state's participation in the war by refusing to vote the government a cent. Republican governor Oliver P. Morton suspended the legislature and ran the state by decree for the rest of the war, using money that Lincoln shipped to him from Washington, D.C.

After the Emancipation Proclamation, disaffection with the Lincoln administration in both Indiana and Kentucky became intense. No less than 2,300 men deserted from Indiana regiments in December 1862, on the eve of the final publication of the proclamation. That was almost a quarter of all the Indiana desertions during the entire war. Around this time, a surgeon wrote a letter describing the impact of the proclamation. He claimed the western army was "demoralized until it is worthless . . . Soldiers are deserting every day."

Democratic newspapers published letters denouncing "Old Black Abe" and his proclamation. The editors saw the document as a perversion of the war's original aim, to preserve the Union. Democrats regarded it as a double cross because Lincoln had previously promised not to interfere with the institution of slavery. This was especially explosive stuff in Indiana, where both Republicans and Democrats had agreed before the war that abolitionism threatened their state with "a black wave" of freed slaves surging across the Ohio from Kentucky. Indiana Republicans managed to swallow the proclamation, though for many of them it was not easy. The Democrats never forgave or forgot. Thereafter Lincoln was known as "Abraham Africanus."

Democrats from neighboring states had similar reactions to the proclamation. Major Henry F. Kalfus of the 15th Kentucky regiment tried to resign when he heard about it. So did seventeen other officers. When the division's general asked why they were resigning, Kalfus was the only one who had the nerve to reply: "I decline to participate further in a war aimed at freeing the Negro." Kalfus was paraded before his regiment, his shoulder straps cut off, and his dishonorable discharge read. Then he was marched out of camp at the point of a bayonet.

Adjutant General Lorenzo Thomas put the entire 90th Illinois Regiment under arrest when he called on them to cheer the president's proclamation and they hissed and booed instead. Their response was symptomatic of the Democratic attitude throughout Illinois. The legislature was dominated by pro-Confederate Democrats who tried to ram through a new constitution that limited the powers and reduced the term of Republican governor Richard Yates from four years to two.

When ten thousand Democrats assembled in Indianapolis for a state convention in the spring of 1863, they found the site of their meeting surrounded by infantry and artillery, with the cannon bearing directly on the speakers' platform. Cavalry roved the town and the state arsenal was under heavy guard.

Whenever Democratic orators attempted to speak, they were interrupted and insulted by soldiers and civilian Republicans scattered throughout the crowd. If a Democrat tried to silence one of these hecklers, an armed detachment would seize the man and hustle him off to jail. A squadron of cavalry yelling like demons circled the crowd, frightening those on the periphery.

When U.S. senator Thomas Hendricks, a leading Democratic opponent of the war, tried to speak, eight or ten soldiers with bayonets fixed and rifles cocked advanced on the platform. A detachment of cavalry with drawn sabers also headed for him. Hendricks abandoned the platform, along with everyone else, and the crowd dispersed in panic. The convention collapsed and most of the Democrats headed for the railroad station to go home. As the trains pulled out, the Democrats began firing pistols out the windows into the city. Federal soldiers stopped the trains and confiscated hundreds of weapons. Several hundred more guns were collected from a rivulet beside the tracks.

Back home, the infuriated Democrats were told by one local newspaper to arm themselves and be ready to defend constitutional liberty. The alternative was submission to "degrading despotism." Indiana was drifting rapidly into a civil war within the bigger civil war. The same thing was happening in Kentucky. The catalyst was an organization called "the Sons of Liberty."

The Sons had antecedents in an earlier secret society, the Knights of the Golden Circle. The very name tempts one to smile and not a few historians have dismissed it—and the Sons of Liberty—as a bunch of malcontents who talked big and loved passwords and secret handshakes and similar hocus-pocus. The Knights were founded in 1854 by a somewhat dubious character named George Bickley. Their purpose was filibustering expeditions to Mexico and Central America, with the goal of expanding slave territory.

Bickley announced two invasions of Mexico, in 1859 and 1860, but neither materialized, although by this time he claimed the Knights had 65,000 members. At this point there was nothing treasonable about the KGC, as contemporaries called it. But the secession crisis transformed the order. Bickley was ardently pro-Confederate and threw all his influence behind a separate Southern nation.

Soon worried Kentucky unionists were claiming that there were hundreds of secret "castles" of the order throughout the state, planning a coup d'état. In May 1861, a legislator called for an investigation of the conspiracy. The hard-nosed editor of the *Louisville Journal* put some reporters to work and concluded the KGC was a bogeyman that existed mostly in Bickley's head—and the heads of paranoid Republicans, who were using it to smear innocent Democrats. An investigation by the Illinois state legislature produced similar conclusions. There, the chief smear artist, a right-hand man of Governor Yates, was forced to confess he had no evidence to substantiate his charges.

For a while there were reports of 125,000 Knights in Indiana and 1.5 million in the entire country. Counties with Democratic majorities were especially suspect. Republicans regularly called them "nests of traitors." Governor Morton got into the act, informing Secretary of War Edwin Stanton of the existence of "evil, awful and dangerous combinations" in his embattled state.

Confirming this statement was another questionable character in this tangled tale, Colonel Henry Carrington, who served as the governor's chief military adviser. Known as "the hero of the Home Brigade" for his disinclination to go near a battlefield, Carrington said the Knights infested all but seven counties of Indiana and had 92,000 members between the ages of sixteen and seventy.

An Indianapolis grand jury investigated the KGC and reduced Carrington's numbers to 15,000. They indicted sixteen men as KGC conspirators but could not get one of them convicted. The Democrats gave the Republicans the political horse laugh and used the outcome to win votes in the 1862 state elections. They accused the Democrats of creating scarecrows and telling Munchausen stories. They consistently denied that the KGC and/or disloyalty had anything to do with the Democratic party.

That was probably true at this point in the war. But every Knight was a Democrat. Their chief motivation remained mutual protection against the Republican penchant for unlawful arrests. As Indiana soldiers began to desert, some KGC chapters tried to conceal the runaways. The Union Army sent detachments into counties where deserters were reported and, on the mere say-so of "ultra" Republicans, often arrested men for harboring them. This sometimes led to gunfire and sudden death on both sides.

In December 1862, Bickley was arrested in Tennessee with a woman who said she was his wife. It soon transpired that he had another wife in Cincinnati. There he was described by neighbors as a born confidence man. Indicted in Louisville, he was never put on trial. Instead, with that marvelous indifference to the Constitution that Lincoln regularly displayed in the Midwest, Bickley was shipped to Fort Warren in Boston and kept there for the rest of the war in solitary confinement.

Disgusted with Bickley and the KGC, leaders of the Democratic party in Indiana and Kentucky began exploring the idea of forming a secret society that would have a direct influence on the war. Out of this ferment came the Order of American Knights, better known as the OAKs. Their long-range purpose was to prevent the Republicans from using force to win the election of 1864, when Abraham Africanus would run for a second term. "Protection of the ballot box" was their avowed aim.

As the war dragged on, more treasonable ideas came to the fore among the OAKs. A number of historians have linked General John Hunt Morgan's famous July 1, 1863, foray across the Ohio into Indiana to a plot between this headstrong cavalryman and the secret societies. A great many things went wrong with this adventure. Perhaps the most important was Grant's triumph at Vicksburg and Lee's failure at Gettysburg on July 4, 1863. If Lee had won and Vicksburg had held out, the argument goes—and it is not a bad argument—the OAKs and Knights might have turned out in force to help Morgan try to subdue the Midwest. But the telegraph that chattered the news of these twin defeats sealed Morgan's fate.

This in turn may explain the atrocious behavior of Morgan's troopers, who looted Unionists and Southern sympathizers indiscriminately. If anything, they were harder on the Southern sympathizers, whom they seemed to despise as cowards. All this ties in with the theory of a collapsed uprising. At Corydon, Indiana, when members of the Knights of the Golden Circle displayed the order's lone-star flag in their windows, they were shown no mercy by the raiders. "Give for the cause you love so well," the gray troopers sneered, and looted chickens, hogs, jewelry, and cash.

What if Morgan had been a shrewder, more coolheaded leader? He might have tried to restrain his troops and win sympathy for an underdog effort at victory, in spite of the bad news from the east and west. He also might have had a plan of attack. At one point he was within fifty miles of Indianapolis. If he had been able to seize the state capital and liberate 6,000 Confederate prisoners in nearby Camp Morton, he might have created an army strong enough to do some serious harm to the federal war effort. His prime target, once he had a real army under his command, would have been Cincinnati. What a wrench that would have thrown into the Lincoln war machine! It was even more important than Louisville as a transportation and manufacturing hub that sent food and war matériel streaming through Kentucky to Union armies in Tennessee and Mississippi.

In the course of Morgan's rampage, Colonel Carrington acquired a reputation as a prime coward. Arriving in southern Indiana with two regiments, Carrington learned that Morgan had headed east toward Ohio. The heroic colonel got drunk and marched his men in the opposite direction. Better soldiers soon defeated and captured most of Morgan's men.

Around this time, the Republicans made headlines by arresting dozens of OAK leaders in Missouri, accusing them of treasonous intentions and rampant disloyalty. The scandal influenced Indiana and Kentucky OAK leaders to change the name of the organization to the Sons of Liberty. The title, of course, suggested that they were identifying themselves with the men who had opposed the tyranny of George III. They elected Clement Vallandigham as the supreme commander. The elaborate rituals of the OAKs and the Knights were simplified; there was less mumbo jumbo and more emphasis on Jeffersonian states'-rights philosophy.

Basically, an applicant to the Sons of Liberty swore allegiance to straight Confederate doctrine, which claimed that the authority of a government was derived from the people. Since the Southern people had withdrawn their allegiance, the federal government was null and void in the South. The same principle would apply in the Northwest Confederacy.

Harrison Dodd, a prominent printer in Indianapolis, was among the first to use the term "Sons of Liberty" to describe the organization. In a speech in 1864, Dodd declared he had opposed the war for every day, hour, and minute since the opening Battle of Bull Run. Another leading Indiana Sons of Liberty figure was Dr. William A. Bowles of French Lick. For Bowles, the Mexican War was a turning point in his life. He commanded the 2nd Indiana regiment at the Battle of Buena Vista, a seesaw struggle during which he ordered his troops to retreat to better ground. The retreat turned into a stampede to the rear. The mortified Bowles seized a rifle, joined a Mississippi regiment commanded by Colonel Jefferson Davis, and fought the rest of the battle as a private.

A court of inquiry found Bowles guilty of bad judgment. Colonel Jefferson Davis thought otherwise and presented Bowles with the rifle he had used in the battle as a trophy of his valor. The commanding general, Zachary Taylor, also blamed the soldiers of the 2nd Indiana for the rout. This disagreement caused a huge dustup in Indiana, where most people salvaged the good name of the state by deciding Bowles was incompetent, cowardly, or both.

The scandal had a disastrous impact on this big handsome man, souring his temperament and shifting his allegiance to the Southerners who had defended him in his hour of need—especially Jefferson Davis. From the day the war began, Bowles was an ardent supporter of the Southern cause. By 1864, he boasted of spending all his waking hours drilling members of the Sons of Liberty. He also donated large sums of money to the organization.

Another major figure in the Sons was Lambdin Milligan, a very successful lawyer in Huntington County, Indiana. He lived the life of a gentleman farmer, with a stable of blooded racehorses. Six feet four, Milligan looked and acted like a leader of men. He liked to say he was the first man in Indiana who denounced the Civil War as unnecessary, unjust, and infamous. He had an abiding hatred for New England. He claimed the money-grubbing Yankees had started the war to reduce the South to "pecuniary vassalage to the commercial and manufacturing interests of the East."

In Kentucky, the leading Sons of Liberty leader was Judge Joshua Fry Bullitt, chief justice of the state's court of appeals and a member of one of Louisville's oldest families. Republicans forced Bullitt to resign from the bench because of his pro-Southern views. The judge was ably assisted in his plotting by ex-major Henry F. Kalfus, who had been received in Louisville as a hero after being dishonorably discharged for opposing the Emancipation Proclamation.

So we come to the summer of 1864. Never had things looked more promising for the Northwest Confederacy. In Kentucky, guerrilla war raged and the Union commander, General Stephen Burbridge, resorted to terror tactics to suppress it. For every Union soldier or sympathizer killed, Burbridge began executing four captured Confederates. Outrage simmered from the Bluegrass to the Ohio. In Indiana, the Democrats were equally infuriated by Governor Morton's continued suppression of the legislature and rule by executive fiat.

The South had sent supposed peace commissioners to Canada to confer with Northerners who might be willing to discuss terms. These gentlemen had more than negotiations in mind. They brought a great deal of money with them—the estimates range from six hundred thousand to several million dollars. They picked up a lot more cash from Confederate guerrillas who looted banks in Kentucky and Tennessee. Their main purpose was to finance the Sons of Liberty uprising.

A key figure on the Confederate side was Captain Thomas Hines, one of Morgan's officers, who had escaped with him from the Ohio Penitentiary in Columbus, where they had been confined after their capture in 1863. Hines was the brains behind the escape. He was an incredibly handsome daredevil, with a striking resemblance to John Wilkes Booth.

Hines combined espionage with cavalry warfare before his capture. Many people think he carried the secret orders that sent General Morgan across the Ohio, overriding the cavalryman's commanding officer, General Braxton Bragg, who had specifically forbidden Morgan to make such a reckless foray. It was, among other things, evidence of Jefferson Davis's dwindling confidence in Bragg.

A full-time spy by 1864, Hines brought the Sons of Liberty leaders in Kentucky and Indiana the plan for the uprising. Colonel Adam Johnson, commander of Morgan's partly rebuilt cavalry division, was to invade Kentucky from western Virginia with 1,200 men to support the revolt. By this time Morgan was dead, killed in an ambush in Tennessee.

Johnson and thousands of Kentucky Sons of Liberty from counties along the Ohio were to cross the river and join Indiana's Sons in a march on Indianapolis. Their goal was the liberation of those 6,000 Confederate prisoners of war in Camp Morton. Equipped with guns from the state arsenal, they would provide a backbone of veterans for the Sons' largely amateur army.

Simultaneously, Captain Hines was planning to be in Chicago on or shortly before August 20, the date set for the opening of the 1864 Democratic Convention. Inside the city were supposed to be two full regiments of the Sons of Liberty, well armed and spoiling for a fight. The city would be swarming with Democrats who would be willing to join the uprising if they were offered guns—and Hines planned to have the weapons on hand. Once Chicago was secured, there would be a march on Camp Douglas, where at least 5,000 Confederate veterans were waiting to be freed and armed from captured arsenals. They were guarded by only 1,600 second-rate Union troops. These soldiers would in turn free thousands of captives at Rock Island, Illinois.

If all went well, there would be two armies in the field, composed of the Sons of Liberty and the freed Southern veterans, numbering at least 100,000 men. To equip them, the Confederate commissioners sent agents to New York, where gun merchants began shipping thousands of revolvers and rifles to Indiana. They also spent $25,000 to buy the support of the former mayor of New York, Fernando Wood, and his newspaper, the *Daily News*. If the conspiracy succeeded, Wood and the paper were ready to rush into print with statements calling for recognition of the Northwest Confederacy and an immediate end to the war.

It was a stupendously ambitious scheme. If it had been launched on schedule, at the very least, it would have badly disrupted the Union Army's timetable. The battle of Atlanta would never have taken place. Sherman would have been forced to detach thousands of troops from his army to deal with the uprising. Grant might have been forced to make similar detachments. Almost certainly the revolt would have triggered uprisings in other border states, such as Missouri, where Southern sympathizers were numerous.

What if Dodd, Milligan, and the other leaders of the uprising managed to create a government at Indianapolis or Chicago and actually brought the Northwest Confederacy into being? If Confederate forces coordinated attacks on Sherman's reduced army, and the Sons of Liberty's armies, reinforced by the liberated Confederates, fought well, the demoralized Federal government might have been forced to ask for terms.

The war had generated a strong sense of separate identity throughout the Midwest. There was a widespread opinion that the two original sections of the country were jointly responsible for the ruinous conflict, with most of the blame cast on New England. It was frequently said that soldiers in Sherman's army would rather shoot an abolitionist than a rebel. America might have ended the war with three separate countries on the map—a long step toward the kind of disunion that has plagued South America.

Even if the Union Army succeeded in smashing the rebellion, it would almost certainly have been forced to resort to ruthless tactics. The bloodletting would have further damaged Lincoln's already dim prospects for reelection. The vast war-weary majority of the electorate might well have concluded that Lincoln and the Republican party were divisive warmongers and voted Democratic en masse in a demand for an immediate peace.

If the struggle in the Midwest lasted several months, the elections of 1864 would have been suspended, and Lincoln would have been a president without legitimacy, ruling by executive fiat. Democratic newspapers would have called on him to resign and demanded the appointment of some neutral figure, perhaps a justice of the Supreme Court, to negotiate an early peace. The British, already alarmed by Napoléon III's installation of the puppet emperor Maximilian in Mexico, might have decided it was time to intervene on the South's behalf and let Whitehall mediate a settlement that would give them enormous influence in the future of North America.

These were the possible outcomes as the Sons of Liberty drilled their men and gathered their weapons for the day of Democratic deliverance from Republican tyranny. But inside the Sons was a spy who unraveled all these looming possibilities.

Felix Stidger was a former officer in Henry Kalfus's regiment. When the major was dishonorably discharged, Stidger had loaned him his horse to ride home. Out of the Army by 1864, Stidger persuaded Colonel Carrington to hire him as a secret agent. He headed for Louisville and soon met Kalfus, who greeted him as an old friend. In just a few weeks Stidger had convinced Kalfus and Bullitt that he was a devoted Sons of Liberty man. They used him as a messenger to Dr. Bowles, Lambdin Milligan, and Harrison Dodd. Soon Colonel Carrington and Governor Morton in Indianapolis knew the names of dozens of the top leaders in the Sons of Liberty and the date of the planned uprising, August 16, 1864.

Meanwhile, inside the Sons, a dispute had erupted between the fighters and the voters. The top Democrats in Indiana began to question the point of an armed uprising. Lincoln looked as if he could be easily beaten at the polls. Why stage an uprising and give the opposition a chance to smear the Democratic party as disloyal? The furious dispute proved to be unsolvable. A fairly large number of prominent Democrats decided to go to the Chicago convention rather than stay home and fight, depriving the Sons of important leaders at the regimental level.

In Chicago, Hines and a handpicked group of ex-Morgan cavalrymen met nothing but disappointment when they attempted to organize the two regiments of the Sons of Liberty for action. Barely five hundred men showed up and they showed no enthusiasm for risking their necks. They said they were only willing to fight if the Lincoln administration tried to break up the convention. When no such attempt materialized, even though the exiled Clement Vallandigham made the keynote address, they claimed there was no motivation for an uprising, and no reason for one, because they were going to be able to beat Old Abe at the ballot box. Hines wheedled, pleaded, bribed, but got nowhere. The men in Camp Douglas, who had been told of the planned uprising, waited in vain.

In Indiana, meanwhile, General Carrington sent cavalry ranging through the state, arresting Dr. Bowles, Dodd, Milligan, and dozens of other Sons of Liberty leaders. More than thirty thousand rifles and pistols were seized, along with tons of powder and ammunition. In a few weeks between three and four hundred minor leaders were under lock and key in the Soldiers Home prison in Indianapolis.

In Kentucky, Judge Bullitt and Major Kalfus heard that General Burbridge was about to strike and fled to Canada. Adam Johnson and his cavalrymen invaded the state on schedule but they were quickly routed. Johnson was blinded for life by a bullet in the head. Bereft of leadership, the August 16 uprising never took place.

Stidger's role in this debacle was crucial. One wonders what might have happened if he had been detected. Almost certainly he would have been murdered. The gutless Carrington would have been left to deal with the reality of thousands of armed and angry men in the field. The chances are good that his behavior would have matched his performance during Morgan's raid. If the Indiana and Kentucky wings of the conspiracy had taken the field, there was more than an even chance that Hines could have persuaded the footdraggers in

Chicago to join them. The great explosion might have taken place on schedule.

A few of the Indiana conspirators, notably Dr. Bowles, smuggled letters out of jail, urging those in the lower ranks to start the revolt without them. But on September 1, an event in distant Georgia took the heart out of the Northwest Conspiracy. General William Tecumseh Sherman sent President Lincoln a telegram announcing: "Atlanta is ours and fairly won." Instantly, Lincoln's chances for reelection went from zero to 98 percent.

Thomas Hines and his Confederate colleagues continued to operate under cover in Chicago and its vicinity for the next few months. But they were never able to organize enough men to make an attack on Camp Douglas or the Rock Island prison camp. By this time Hines's identity was well known and he had several close calls as federal agents swarmed in his wake. He finally fled to Canada, after a stopover in Kentucky to marry his sweetheart. He was one cool customer.

The Republicans used the Sons to bolster their 1864 election campaign. When federal agents seized a large number of pistols in Harrison Dodd's printing firm, that very night a Republican speaker brandished one of them before a party meeting and called it "one of the arguments for peace."

The *Indianapolis Journal* predicted that the "northern wing of the southern confederacy" would supply speakers with material that would elect the whole Republican ticket. Colonel Carrington exhorted the voters: "Traitors intended to bring war to your homes. Meet them in the ballot box while Grant and Sherman meet them in the field."

The *Indianapolis Journal* boldly called the Democratic presidential candidate, General George McClellan, the commander of an "insurrectionary army" that had plotted to bring the war into the peaceful precincts of the upper Midwest. Another paper called for victory over "the McClellan, Vallandigham, and Dodd party." It all added up to a propaganda triumph for the Republicans. For years they had been trying to smear the Democrats with the treason label. The Northwest Conspiracy seemed to prove it.

While the campaign raged, the Indiana leaders were tried by military commissions like the one that had convicted Clement Vallandigham. Felix Stidger was a star witness in these trials. There are grounds for suspecting he made up a lot of what he said. He seemed to have a capacity to recall in detail conversations six months old. No one stopped him, because the judge advocate general continued to be both the prosecutor and presiding judge, who could rule any and all objections out of order and bar testimony whenever he felt like it.

On October 7, in the middle of his trial, Harrison Dodd escaped from prison and made it all the way to Canada, disguised as a woman. The Republicans promptly put Bowles, Milligan, and two other leading Sons of Liberty on trial to replace him.

On the stand, Felix Stidger repeatedly claimed there was an intimate connection between the Sons of Liberty and the Confederate government. Most of this was based on Dr. Bowles's boastful statements about his friendship with Jefferson Davis. Captain Hines, who demonstrated the Southern connection by his words and actions, did not come under discussion, because the Republicans never caught him.

From a legal point of view, the trials were a farce. The judge advocate general regularly accepted hearsay testimony against the defendants and overrode defense objections. When a clergyman attempted to testify as a character witness for Milligan, he was subjected to innuendo and insulting references to his loyalty to the Union.

The more or less foregone Indiana verdicts were: guilty of all charges. Bowles, Milligan, and another man were sentenced to hang. A fourth conspirator got off with hard labor during the war. The executions were not immediately carried out for several reasons. Governor Morton feared that the cases were weak and there was grave potential of a backlash that might ruin his political career. Lincoln was also involved. There seems to be a near certainty that he sent word to the military commission that he would not carry out a death sentence and would free the condemned men after the war. This emboldened the judges to vote for the noose to teach a loyalty lesson to the lower ranks of the Sons of Liberty.

This plan went badly awry when Lincoln was assassinated on April 14, 1865. His successor, Andrew Johnson, knew nothing about the postwar pardon arrangement and ordered the condemned men executed. Governor Morton rushed emissaries to Johnson to plead for their lives. The political backlash would be even worse now. But Johnson declined to cooperate. On May 9, the War Department ordered the executions without further delay.

By this time, with Morton's help, an appeal had been submitted to the federal district court in Indianapolis. Arrangements were made to forward it swiftly to the U.S. Supreme Court. Johnson reluctantly commuted the condemned men's sentences to life imprisonment and they were sent to the federal prison in Columbus, Ohio. There they spent another unpleasant year. To humiliate them, the jailers frequently made them eat with Negro convicts.

On April 3, 1866, in a verdict known as ex parte Milligan, the Supreme Court ruled the convictions were void because the military commission had no jurisdiction in a part of the country where the civil courts were still open. The judges threw in an opinion that the defendants were disloyal scoundrels and deserved hanging. That was a sop to the Radical Republicans who were thirsting for the condemned men's blood.

Thereafter, except for retaliatory lawsuits for false arrest by Milligan (he won $12 in damages), the conspiracy to found a Northwest Confederacy sank into oblivion. But it remained a potent source of election campaign material, without its name. The accusation that the Democratic party was disloyal remained a favorite cry for Republican orators until the Spanish-American War.

The conspiracy reveals a dark side of the Lincoln administration and the Civil War that few historians have been willing to look at. Most Lincoln biographers give him a free pass on the brutal tactics of the

Republicans in Kentucky and Indiana, their gross disregard for civil rights and the processes of law. But there is evidence aplenty that Lincoln was involved in these messy operations to his eyeballs. The president was closely involved in Vallandigham's trial and never said a word against General Burnside for his role in it. One of the worst offenders against civil rights in Kentucky, General Eleazar A. Paine, was a personal friend.

At a deeper level, this forgotten patch of our past reveals the arbitrary side of the Civil War, the way the abolitionists fomented the cataclysm, and then used the machinery of the federal government to shift the war from a struggle to save the Union to a war to free the slaves. This switch was too much for a great many Democrats to swallow, and the result was widespread alienation and resentment. Coupled to this resentment was the growing sense of the Midwest as a separate section of the nation, distinctly different from the East. It is a state of mind that persisted into World Wars I and II. In both wars, there was great resistance to the sentiments of the more bellicose, Eurocentrically minded East.

In the Civil War, this attitude was compounded by a primal fear of an African-American revolt such as the one Nat Turner launched in Virginia in 1831, where no quarter was given to whites, whether they were aged men, women, or innocent children. This fear of a race war was implanted in the Southern consciousness by the events in Haiti at the turn of the nineteenth century. There such a war resulted in the extermination of the white population.

Slavery was not a pretty institution. But in 1860, a great many whites thought the alternative—abolition—was far worse. At the deepest level, this fear of the African-American was the driving force behind the South's rebellion and the midwestern Democrats' Northwest Conspiracy. Many if not most of the conspirators were, like Lincoln, only a generation removed from Kentucky, Virginia, or the deeper South. It was easy to see why this racial paranoia infected the minds and hearts of Southern sympathizers in the border states to an egregious degree.

This dolorous fact is especially visible in the October 1864 Battle of Saltville. There the Army of Kentucky, led by the hated General Burbridge, assaulted an important Confederate saltworks in the mountains of western Virginia. Confederates, some of them from Morgan's old division, repulsed the foray, which demonstrated Burbridge was a fifth-rate general. In the assault were several black regiments. After the Union army withdrew, the Confederates came out of their fortifications and shot every wounded black soldier on the battlefield.

Not a word of criticism of Confederate conduct at Saltville appeared in any Democratic newspaper in Kentucky, Indiana, or Illinois. Would that sort of hatred have been perpetuated by the creation of the Northwest Confederacy and a resultant Union defeat? Almost certainly, the answer is yes. All in all, there would seem to be no need for us to shed tears over the collapse of the Sons of Liberty's dreams of glory.

JAY WINIK

BEYOND THE WILDEST DREAMS
OF JOHN WILKES BOOTH

The subtitle of Jay Winik's best-selling April 1865 *is* The Month that
Saved America. *It's an apt description of those final days of the Civil War
and its hectic sequel, a chronology of an imploding lost cause. The Confederate capital, Richmond, fell on April 13. On April 9, Robert E. Lee surrendered his hungry and exhausted Army of Northern Virginia to the federal
forces of U. S. Grant at Appomattox, Virginia. Five days later, the actor
John Wilkes Booth assassinated President Abraham Lincoln at Ford's Theater
in Washington, D.C. On April 26, Joseph Johnston, resisting the orders of
the Confederate president Jefferson Davis to fight on, surrendered what was
left of his Army of Tennessee at the farmhouse of James Bennitt, near
Durham, North Carolina. It was the same day that the fugitive Booth was
trapped by Union troopers and shot down in a Virginia tobacco shed.*

*That was drama enough, but as Winik writes, an even greater potential for
upheaval lurked in the wings. What if Vice President Andrew Johnson had
also been assassinated, as Booth and his fellow conspirators had planned?
What if the intended killer had not lost his nerve? John Tyler may have established the precedent of presidential succession, but the framers of the Constitution had neglected to contemplate what might have happened had both the*

president and vice president died. As it was, the killing of Lincoln made Reconstruction that much more difficult.

One of the central moments of the American story has to be the meeting of Lee and Grant in the parlor of the McLean House in Appomattox, just after 1:30 in the afternoon of the ninth. "What General Lee's feelings were I do not know," Grant later wrote. "As he was a man of much dignity, with an impassible face, it was impossible to say whether he felt inwardly glad that the end had finally come, or felt sad over the result, and was too manly to show it. Whatever his feelings, they were entirely concealed from my observation . . ." Was Lee perhaps thinking back to a conference with his generals earlier that morning? When Lee broached the subject of surrender, one of his subordinates, E. Porter Alexander, made a countersuggestion: that Lee's troops scatter "like rabbits and partridges" and fade into the landscape to become guerrillas. But Lee would have none of it.

But what if he had accepted Alexander's despairing idea? What would the consequences have been? Just suppose that in the anarchy resulting from the deaths of both Lincoln and Johnson, Lee had had second thoughts.

JAY WINIK is the author of *April 1865*. After a distinguished career in government, he is now a senior scholar at the University of Maryland's School of Public Affairs. He is also the author of *On the Brink*, an account of the end of the Cold War. Almost all the quotes he uses in the chapter that follows were taken from actual sources.

Finally, the moment of maximum peril for the North seemed to be over. It had been a long time coming.

At several points during the war, it looked as though the Confederacy could, or even would, win, or at least wouldn't lose, which amounted to much the same thing. The dark days of 1864 were the worst: as U. S. Grant lost a horrific 52,000 men in the six-week Wilderness campaign (a stunning 7,000 to 8,000 in one hour alone at Cold Harbor, a far higher toll than at Pickett's charge at Gettysburg the year before) and then settled down to a maddening siege, a pall of gloom had settled over the Union psyche. Surveying the carnage and the stalemate, Abraham Lincoln himself, head bowed and pacing the halls of the White House, morosely declared the "heavens are hung in black." Northern Democrats agreed, glumly proclaiming that "patriotism is all played out" and deriding Grant as little more than a "butcher."

The Union literally had begun crying out for peace: Northern morale sharply plummeted, the peace movement gained steam and so did fervent antiwar rallies, and some 200,000 men would desert the federal army. "Disgust with our government is universal," declared one critic. It was more than disgust. Ominously, the famed journalist Horace Greeley seemed to be speaking for much of the North when he memorably declared: "Our bleeding, bankrupt, almost dying country longs for peace."

But even as a deathly weariness settled over Lincoln ("I must have some relief from this terrible anxiety," he moaned, "or it will kill me"), his perseverance eventually paid off. William Tecumseh Sherman and his army, like a tribe of thundering Mongols, took Atlanta and burned it ("but good"), presented Savannah as a Christmas present to the president, then lunged into South Carolina, leaving a 425-mile corridor of destruction, right up to the burning of Columbia. And by April 1865, Grant's mighty Army of the Potomac, fighting with greater alacrity than it had in the entirety of the campaign, was now prepared to drive into the heart of the Confederacy itself, into Richmond, and into Lee's vaunted Army of Northern Virginia.

Never was this more evident than on April 2, when the nine-month siege around Petersburg and Richmond came to an end. The Confederate lines had been broken; Robert E. Lee had abandoned the crown jewel of the South, Richmond, the Confederate capital; and the Army of Northern Virginia began a frenetic retreat to hook up with another Confederate general, Joe Johnston. Still, Lincoln, who saw the crisis clearer than anyone else, knew that even if this was the "beginning of the end," there would still be profound challenges for the Union.

For one thing, how would the end of the war unfold? Even as the Confederacy was coming to pieces, Lincoln saw indications that the war could drag on for several more months of murderous fighting, even a year, and how much more could the country take? He knew that for every Union success, he could still count a time when Lee had been within his grasp and eluded his generals; and now he worried about the unthinkable, the specter of Lee and his men slipping into the western mountains (where Lee once said he could hold out "for twenty years") to wage a campaign of prolonged harassment. And finally, he knew that the glory of a restored Union must be built on more than butchery, revenge, and retribution; somehow, the country would have to be reunited, not just in fact but in spirit, and a genuine peace made. No wonder he was the most "tired man" in the world.

And that was largely due to one adversary: Robert E. Lee. Lee had foiled his enemies before when the odds were at the longest, and he planned to do so again. Things could always go awry, and indeed they did: while Richmond and Petersburg fell, the North's long-awaited victory was marred as the ultimate prize once again evaded Lincoln. Under the cover of darkness, Lee had escaped, stealthily crossing the Appomattox and forging westward. He had a one-day jump on the federals.

It was now a race.

True to form, Lee was still hoping to cheat fate. More than that, he was full of fight. Early in the week, he urged his men "to fight to the last." By April 8, with Grant's army increasingly surrounding the vaunted rebel army, this had not changed; Lee remained as aggressive as ever, thundering coldly to his men, "We must all determine to die at our posts." And Grant learned this the hard way: when he sent a tactful communiqué stating that "peace" was his "great desire" and calling on Lee to surrender, the rebel general would have none of it. Instead, Lee sent back a brash response. Grant, having misread his opponent once, wouldn't make the same mistake again. He muttered gravely to an aide, "It looks as if Lee still means to fight."

Lee did indeed. On the fog-filled morning of April 9, he ordered his generals to probe for a hole in Grant's slumbering army and lead a breakout. His cavalry fought with a special fury, but they were stymied by the mathematics of war: a solid wall of blue, some two miles wide, of advancing Yankee infantry. Quipped one soldier: "Lee couldn't go forward, he couldn't go backward, and he couldn't go sideways."

One other course, however, remained. Lee summoned his top generals. The council of war became a council of peace, until E. P. Alexander, one of Lee's most trusted men, proposed a third option. "A little more bloodshed now makes no difference," Alexander said, instead suggesting a Confederate trump card, one that a fleeing Confederate president, Jefferson Davis, had already called for: that the men take to the woods, evaporate, and become guerrillas, the specter most feared by Lincoln, Grant, and Sherman. "We would be like rabbits and partridges in the bushes," he tantalizingly suggested, "and they could not scatter to follow us."

In fact, two elite artillery units had already destroyed their gun carriages and headed to the hills, while hundreds more infantry had vanished into the empty, largely unsettled countryside. Now, they waited for word as to what to do next. In this fateful moment, as Lee weighed the course he would accept and the course he would reject, the aging general would alter the nation's history for all of time.

Here, surely, was temptation.

There were no more miracles to be performed, but there were clearly still options; and this option—guerrilla war—was not lightly to be ignored. As military men have too often learned the hard way, and as every American saw frightfully in Vietnam, guerrilla warfare does the job. By luring their adversaries into endless, futile pursuit, guerrillas erode not just the enemy's strength but, far more important, the enemy's morale as well. Throughout history, a number of world powers, large and small, have been humbled by guerrilla tactics. By the time of the Civil War, even as the emphasis remained on large armies and full-scale battle (as one Prussian general put it, "the small war was swallowed by the big war"), guerrilla efforts were well established as a viable mode of warfare. Much of this Lee would—and did—know about.

The actual word "guerrilla" came from the Spanish insurgency against France in the early 1800s, to which Jefferson Davis frequently referred (for his part, Napoléon, in a fit of pique, grumbled that this guerrilla war was his "Spanish ulcer"). And by then, the French fatally referred to guerrilla battle as a war of extermination requiring *un peu de fanatisme*. But equally familiar to nineteenth-century Americans were the Thirty Years' War ("a killing field") and French religious wars; the partisan war against revolutionary France in the royalist Vendée; the Netherlands against the Spain of Philip II; Switzerland against the Hapsburg Empire; and the Polish uprisings in 1831 and 1861, to name a few. And then, of course, there was the most honorable example of them all, the American experience in employing guerrilla tactics against the British in the War of Independence; Lee's own father had fought the British as a partisan.

The day after Richmond fell, Davis called on the Confederacy to shift from a static conventional war in defense of territory to a dynamic guerrilla war of attrition ("we have now entered upon a new phase of a struggle the memory of which is to endure for all the ages . . ."). Years later, Charles Adams, descended from two presidents, remarked balefully: "I shudder to think of what would happen" if "Lee was of the same turn of mind as Jefferson Davis." But was he?

From a military point of view, the plan had considerable merit: the Confederacy was well supplied with long mountain ranges, endless swamps, and dark forests to offer sanctuary for determined partisans; its people knew the countryside intimately and had all the talents necessary for adroit bushwhacking, from the shooting and riding, right down to the sort of dash necessary for the nomadic hit-and-run lifestyle. And it had the fighters, many of whom were as legendary as they were feared: fierce cavalrymen like Nathan Bedford Forrest ("the Wizard of the Saddle") and the plucky and daring John Mosby; and it had dreaded terrorists like William Quantrill, Bloody Bill Anderson, Sam Hildebrand, Champ Ferguson, Marcellus Clark, and, of course, the youthful James boys. Adams said that guerrilla war would have reduced the Confederacy to a "smoldering wilderness." Retrospectively, it is easy to see how guerrilla war could easily have led to the Vietnamization of America or, even more ominously, the Middle Easternization of America, with the cities becoming nineteenth-century versions of Belfast or Beirut. For their part, the Union Army would be forced to undertake the onerous task of occupying the entire Confederacy—which would entail federal forces having to subdue, patrol, and police an area as large as all of today's France, Spain, Italy, Switzerland, Germany, and Poland combined.

In a guerrilla conflict, there would be no real rest, no real respite, no true amity, nor, for that matter, any real sense of victory. The North, deprived of the fruits of closure, deprived of the legitimacy that all victors clamor for, would, as a democracy, at some point reach a moment of reckoning: how much longer would it countenance sending men into war? The sweeping executions? The collective expulsions? Or being an occupying force? The molestations of the North need not even be constant or kill many people: terror would be the watchword, and all the Union would have to do was wait . . . and wait . . . and wait. As Marx later commented on the French guerrilla experience, it would be like "the lion in the fable, tormented to death by the gnat."

Indeed, in Missouri, the Union had already gotten a bitter taste of this. There, a full-scale guerrilla war was already taking place. The patchwork plans of the North had failed dismally to curb the guerrillas; General John Sanborn, who had served under Grant, put it this way: "No policy worked; every effort poured fuel on the fire." One of Lincoln's advisers, the famous legal scholar John Lieber, expressed it more fearfully: "Where guerrillas flourish, they create a slaughterfield." Even Confederate generals were dismayed at the wanton carnage; said one military man in Richmond: "They recognize the life of a man less than you would that of dog killing a sheep."

Missouri was something never before witnessed on American soil, and federal policies were at once muddled, incoherent, and ineffective. A collective sociopathy reigned in the state; the very fabric of civil society was torn apart; all morals disintegrated, and in terms of savagery, bloody Missouri rivaled the worst civil wars twentieth-century man has had to witness. This, then, was another face of guerrilla war for Lee to consider.

But, but, but. If Lee were somehow to succeed with guerrilla war, his place in history would be assured. Yet, in the end, he said no to guerrilla war, reasoning that it would set brother against brother, as killers and marauders, and presciently noting that the effect on "the country" would be too great. Lee's historic decision, sparing the nation a nasty, divisive guerrilla conflict that could well have changed this country for all of time, would in turn be met by an equally historic effort: the generosity, dignity, and magnanimity of U. S. Grant at the Appomatox surrender. Grant's gestures, which would come to be known as the spirit of

Appomatox, would go against the grain of sentiment sweeping the North, which had been burning for revenge and retribution. Revealingly, the very day that Grant would salute Lee as a brother and an honored foe, while tears ran down the cheeks of men on both sides, the *Chicago Tribune* would recommend that Lee be hung.

Yet for all the promise of April 9, as Lincoln knew too well, dire questions remained. For starters, the war was not quite over: Florida and Texas remained in rebel hands, and so did vast tracts of the Confederacy; over 175,000 men, in three extant armies, were prepared to fight on; Davis's government was racing deeper into the South, calling for partisan war. And no less than Mary Custis Lee, Robert E. Lee's wife, would ominously note: "The end is not yet. Richmond is not the Confederacy. General Lee is not the Confederacy." The situation, then, was still quite volatile. How much longer would the war last? A week? A month? Six months? Throughout history, such brief time spans have been enough to form military alliances, declare and win wars, unseat great dynasties, shift the momentum of conflicts themselves, or complicate any reconciliation to come. Which is precisely what happened.

Five days later, at 10:15 P.M., three assassins fanned out in the Union capital of Washington, D.C., to decapitate the Union government. The first, Lewis Powell, would stab five people at the secretary of state's home, en route to stabbing Secretary William Seward five times. His throat was cut "on both sides." Three times his neck was stabbed. Seward would tumble helplessly off his bed in a trail of blood, and by morning his wife would be screaming hysterically: "They have murdered my son; they have murdered my husband." (Actually, though hanging by a thread, Seward and his son would live). This was but one of three coordinated assaults set to take place across the city. According to plan, the vice president, Andrew Johnson, was to be murdered. And so was the president, while watching a play that evening at Ford's Theater.

John Wilkes Booth shoots President Abraham Lincoln in the back of the head as Mary Lincoln looks on, aghast. Booth and his fellow conspirators also planned to kill Vice President Andrew Johnson. Had they succeeded, there is no telling what amount of history-altering chaos they might have unleashed.
© PictureHistory

Johnson had been invited to Ford's as well, but begged off because he was tired. He wanted to turn in early, not realizing that on the floor above at his hotel was the other assassin, George Atzerodt, who, at 10:15, planned to plunge a bowie knife into Johnson's heart. But at the last second Atzerodt got cold feet, and by dumb luck Johnson escaped unscathed. Not so for Lincoln: he was shot by the actor-turned-assassin, John Wilkes Booth, also at 10:15, and by 7:22 the next morning was dead.

As word of the vicious multiple attacks quickly seeped out, the Northern capital was nearly paralyzed by fear. People worried about being murdered in their beds, and martial law was immediately declared. Never before had a president been assassinated—or died while a war was under way. And never before had the still largely amorphous mechanism of presidential succession been tested in a crisis. The Constitution was unclear about how this would work, and current laws only stated that, if both the president and vice president died, electors would convene in December, a full eight months away, to elect a new president. And now a host of other fateful questions remained. Would the three Confederate armies in the field, however tattered, seek to take advantage of the chaos gripping Washington? ("If the Emperor NAPOLEON had been assassinated," warned *The New York Times*, "all France would have been in bloody revolution before 24 hours passed away.") Was this now the time for the South to resort to guerrilla warfare? Would the cabinet resort to a regency government, or cabinet-style government, or even a military-style intervention? (Already some in the cabinet feared that a Napoleonic-style coup was under way and believed that, of all people, the Union general William Sherman was behind it). And finally, would Lincoln's legacy of healing devolve into nothing more than an orgy of retribution?

And other, larger questions loomed: How did all the chaos and turmoil resolve itself? How did America avoid the cruel chain of history that consigns far too many civil wars to more turmoil and more bloodshed? How did America not become like the Balkans, or Northern Ireland, or the Middle East? In the end, defying the odds of history, all the pieces would tumble into place: after running the government for nearly a day, the secretary of war and the cabinet, would show remarkable discipline and foresight and turn the government over to Andrew Johnson of Tennessee, a man widely written off as a drunk and buffoon, and a man whom nobody had ever thought of as being presidential material. Robert E. Lee, now safely back in Richmond, would again, quite publicly, spurn any temptation for guerrilla war; rejecting it for all the Confederacy to see, including Davis, he instead called on all Southerners to become good Americans (in short order, the remaining Confederate generals in the field, as well as guerrillas, would follow Lee's example, and not that of the bitter-ender, Jefferson Davis). Lincoln's call for magnanimity and the spirit of Appomatox would prevail over the calls for harshness and revenge; in short order, America would become one.

But it had been so close. But for one or two other events . . .

It's just as plausible to conjecture that assassin George Atzerodt had decided to go drinking an hour earlier, and rather than losing his courage, he instead found himself fortified by several stiff whiskeys. Making his way to Johnson's hotel room at Kirkwood House, his heart pounding, he stood there, lost in thought, for several minutes. Then he knocked, tentatively at first—then forcefully. The unsuspecting vice president, clad in his nightwear, sleepily opened the door—it was 10:21. Atzerodt pushed the vice president into the room, catching him off balance, closed the door, and plunged the knife into Johnson's heart. Johnson never had a chance. Unlike Lincoln's high-profile murder, Johnson's body was not discovered until forty-five minutes later, when a military messenger arrived at his hotel room to find the vice president's body lying in a thick pool of blood. The messenger raced back to War Secretary Edwin Stanton at Peterson House, where Lincoln lay dying. Inside, the mood of vengeance and fear deepened.

Talk of the streets running red with Confederate blood was everywhere. Citizens poured into the streets as rain drummed against windows, a hostile and growing crowd muttering, "Kill them. *Kill* the goddamn rebels!" Government departments and business houses were immediately closed; the city itself was cordoned off. But even though the government was for all purposes headless, it did not come to a standstill. Never was this more apparent than when Lincoln finally died several hours later.

Stanton, brusque, humorless, authoritarian, slightly paranoid, and deeply devoted to Lincoln, had spent the evening literally becoming the U.S. government, issuing orders, military and civil, assuming all police control, taking depositions, arresting suspects, and tending to the security of the Capitol. And he was a questionable man for the job: overwrought with exhaustion, several weeks earlier he had suffered a panic attack in Savannah. But that morning, as the rest of the cabinet gloomily assembled in Peterson House, he became the de facto leader of the United States.

"Gentlemen, we are at a terrible Rubicon," he said early in the morning to his exhausted colleagues. "The country is crying for blood at the deaths of our president and vice president; our colleague William

Seward's life hangs in the balance. None of us can know how grave the threat is to our security, or who is really behind these terrible attacks." The cabinet nodded in assent. "And the equally grave matter is how the country should be now governed. As you know, the Founding Fathers did not anticipate events such as this. Our laws state that in December, eight months hence, we will have a new election to decide our new president and vice president. But until then, how do we navigate the country through this terrible ordeal we have just been thrust into? We have a war to finish; I have already sent for General Grant. May God have mercy on the South for what they are now about to suffer. We may have seditionary elements to deal with in our own midst. We have a nation to keep from being plunged into chaos."

After nine hours of frantic, sleep-deprived discussion, the cabinet made a fateful decision: it would rule the country as a regency until a new election; civilian control of the military would remain in effect. A shaken chief justice, Salmon Chase, quickly blessed the whole affair. But like the three-man council that governed America during the Articles of Confederation, and the Directory that ruled France after the Terror, in the tension-filled days that followed, the cabinet discovered how difficult such a task is. And with Lincoln gone, there were no longer any restraints on the revenge-minded Union.

"Our nation longs for vengeance for the death of our beloved Abraham Lincoln," wrote Horace Greeley, summing up the views of the North. "More than ever, these rebels must feel our hard hand of war." The loudest voices in Congress agreed: a grieving Charles Sumner of Massachusetts, who had wept at Lincoln's bedside, cried out that the deaths were "the judgment of the Lord" and that "the time has come when all must understand that treason is a crime and not a mere difference of political opinion." Representative George Julian of the Joint Committee on the Conduct of War agreed, calling on the House to hang Davis when he was found ("in the name of God"), and Lee, and not to "stop there."

Soon, such calls would be echoed across the land.

. . .

In the next two weeks, with massive anti-Confederate rallies and riots in New York City, Boston, New Haven, and Philadelphia, the calls for Lee to be hung would reach a crescendo. Watching this furor grow, a nervous Southern diarist, Mary Chesnut, wrote sadly, "Yesterday these poor fellows were heroes. Today, they are only rebels to be hung or shot at the Yankee's pleasure." The Northern cabinet met to figure out how to contain such furious public sentiment. On April 27, fearing that events were now spinning out of control in former rebel territories and that they must be responsive to "the people, " the cabinet convened in emergency session. To mollify a public fury spinning out of control, they debated whether Lee should be arrested and tried for treason. But it was already too late.

As they agreed, ordinary Northerners took matters into their own hands. A gathering mob of ten thousand from New England to New York, Ohio to Illinois, many walking hundreds of miles, descended upon Richmond in fury of protest. Holding pickaxes and clubs, ropes and sticks, they made their way to Robert E. Lee's house in Franklin Street. The Union officer in charge, General Godfrey Weitzel—who remembered Lincoln's words weeks earlier that he should let the rebels "up easy"—anxiously placed Lee in the old Libby prison "for his own protection."

His well-intended effort would backfire; after setting fire to Lee's home, the mob was undeterred.

"To the prisons!" shouted one man.

"To the prisons!" the crowd answered.

Another man raged, "Let's hang Lee!"

"Let's Hang Lee! Let's hang him twenty times!" answered the crowd.

In a frenzy, they were on the move once again. Later accounts in *The New York Times* would compare this march to Lee's prison with the historic storming of the Bastille in France.

Union troops tried to stop the mob, but unwilling to fire on their own people, they proved to be hapless bystanders. The mob, cheering

and shouting and thirsting for blood, made its way to the prisons, push-
ing them aside. But now it was met with stiff resistance, a cordon of
rebels from inside prison itself as well as from the city at large. Word had
rapidly spread among Richmonders that Lee was imprisoned and a mob
intent upon hanging the great general was taking the law into its own
hands. For the first time since occupation began, white Richmonders
came out in droves to protect their beloved general. Amid the dust and
cobblestones, a terrible scuffle took place. Then a shot rang out; but
from where? Now a body was writhing on the ground. Then another
shot. Soon, a blizzard of shots was fired, this time by the Union troops,
and in the end, eighty Southerners were dead, with ten of them hacked
to death by the Northern mob. The injured were in the hundreds. For
their part, twenty Northerners were dead and forty-five injured. Perhaps
most inflammatory of all was the fact that a radical fringe of the mob
tried to get to Lee himself; he would escape—barely.

Two of Lee's military guards were attacked with knives and clubs and
killed; then the mob, now carrying the keys to Lee's cell, lunged for Lee
himself. A struggle broke out and the general was violently shoved to
the ground. Lee's panicked jailers and remaining guard detail drew their
gun and began to fire, and the aging commander (the fifty-eight-year
old was already not in good health) was hustled to a waiting horse
escort, where at full gallop he was taken to a safer venue. But in the
process Lee, having escaped four years of war without being wounded,
suffered injuries.

Back in the North, the cabinet moved quickly to restore order. After
having met with U. S. Grant in North Carolina, Bill Sherman (cleared
by his old friend of conspiracy and sedition, as initially feared by the
cabinet), was ordered to Richmond to "put things back in order"; he
would, he declared, deal with the remaining remnants of Joe Johnston's
rebel army later. Upon hearing this, the truculent Ohio senator Ben
Wade boasted, "By the gods, there will be no trouble *now* in running
the government down there." Sherman, however, would disappoint.
Worried "sick" and "feeling powerless" about the "renewed civil and

anarchical war" as well as the "disjointed elements of the government" he diligently worked hard to prevent another lawless occurrence that could inflame Richmonders.

His efforts were too late.

Across the South rose an inflammatory cry: "Remember the Richmond eighty!" Lurid tales of how "Bobbie Lee" was almost lynched ("like a common house boy"), and was only saved by Richmonders themselves, rippled through all corners of the original Confederacy. For his part, Lee, now back at home (where he was now surrounded by a crack detail of Sherman's troops) and recuperating from his injuries, including a nasty cut on his head and a broken arm, was badly shaken. It was as if Appomatox had never happened. Two days later, one of John Mosby's riders, a young cavalry scout, called upon him, telling the general that many wanted the South to rise up again and undertake guerrilla resistance "for honor." His men were waiting for word as to their next moves. Would Lee bless their actions?

The general, courtly as always, leaned back in his chair and closed his eyes. He had been against guerrilla war, bitterly so; he had given his word to Grant. He had seen what happened in Missouri. But that seemed a lifetime ago. Grabbing his sword, he looked at the inscription: *Aide-toi et Dieu t'aidera* ("Help yourself and God will help you"). Now he pulled himself forward and, in a soft, almost anguished whisper, told Mosby's boy: "Get the word out. It is the will of Providence."

Then he added: "The time is now."

The country was never again the same. With a renewed zeal and purpose that had often been missing in the early months of 1865, Confederate forces, with Lee's sanction, now regrouped. Earlier in the month, the prominent Maryland (and pro-Confederate) journalist William Wilkins Glenn wrote in his diary: "Nathan Bedford Forrest has genius, popularity, and power. If his army and Joe Johnston's join and fall back to Texas . . . with an army of 50,000 men, with plenty of grass for horses and mountain ranges for defense . . . they could work miracles." The

Southern generals were of essentially the same turn of mind. Forrest, Johnston, and Jeff Davis successfully escaped to Texas and were soon joined by other commands led by a number of other generals, including the articulate Richard Taylor (son of former U.S. president Zachary Taylor), the boisterous General E. Kirby Smith, the audacious Sam Jones, and Jeff Thompson.

A new rump government was established, and an organized plan for a partisan campaign, under the direction of the fearless Nathan Bedford Forrest, was set up. Their planning and strategizing began. That summer, Lee was indicted for treason. That was when the guerrillas struck, first along the frontier and in smaller places as far north as Vermont, torching buildings, row houses, and stables, robbing and dynamiting banks, and waging cavalry raids on marketplaces. (Never did they strike newspapers; it quickly became apparent that they saw a weary Union press as their ally.)

But when the aging general unexpectedly died in prison—from a heart attack—out came a new cry: "Remember Bobbie Lee." Now, guerrillas ran wild: in New York City and Illinois, in western Pennsylvania and Boston, in Baltimore and even Washington, D.C., they struck with a special fury.

And all across the South, enraged Southerners, as a sign of protest, wore little pins with Lee's likeness on them.

In upcoming months, fringe elements in the North began calling for a military government to restore order. But, true to its word, the regency government allowed an election to take place. Eight months after Lincoln was assassinated, U. S. Grant was elected president, in a bitter campaign, by a hair, replacing the hapless cabinet that had brought the country neither peace nor outright war, only this low-level fever of harassment. By then, a renewed peace movement had emerged in the North, led by second-time Democratic party candidate General George McClellan. It clamored to let the South go its own way (boasted one campaign slogan: "A General who has the courage to make the tough decisions"). Grant, by contrast, promised to end the war in a half a year, stop the terrorism, demobilize the Union army, and unify the country.

But within two years, Grant had accomplished none of his aims. Even worse, this brilliant general proved to be an ineffective politician, and his scandal-ridden administration brought him increasingly under personal attack. This was the least of his problems. It was his failure to quell the guerrilla conflict and reunify the country that was the most problematic. One spring day at the beginning of April 1868, Grant's chief of staff, John Rawlins, found the president with his head slumped down on his desk; he had nearly broken from the strain of events. By his side was a long commentary from *The New York Times*, normally a staunch ally of the Republican party:

At what point are the agonies and cruelties of this guerrilla war going inevitably to pervert our identity as a republic? At what point are they no longer sustainable for some unattainable belief in Union? The Union army has been unable to demobilize the army, which is always problematic for democracies (we remind our readers that since the beginning of this republic the people have been against standing armies). We wonder: Against this willful guerrilla onslaught, how will President Grant ever be able to pacify the entire South, without addressing their core grievance, which is independence? Make no mistake; we agree with the President that the cause for which this war first began was the "worst ever." But we are realists. Over time, our country is coming to resemble a large maze, with much of the country under Union control here, with pockets of confederate resistance there, and ambiguous areas in between. There are days when even our cities feel like embattled garrisons. At times we wonder, who feels more under siege: the largely victorious Union or the hardened guerrillas? We fear that our whole identity as a great republic is being undone.

We should have learned from bloody Missouri. Our actions there were ineffectual, and the mass executions and expulsions only created more guerrillas and undermined democracy. We know what the French once said of a comparable experience. Their columns sought to put down [the] guerrilla resistance of Abdelkader in North Africa in 1833. As one dispatch to King Louis-Philippe sadly stated: "We have surpassed in barbarity the barbarians we came to civilize." Is this the price Americans are willing to pay for the Union? Increasingly, we think not.

For now, we will stick with the policies of President Grant, but with great trepidation. And the clock of our support is ticking. We know this stage of the conflict was not of his initial making. We know that it stems from that most awful of months in this nation's glorious history, April 1865. We know that the regency cabinet badly managed events. We know we cannot bring back the great, the beloved Lincoln. However, our patience is running out. We also feel the wholesale tragic neglect of the freedman—uneducated, poor, and unfortunately, now resented bitterly, all a result of a country obsessed with this guerrilla war—and our efforts to bring him back into the fold cannot be delayed much longer without its own tragic moral and economic consequences.

We leave you, our readers, with these three questions, which loom larger, above all others, on the tongues of all Americans: Is it worth it? When will it end? And cannot the Union be just as precious without the rebel South?

Rawlins walked quietly over to the president and read the editorial. With tears in his eyes, the embattled Grant looked up and said firmly: "God help me, I just don't know."

CECELIA HOLLAND

THE REVOLUTION OF 1877

For the United States, the 1870s were a time of mixed fortunes. The Civil War was a decade behind the nation—which, in 1876, celebrated its Centennial in a gaudily mammoth exposition in Philadelphia. The exposition featured (among other things) Alexander Graham Bell's new invention, the telephone, a half mile of sewing machine exhibits (the sight of which left the novelist William Dean Howells with a deep sense of oppression), a steam engine with twin vertical cylinders that soared above the heads of spectators who came to view it by the thousands, soda water stands of white or colored marble, and a building the size of a football field (already the rugbylike form of the game was developing) devoted entirely to women and their work, notable for a relief bust of a dreaming maiden molded entirely from butter (in the days before air-conditioning, it had to be kept on ice). The whole exposition, as well as the celebrations that took place everywhere that summer, seemed to symbolize Abraham Lincoln's vision of "one nation indivisible."

But it was also a time of unease. The administration of U. S. Grant, just ended, was ripe with scandal. The country weathered a presidential election that was not decided until two days before the inauguration. The winner was Rutherford B. Hayes, the former Republican governor of Ohio and a man Henry Adams described as "a third-rate nonentity." The price of victory was

WHAT IFS? OF AMERICAN HISTORY

the official end of Reconstruction and the withdrawal of federal garrisons from the South. The nation was in the midst of a prolonged depression in which everyone but the very rich suffered. One out of every four workingmen in New York City was unemployed; the pressure of hard times crushed the nascent trade union movement. Wandering job seekers joined the legions of tramps. Even as the captains of industry cut wages of the workingmen who were already dangerously underpaid, they still managed to congratulate themselves on their leadership acumen. At an 1877 dinner in honor of the banker Junius Morgan (J. P.'s father), the losing presidential candidate, Samuel J. Tilden, could invoke "a consciousness that human society is better because we have existed."

Howard Mumford Jones has called this period "at once depressing and brilliant." As he went on to note:

We did not, as did Mexico, experience either a dictatorship or a genuine class war. We did not, as did China, break up into shards and fragments of power, each under a warlord. . . . We were not, as was the Austro-Hungarian empire, held together by habit because nobody could think of any better way of getting along.

That none of these things happened, Cecelia Holland points out in the following chapter on the great strikes that spread across the nation in the summer of 1877, was surprising; they very well could have done so. The split would not have been along sectional lines, as was the case in the Civil War, but along class ones. At the very moment when the nation at last seemed to be uniting, it would come as close as it has ever been, or would ever be, to a worker's uprising.

CECELIA HOLLAND, one of our most acclaimed and respected historical novelists, is the author of more than twenty books. She lives in northern California.

THE CENTENNIAL EXHIBITION, held in Philadelphia in 1876, put America on a world stage in the year of her hundredth birthday and demonstrated in lavish detail her right to be there. The enormous grounds with their splendid buildings presented a startling array of American ingenuity, new inventions like the sewing machine, the typewriter, and the brand-new Bell telephone, technology that would knock down age-old obstacles to progress and throw open the doors of utopia. Millions of people came to see and cheer the nation's productivity and resourcefulness and bask in the promise of a glorious future. Yet under the calliope gaiety and the red-white-and-blue boasting, even the most loyal American must have felt a sinking feeling of foreboding when she contemplated the years to come.

The country was in a deep economic crisis in which millions suffered at the edge of starvation. The Grant administration, at last coming mercifully to a close, had plumbed new levels of corruption and ineptitude in Washington. The wretched living conditions of many working people bred scattered but dangerous violence in every major city and throughout the backcountry. Farmers were being driven off their land as prices for their crops kept falling. Thousands of people were homeless and on the tramp.

Even the U.S. Army, which only a few years before, at one million men strong, had been the finest in the world, was in steep decline; in June, with the gaudy celebrations of the Centennial in full swing, the news broke that Sioux warriors had utterly destroyed George Armstrong Custer's Seventh Cavalry at the Little Bighorn.

The United States had lasted one hundred years. The Centennial ballyhooed a glorious future of wonderful machines and overflowing abundance. But the loyal American might now wonder if reality wasn't pointing in another direction. For all the inventiveness of its people, the American Republic was sagging under fundamental structural failure. The economy was outgrowing its existing institutions with new solutions nowhere in sight.

There were positive signs. The Civil War, now more than a decade gone, had removed the great burden of slavery from the working class. The rapid growth of railroads meant that goods would reach almost any market, and as the Centennial showed, new products were appearing all the time.

But banking and the money system were both still in a backwoods mode. While a steady flood of immigrants brought in plenty of workers, the banks staggered under the strain of financing the gigantic projects necessary to build a national infrastructure, and there wasn't enough money in circulation to pay for the goods potentially available. When in 1869 the railroads spanned the continent, making a national market possible, the structure to support such a market didn't exist.

Before the Civil War, most industrial labor was part-time or temporary. Factory wages supplemented income from farms rather than forming basic support for families. The factories of Lowell, Massachusetts, depended on the farm girls who came into town to work for a year or so, earn their trousseaux, and then go home to marry. Other workplaces used children and slaves, and especially on the frontier home crafts dominated.

The amount of money coined depended on how much gold and silver was available; with the Gold Rush over and the Comstock Lode worked out, both these supplies declined throughout the 1870s. Barter and payment in kind were still very prevalent throughout the country. People weren't used to working for money and there wasn't enough money anyway to pay them, and since they didn't get paid they couldn't buy anything, no matter how wonderful the goods. Yet more people poured into the United States every day, most into the cities, immigrants who were desperately poor and hungry, needing not telephones and sewing machines but food, shelter, and jobs.

The antiquated banking system gave way in 1873. Jay Cooke's speculation in railroad bonds broke his bank and the subsequent panic precipitated the country's slide into depression. For the next three years, unemployment in New York, Philadelphia, Pittsburgh, and other cities pushed 25 percent while many of those people who had work didn't make enough to live on. In the packed slums, with their airless tenements reeking of filth and disease, families lived two and three to a single room, garbage rotted in the hallways, privies drained into the drinking water, children were eaten by rats. At the same time, a few men in the position to control the explosive growth of infrastructure— railroad men, at first—were becoming obscenely rich.

In 1876, the year of the Centennial, there was an election to determine who would preside over the upcoming explosion, and it was as contentious as the condition of the country.

The Democrats, who were expected to win, ran Samuel Tilden of New York against Republican Rutherford B. Hayes of Ohio. The vote was extraordinarily close, with Tilden winning the popular election by 250,000 votes out of a total of almost ten million. The situation in the electoral college was closer yet and heavy with problems. Sneaky dealings took place on both sides and each party accused the other of fraud. Most of the Southern states had already finagled their way out of Reconstruction but the four still grappling with the federal program each sent two rival slates of electors to the convention. The controversy dragged on for months, until at last a deal with Southerners wanting an end to Reconstruction and a railroad through their states gave the highest office in the land to Republican Rutherford B. Hayes. The man who now assumed the presidency of the United States was a stout citizen of the upper middle class, whose intelligence, wealth, affability, and excellent connections had supported a long and successful political career. He was religious without belonging to any church. Besides God, he believed in hard money, temperance, and justice for the ex-slaves; he thought the way to improve the poor was through education. His wife, Lucy, was the first president's wife to be a college graduate, a champion of temperance dubbed "Lemonade Lucy" in the press.

Hayes had served in the Union Army during the Civil War, fighting through long campaigns of small fighting, not much glory but a lot of experience. A successful lawyer and investor, he might have been the richest president in the nineteenth century. He had been governor of Ohio three times, and he had a reputation for winning close elections. In 1876 he won one without even getting the most votes.

Hayes was pronounced president in March of 1877. The crisis that would stagger the Republic was already unfolding before him.

The great rail system that symbolized the American destiny was falling apart, a victim of the dysfunctional economy. In the year before Hayes assumed office, seventy-six railroads were run into bankruptcy by low demand and high costs, expanding overhead, and rate wars. Trying to stay in the black and protect their stockholders' dividends, manage-ment cut wages and piled on the work until the workers could take no more. The railroad brakeman was the epitome of the overworked, under-paid, and critically important labor the bosses of the Gilded Age ignored at their peril. For dashing around on top of, between, and sometimes under moving railroad cars, with no benefits and no job insurance, he got $40 a month—barely enough sometimes to pay his expenses, much less support him and his family. Meanwhile, in San Francisco, Leland Stanford, one of the Big Four bosses of the Southern Pacific Railroad, spent one million dollars in a single year to build a house. To the brake-man, the 10 percent pay cut must have seemed insult as well as injury.

As Hayes settled into office the country was still rocking from a demonstration of how powerful these class tensions were. At the insti-gation of an ambitious union buster, a Pinkerton detective had infil-trated a group of discontented Irish coal miners, who were supposedly responsible for such a reign of terror throughout the Pennsylvania mining country that it was a wonder anybody was left alive there—even more, that nobody had really noticed the slaughter until the Pinkerton agent revealed it in a sensational trial. But most people expected the working class to be in a murderous rage. The Molly McGuires were a powerful symbol of the class hatred and suspicion simmering in America. Ten of the Mollies, who may only have been talking up their resentments over a beer, were sentenced to hang on June 21, in the heat of the summer. As the date approached and tensions rose, gangs of other workmen vowed to free them, but never did. In the end, the gruesome ritual went on and the men died.

The hangings accentuated the general sense of threat. The excesses of the Paris commune still lingered in people's minds and the uproar of 1848 wasn't that far gone. Jittery, perhaps guilty well-to-do businessmen saw red communism in every workman's gripe, every labor association. Some of the better-off saw and agonized over the condition of the poor. How long, many were asking in the grim spring of 1877, before the streets of New York and Philadelphia and Pittsburgh rang with cries of bread or blood?

For Rutherford B. Hayes, who arrived in Washington in March of 1877 in the private railroad car of the president of the Pennsylvania Railroad, these issues were nothing new. As governor of Ohio, he had used state militia troops to break up a strike among coal miners. Now, less than three months after he reached the White House, he was facing labor unrest again.

On June 1, when the Pennsylvania Railroad's 10 percent wage cut went into effect, many expected an immediate strike on the road but nothing happened. Emboldened, the other great trunk-line railroads announced cuts—including the Baltimore & Ohio, which would hammer wages down on July 16.

The railroad men had to resist. They were starving on what they had been paid before the cut. Nor were they alone. Working-class people generally were suffering from the terrible inequity in the distribution of wealth. They were building the greatest industrial machine the world had ever known but they were getting nothing for it but crumbs. They had no national leadership. No one spoke for them in the boardrooms and conference rooms and caucuses. But common desperation gave them a single purpose, and magnified by their numbers the acts of ordinary men had national effects.

On July 17, the day after their wages went down, B&O brakemen in Martinsburg, West Virginia, a key junction point, uncoupled the engines from their trains and gathered in the yards to prevent anyone else from using them. Happening at a major crossroads in the web of rails serving the whole country, the Martinsburg strike set off an immediate chain reaction.

The Martinsburg strikers knew from previous experience that an action would be effective only if they could keep the bosses from bringing in strikebreakers. They gathered in droves around the railroad yard to prevent replacement crews from reaching the trains, and sympathetic onlookers, many workmen from other industries but also street people and idle boys, swelled the crowds.

The governor turned out the militia, recently reorganized into something called the National Guard, but the soldiers were mostly local men, many of them were railroad men themselves, and most understood the plight of the strikers. After a single brief, nasty incident, the guard disbanded. In twenty-four hours the trains were backed up for miles around Martinsburg, and the boatmen on the Chesapeake & Ohio Canal had joined the strike.

The issue was polarizing. On one side were hundreds of thousands of working people and their families, struggling just to keep their babies fed and their rents paid. On the other side was a little group of very rich men, who many thought had just bought the federal government, and who acted as if that same government was their instrument for protecting and augmenting their wealth. Looking anxiously on was a larger group, maybe the majority, not rich, not yet desperate, but suffering under the depression, many sympathetic to the workers, all dependent on the railroads. These people distinguished between strikers, whom they often supported, and rioters, whom nobody liked.

Pittsburgh mobs watch the burning of the Union Depot and its adjoining hotel during the railroad workers' strikes that spread spontaneously across the nation in July 1877. Never would the United States come so close to open class warfare. © CORBIS

The strike at Martinsburg hit the bosses where they hurt. With the freight cars idle on the tracks, the railroads were losing money every moment. The bosses began to clamor for government help. In Baltimore, the governor ordered the Maryland National Guard to go to Martinsburg to break the strike and get the trains rolling again.

On July 20, the National Guard's 5th and 6th Regiments marched through Baltimore toward Camden Yards depot to board trains for West Virginia. A mob awaited them in the streets. Baltimore had been simmering since the Civil War, a stew of oppressed working and unemployed people, tramps and boys with time on their hands, heavily flavored with resentment and rage. They had rioted before to show their displeasure and they were displeased now.

As the Guard regiments approached the train depot the mob assaulted them with volleys of stones, bricks, and bullets. The terrified troops fired back. In the riot that followed, which lasted for hours, scores of people were hurt and killed, the train station went up in flames, and Baltimore came to a stunned halt. And now, fueled by the energy of class warfare, the strike was spreading fast.

In Pittsburgh, a city of steel mills and foundries sometimes described as "hell with the lid off," railroad workers shut down the freight yard and the trains backed up on the tracks. Food began to spoil in the stalled cars. When the police came out to enforce order, a steadily growing mob attacked them with stones and guns.

A train from Philadelphia brought in the Pennsylvania National Guard, which advanced in formation to clear the mob from the tracks. The packed crowds resisted the orders to disperse—jammed onto the tracks, they actually could not move out of the way—and when some children threw a handful of rocks the Guard panicked and rolled out Gatling guns and sprayed the mob and the onlookers indiscriminately with bullets.

Their fire killed and wounded dozens of people, many of them innocent bystanders, including small children. As news spread through Pittsburgh of the slaughter, the Guard took refuge in a railroad roundhouse, and the mood of the mob turned murderous.

Most local people already sympathized with the strikers, and they had a long and deep enmity with Philadelphia. A furious crowd surrounded the roundhouse where the Guard huddled and began rolling flaming boxcars down into it. Soon they had set the whole place on fire. When firemen appeared to fight the blaze, the rioters cut their water hoses. While the railroad's property blazed, the rioters turned to systematic looting; all through the night, lines of people hurried up and down the city's streets, carrying crates and bales and boxes pried out of trashed freight cars.

The next morning the Guard managed to escape from the blazing roundhouse, fought their way through packed and hostile streets, and fled Pittsburgh. And still the strike was spreading.

The nation's capital, however, was quiet. Washington, isolated in its marshes on the margin between North and South, had few industrial workers; it was not a railroad junction; there was no real tinder to spark a local conflagration. As the violence swept across the country—as Chicago went up, New York, a dozen smaller cities in between, and even far-distant San Francisco—the plutocrats screamed for help from Washington, but in Washington, nothing happened.

As Pittsburgh and Baltimore erupted and the turmoil spread to Chicago and New York, probably the worst of it was the uncertainty. Nobody knew where this would end. Many in the besieged privileged class believed a great conspiracy was afoot—a revolutionary, communist conspiracy, which would destroy everything that mattered to them, and which only concerted effort by the federal government could put down. Karl Marx himself weighed in on the strike, predicting it would be suppressed, but still, "a nice sauce is being stirred over there." He wondered wistfully if the leadership of the working-class revolution might not be transferred to America.

There was in fact a communist political party in the United States, although minuscule. In 1876 the First International Party had officially died when only eleven delegates turned up for their convention, but the remnants coalesced into the Workingman's Party of the United States, or WPUS, which had about 4,500 members.

As the strikes swept across the country, the WPUS did try to get out in front and lead. In Chicago, as Pittsburgh was rioting, gangs of WPUS men went up and down the streets for two days, shutting down shops and factories and calling the workers out into the streets. On the third day, policemen formed their own gangs and began attacking the strikers. There followed two days of shooting, rock throwing, and the crunch of billy clubs on skulls. At least eighteen died and far more were wounded in what was later officially called at least in part a police riot.

The WPUS was even stronger in St. Louis, where, as the East boiled and Chicago stewed, the party managed to coordinate a general strike. For days great crowds turned out to hear radical speakers, who called for calm, although with an eight-hour day and benefits. The local railroads helped by rescinding their pay cuts; the Missouri Pacific even restored wages from previous cuts. The city trembled in a state of high excitement for days but there was no violence.

In San Francisco a few days later the WPUS held another rally and again appealed for calm. Instead the mobs attacked the local Chinese population, burning laundries and boardinghouses. A mob assault on the Pacific Mail Dock led to a pitched battle between rioters and the pick-handle–wielding fighters of a vigilante committee led by local businessmen. The dock burned but in the end the vigilantes ruled San Francisco. The loyal American could well wonder whom the WPUS was leading, and where to. Meanwhile, the cries of insurrection rose, as did rumors of revolution and calls for federal troops to put down the mobs and get the trains running again. The pressure mounted on the president to act. And how Rutherford B. Hayes responded would change everything. Of course he had a range of possibilities. For instance, he could have chosen to crack down, to obey the imperious demands of the railroad bosses who believed he owed his election to them, to give an ear to the newspaper editors that naked communism was at work here and only brute strength would save the Republic.

The question then would have been how to do this cracking. There were only 25,000 soldiers currently serving in the U.S. Army, and in the summer of 1877 most of them were off on the frontiers, haplessly chasing down Indians. Cognizant of that, many politicos and railroad men were demanding that Hayes issue a call for volunteers to fight the "insurrection" and break the strike. After all, in a number of places, San Francisco the best known, such vigilantism worked.

Hayes resisted. But suppose the rioting had spread to Washington, only a few miles from Baltimore. What if?

In the few days after the Baltimore riot, although nervous Washington is quiet, police notice an increasing number of people in the streets— some native Washingtonians: Washington then as now a city of slums and poverty—but strangers also, people filtering in from Baltimore and beyond, and who are milling around near the Capitol, gathering in

Lafayette Park across from the White House. They seem to have no leaders but here and there men are climbing up on soapboxes to orate, passionate liquorish words that open up old wounds in growing, restless crowds.

They seek redress of grievances, their right under the Constitution. More broadly, they want their lives made right. The federal government should refrain from defending the bosses, and, more, it should work to get them better living conditions and decent wages for their work. The dreams proliferate. No one can speak against them—wasn't the bedrock reason behind the Civil War that a man should own the fruits of his own labor? Increasingly, the men on the soapboxes talk of seizing power, as in Europe working people struggle to seize power.

The idea builds of a worker's paradise where everybody has a job and nobody takes orders from a boss. Some of these visions seem so near, so real. In the crowds, people are sharing food and water, are helping each other, are loving and peaceful in spite of their high excitement; surely it's all possible, surely the only thing holding it back are the evil men in power.

The crowds are also sharing moonshine. Wild rumors accumulate— Pittsburgh is in flames, the federal troops are on the run. Mobs have seized control of Chicago, of St. Louis. The bosses are demanding Hayes set federal troops on the people. An army of workingmen is even now marching on Washington. The Guard has been called out everywhere. There are guns everywhere. The supply of food is running out.

Adventurous rowdy boys, tramps, all sorts of footloose eager people, are coming in from outside the city, sensing a climactic moment. The crowd begins to coalesce, swarms through the streets toward the Capitol, surrounds the noble white buildings. The police, struggling to keep them back, are overwhelmed, cannot establish lines. A few men break into gun shops and steal weapons. The police send for help. They are losing control of the city.

Hayes snaps. Under pressure by his whole party, and especially from the great industrialists who see their power crumbling, he calls up not only the handful of local troops but sends out a general order to the U.S. Army to come defend the nation's capital from insurrection. And he suspends the Constitution and declares martial law. In reality, the entire strike, flaring up here and dying down there, lasted only nine days. If the president takes these steps, his actions, announced around day five or six, would be gasoline on a flagging fire, fueling the strike with a new sense of purpose.

Wherever they come from, any volunteers the government can throw into the struggle only escalate the level of the street war, bring in personal grievances, old scores, race and ethnic issues, turn the mobs even uglier, deepen divisions, and create rancorous bad blood enough to last generations. The president's policy pits working people and their aspirations against the federal government. When at last the U.S. Army, with the National Guard, manages to establish order in places like Pittsburgh and Reading, there are hundreds dead, thousands more hurt or starving or homeless, millions disaffected and radicalized.

Now death and disease stalk the slums of New York, Chicago, Baltimore. By year's end even the well-to-do are obviously losing ground and in a dozen places mass graves are receiving the dead of cholera and typhoid epidemics and simple starvation. Even with the strikes ended and the trains rolling again the depression deepens. Some fundamental trust is gone, the resilience and hope for a better day that made people keep trying in desperate times. Hayes presides over a country falling apart, an experiment that has obviously failed. The railroads broken, the farmers of the West have nowhere to sell their crops. Factories are going dark all through the Northeast.

Hayes clings to his hard-money stance, to his insistence on education and good morals to improve the people. When toward the end of his term the economy begins to come out of its hole, the Republicans congratulate themselves that they pursued the proper course. They are wrong. The economy stops shrinking but does not improve much.

Hayes's presidency does nothing to slow the decline of the institution, already so wobbly after Johnson and Grant. The power of the federal government continues to bleed away. Some local governments recover quickly from the turmoil of 1877—New York City, San Francisco, and Utah—but vigilante governments pay no attention to the Constitution, and a new sectionalism splits the nation into pieces. Everywhere people have stopped being Americans and instead are rich, or wish they were rich, or white, or black, or workingmen, Irish, Chinese, Southerners, Mormons. The federal government is swamped with their contentions. Everybody hates everybody.

In the decades after 1877, the economy struggles to regain some momentum but stalls repeatedly. The wretched poverty of the working class makes them both unreliable on the job and insignificant in the marketplace, and their resentment generates a constant low-level resistance movement, sabotaging and striking and slowing down the work. Productivity stays low, costs high. Without a mass market to spur growth and innovation, the ingenuity of the American mind expresses itself in toys and gimmicks. Periodically, uprisings in the teeming, filthy cities jolt the economy and spur governments to harsh rounds of reprisals. The federal government, taking a cue from Germany, struggles to set up a welfare state, to stabilize the country, but the economy is operating at the creep, and nobody is going to get very much. The twentieth century will open dark in America. To the loyal American, the promises of the Philadelphia Centennial now seem bitter indeed.

There was no riot in Washington, and Hayes trusted the Constitution and obeyed its rules. Although he sent federal troops to a number of places, he always did so after proper requests from the affected state governments for help in keeping order. There was a very ad hoc feel to his policy. He put out fires, sending troops as required, but never launched any national counterattack to crush the strikers. And he refused over and over to send troops to operate railroads.

This piecemeal policy worked, especially as the federal troops tended to reach their postings after the worst of the violence had died down, and then their very visible presence was enough to keep order. Conditions were improving slightly. Some of the railroads rescinded their pay cuts, a few began reconsidering their pay policies. The strike faded away, and people returned to work. Slowly the country got back to normal. Yet something had changed.

It was a small move, but vital. If Hayes had sent in troops to run the trains, to break the strikes, he would have recharged the old spirit of sectionalism that had led the country to the Civil War, but this time with social classes instead of regions. He would have thrown the power of the federal government behind the bosses and cast the workers as outlaws, as Molly McGuires.

But Hayes made the same distinction many others of the middle class made early in the strike, between strikers, who had cause, and rioters, who had none. By bringing the power of the federal government in to suppress the rioting, but leaving the strikers to work out matters with the railroads by themselves, the Hayes administration recognized the legitimacy of the new urban working class. In 1877, the labor movement forced its way in the door and became part of the household.

Of course the railroads still had the upper hand. Decades of more violence, oppression, and rage lay ahead. But the struggle looked to be winnable, and beyond lay the promise of the Centennial, real freedom, abundance, and prosperity for all. Taking that long look ahead, the loyal American could be grateful to Rutherford B. Hayes.

ANDREW ROBERTS

THE WHALE AGAINST THE WOLF:
The Anglo-American War of 1896

Grover Cleveland was a master of saying no. Not even John Tyler had exercised the veto more often. That quintessentially negative document known as the Monroe Doctrine seemed ready-made for him. "The American continents," said President James Monroe in 1823, ". . . are henceforth not to be considered as subjects for future colonization by any European powers." A no trespassing warning rarely invoked, the doctrine would nevertheless become a cornerstone of American foreign policy. In the 1840s, for example, Tyler cited it in warning Great Britain not to meddle with Texas; it became a principal justification for annexation. The U.S. government also raised the specter of the doctrine to thwart European interventions in Latin America—though the nations supposedly protected remained wary of American intentions, often with good reason.

Which brings us to Grover Cleveland, who was in his second term as president. (He had lost his first bid for reelection to Benjamin Harrison in 1888, but beat him in a return match in 1892.) Another long depression that began in 1893 may not have been of Cleveland's making, but it turned his final four years into an unrelenting disaster and doomed his hopes for a third term. At the end of 1895, he found himself with a second crisis on his hands, this time an international one. It was a boundary dispute between Venezuela and the

163

British colony of Guiana that had been festering for years, a forgotten argument over a seemingly worthless stretch of jungle. Then gold was discovered. Great Britain abruptly extended its claim deep into Venezuela: Venezuela responded by counterclaiming much of British Guiana. Lord Salisbury, the British prime minister, refused to submit the dispute to arbitration. Cleveland, who had trouble delegating responsibility, conjured up the Monroe Doctrine and proposed to determine the disputed line himself. The United States, he added, would resist any attempt by Great Britain to grab new territory in the western hemisphere. Richard Olney, the secretary of state, poured fuel on the fire when he proclaimed what amounted to a new definition of the doctrine: "Today the United States is practically sovereign on this continent, and its fiat is law upon the subjects to which it confines its interposition . . . Distance and three thousand miles of intervening ocean make any permanent political union between a European and an American state unnatural and inexpedient."

In the event, war with the United States was the last thing Great Britain needed. The conflict with the Boers in South Africa was heating up; the Germans were flexing their muscles in Europe. Great Britain backed down and agreed to arbitration. But what if it hadn't done so?

ANDREW ROBERTS is the author of a biography of the earl of Halifax, *The Holy Fox; Eminent Churchillians;* and a biography of the Victorian prime minister, the third marquess of Salisbury, *Salisbury: Victorian Titan,* which won the Wolfson History Prize and the James Stern Silver Pen Award for nonfiction. His latest book is *Napoleon and Wellington: The Long Duel.*

It is very sad, but I am afraid America is bound to forge ahead and nothing can restore the equality between us. If we had interfered in the Confederate War it was then possible for us to reduce the power of the United States to manageable proportions. But two such chances are not given to a nation in the course of its career.

— LORD SALISBURY TO LORD SELBORNE, MARCH 1902

ALTHOUGH NOTHING is ever inevitable in history, in retrospect the Anglo-American War of 1896 was about as predestined an event as anything could be. All the telltale political signs were there that the two great English-speaking nations would clash. Schoolmasters like to outline long-term, short-term, and immediate causes of great conflagrations, and this transatlantic conflict had all three.

The long-term cause was America's burgeoning self-confidence in her hemispherical hegemony and Britain's realization that without war she would one day have to cede superpower status to the parvenu power America. The short-term cause was, first, the discovery of gold in the long-disputed territory, and then President Cleveland's speech to Congress on December 17, 1895, insisting that the Venezuelan boundary dispute with British Guiana be resolved to his immediate satisfaction. Yet the immediate cause that sparked the conflict was the British colonial secretary Joseph Chamberlain's speech to the Canadian Club in London later that month, in which he decried the 1823 Monroe Doctrine and described Great Britain—accurately but unnecessarily tersely—as "an American Power with a territorial area greater than the United

States themselves, and with a title acquired prior to the independence of the United States."

Many great historical events also have coincidence and accident at their genesis, and it was pure chance that President Cleveland's secretary of state, the friendly midwesterner Walter Q. Gresham, should have died on May 20, 1895, to be replaced by the tough railway lawyer and union-busting attorney general Richard Olney only three weeks before Chamberlain became secretary for the colonies. Similarly, the influenza epidemic that laid low Arthur Balfour, the principal dove in the British cabinet, could hardly have been foreseen by those global commentators who watched, aghast, as the two great English-speaking nations dragged each other into war in the opening days of 1896.

Mark Twain—who was arrested at his London home and interned as an enemy alien soon after the outbreak—made perhaps the wittiest and most apposite remarks about the conflict. On the Venezuelan border dispute that was its ostensible cause, he remarked that it made as much sense as two bald men fighting over a comb. For two global great powers to fight over near-worthless territory at the mouth of the Orinoco River, which neither coveted, certainly seemed on the face of it absurd. As the war progressed and the Royal Navy found that it could not directly engage the American Army, and vice versa, it was Twain who memorably dubbed the struggle: "The Whale against the Wolf."

In a rematch, Grover Cleveland, a Democrat, had beaten his Republican rival President Benjamin Harrison, with 277 electoral votes to 145 in the election of November 1892, and by late 1895 he was entertaining the possibility of standing for reelection, with an aggressive newly installed secretary of state at his side. Unlike the deceased Gresham, Richard Olney was acerbic, forthright, and partisan, and was disposed to take seriously the complaints of the Venezuelan government that Britain was behaving despotically over the half-century–long boundary dispute it had been pursuing against its neighbor, Queen Victoria's colony British Guiana. Olney saw an opportunity to tweak the British lion's tail, at a time that his president knew that such a thing would be popular with the voters, especially at a time when the nation was suffering from one of the worst depressions it had yet experienced.

Yet Olney's timing could hardly have been worse. For across the Atlantic had come to prominence a statesman easily as acerbic and thrusting as the secretary of state, in the tall and angular shape of the arch-imperialist Joseph Chamberlain, whose purview as secretary for the colonies included responsibility for British Guiana. When Olney's note of July 20, 1895, was delivered by the American ambassador in London, the pacific Thomas Bayard, the marquess of Salisbury, the British prime minister, was originally disposed to reply to it languorously and belatedly. At a cabinet meeting in his vast room at the Foreign Office, he proposed employing plenty of the irony at which he had excelled both as a journalist three decades earlier and as a veteran composer of state papers.

Yet Salisbury (who took four months to answer) had reckoned both without the *amour propre* of Joseph Chamberlain and the incompetence of the young official at the British embassy in Washington who made an error about the date that Congress would reconvene. Although Salisbury's answer to Olney was ready by November 26, it was not actually delivered before Congress met, and his refutation of the legitimacy of the Monroe Doctrine that it contained—suitably stiffened by Chamberlain in the cabinet—meant that Cleveland was "mad clean through" when he read it, snorting to himself in fury.

If anything, Congress was even more angry than Cleveland, and in the words of the *London Times'* Washington correspondent, it gave the president "the most spontaneous demonstration" of support in the memory of living senators when he delivered his thinly veiled threat of war if Britain did not accept purely American arbitration over the Venezuelan-Guianan border. Cleveland closed with the words: "In making these recommendations I am fully alive to the responsibility incurred and keenly realize all the consequences that may follow."

This was not wholly true, however, because before the president had made his saber-rattling demands, neither he nor Olney had taken the elementary prior precaution of discussing the situation with the secretary for the Navy, Hilary A. Herbert. There were consequences that were about to follow Cleveland's recommendations to Congress—which were supported by a unanimous vote in both houses the very next day—that were not foreseen at the time by anyone other than a few very worried staff officers at the Navy Department in Washington.

Although none could have known it at the time—even the principals involved—a decision made thousands of miles away in South Africa was to have a significant impact on the course of the crisis. On Christmas Eve 1895, the prime minister of the Cape Colony, Cecil Rhodes—who was closely watching the way the Anglo-American crisis was developing—telegraphed his friend and physician Dr. Leander Starr Jameson and told him to postpone the raid they had planned into the Transvaal for five days later. Rhodes's acute geopolitical sense allowed him to spot the fact that back in London the Tory-Liberal Unionist coalition government needed as few distractions as possible in its eyeball-to-eyeball confrontation with the Americans.

Franco-British and Anglo-German relations had not been good in recent months, but President Cleveland's brash enunciation of the Monroe Doctrine, which effectively closed down any European hopes for influence in the Western Hemisphere, threw both Paris and Berlin into the arms of the British Empire over the issue, a fate few would have predicted for them even the previous year. As the French politicians Gabriel Hanotaux and Raymond Poincaré both saw, the dispute had direct correlations for the squabble between French Guiana and Brazil. In his bitter retirement, the former chancellor prince Otto von Bismarck made some growling references to German ambitions in Samoa that reminded his countrymen of the undesirability of the Monroe Doctrine prevailing. He scowlingly referred to it as an "arbitrarily invented principle."

With both France and Germany—albeit probably only temporarily—in the British camp, Salisbury and Chamberlain saw their chance. Unlike Cleveland and Olney, they never allowed the factor of naval dispositions to stray far from their thoughts, and the first lord of the admiralty, Lord Goschen, had been making appropriate arrangements, although in the most sotto voce way, ever since Bayard had somewhat red-facedly delivered Olney's note back in July.

Salisbury had loathed and feared the United States ever since the 1860s, when he had been Parliament's most outspoken supporter of the Confederacy. In those days he had seen Lincoln's Union as a despotic regime, a tyranny of the democratic majority over the Southern minority, and in the intervening three decades he had not seen much to change his mind about the fundamental nature of modern America. He had privately long decried Lord Palmerston's decision not to interfere in the American Civil War on the side of the Confederacy and had always thought of the universal suffrage practiced in America as supremely detrimental to the cause of good government.

Suddenly here was Salisbury's opportunity to take revenge against the forces of democracy that had, thirty years before, so disturbed his mind that he used to sleepwalk in his nightshirt through the corridors of his stately ancestral home of Hatfield House, fighting off imaginary mobs and prompting fears in his wife for his safety and sanity.

Only one man was influential enough in the cabinet to withstand the combined forces of Salisbury, Chamberlain, and Goschen, and that was the prime minister's brilliant young nephew, the leader of the House of Commons, Arthur Balfour. Yet, he was ill, fighting off a heavy bout of influenza hundreds of miles away in his Scottish home, Whittinghame.

If the coast was therefore clear politically in Britain, so was it militarily in America. The eastern seaboard of the United States had virtually no coastal batteries to defend its great cities of New York, Boston, Baltimore, Charleston, and Washington. Other cities that were dangerously exposed to the guns of the world's greatest navy of the day—whose Pacific and West Indies Station fleets almost rivaled its Atlantic one in strength—included New Orleans, San Francisco, and San Diego. As the British naval historian George W. Steevens wrote in a private memorandum to Goschen at the time: "Conquer the United States we cannot—that is an impossibility. But with a few heavy blows at the outset we can sicken them out of the war altogether."

In retrospect, it is astonishing that the chorus of support for war against Britain should have been so loud in the United States, considering these naval vulnerabilities. The Toledo *Blade*, Boston *Evening Telegraph*, and Concord *Evening Monitor* were typical of the hundreds of local newspapers that ran blood-curdling articles with headlines such as "The Coming War with England," "America's Duty in the Venezuelan Crisis," and "Our Legions: Can They Hear the Bugle Call?" Only the American naval historian Admiral Alfred Thayer Mahan seems to have recognized the danger, denouncing what he termed the "Editors' War" even before it broke out.

It was not just journalists; the politicians on both sides of the Atlantic must also bear their share of the responsibility for what happened. In an article in the *North American Review*, Senator Henry Cabot Lodge of Massachusetts announced on December 23 that America was "ready to fight now" for hemispherical supremacy and the Monroe Doctrine. The Democratic chairman of the Senate Foreign Relations Committee, John T. Morgan of Alabama, blatantly pleaded for war. Joseph Pulitzer's *New York World* canvassed the forty-five state governors, no fewer than thirty-seven of whom immediately came out in favor of war. The Hearst newspaper empire clamored for immediate hostilities should Britain continue to refuse American arbitration over the border dispute.

The president of the New York police board, the Harvard-educated thirty-seven-year-old Theodore Roosevelt, made his name by calling for an invasion of Canada, a call that was soon enthusiastically taken up by Senators Cullom of Illinois and Chandler of New Hampshire. Irish politicians in the British House of Commons meanwhile caused an uproar when they promised that an army of 100,000 Irishmen would make their way to America to fight against "the English oppressor." Worst of all for the cause of peace was the pamphlet entitled "British

Aggressions in Venezuela, or the Monroe Doctrine on Trial," which was published by the former U.S. minister in Caracas, William L. Scruggs, and which sold 300,000 copies.

The United Kingdom had imported £89.6 million of United States products in 1895 and only exported £18.8 million, so the net financial loser in any fratricidal war was always going to be America. As British investors liquidated their American equities in early January 1896 and quickly repatriated their money before exchange controls were imposed, the New York Stock Exchange saw a series of heavy falls, which were all blamed on the "wily limeys." The American economy did not respond well to the threat of war. Meanwhile, former prime minister William Gladstone's denunciation of Cleveland's "outstanding folly" was further resented, and isolated attacks against British people and property were reported in the Midwest and on the West Coast.

When it was reported that the Liberal leader Lord Rosebery, the Prince of Wales, the Duke of York, and the archbishop of Canterbury had all refused to reply to American requests for pacific public statements, the situation worsened yet further. Sabers were no longer being rattled; they were being sharpened. In Washington the British diplomat Cecil Spring-Rice wrote a haunting poem entitled "Those Who Are about to Die Salute Thee, Caesar!" which Sir Arthur Sullivan set to music and which was sung in music halls from London to Glasgow.

The terrible risk that Washington was, seemingly uncomprehendingly, embracing can be most starkly illustrated by comparing the relative strengths of the U.S. Navy and the Royal Navy in the first two months of 1896, when the New York *Sun* was calling for "a final reckoning against this arrogant empire" and the New York *Tribune* was predicting that "we'll give Victoria the same medicine we gave her granddaddy." In order to achieve this, the United States had only one first-class battleship—with a further three under construction—two second-class battleships, and one newly launched armored cruiser.

By contrast, the Royal Navy had for years followed the policy of staying larger than the combined size of the French and Russian navies, the world's next two biggest. In all, Lord Goschen controlled 29 first-class battleships, 24 second-class battleships, and 16 armored cruisers, as well as 126 unarmored cruisers, 62 gunboats, and over 300 destroyers and torpedo boats. Of course not all of these could be deployed in a single theater of war without weakening the empire strategically elsewhere, but nonetheless the imbalance between the two countries' naval capabilities was so pronounced that it was almost grotesque for many in the British Admiralty to hear the ever-louder American calls for war, knowing as they did what was likely to happen.

A recently launched first-class British battleship such as HMS *Renown* or HMS *Centurion* carried between six and twenty inches of Harveyized (strengthened) steel on its hull. It weighed around 13,000 tons and had breech-loaded guns of 12-inch caliber that could fire shells over two miles. As the British military journal *The Admiralty and Horse Guards Gazette* warned on Boxing Day 1895, the United States should now back down over Venezuela, "so that the British lion does not one of these fine days get his back up at this recurring tail-twisting process, and determine to lay about him with his very long and sharp claws."

In one area, both geographically and psychologically, the British Empire was highly vulnerable, however, and it was the one that had been spotted by Theodore Roosevelt. Canada comprised five million subjects of the Crown, as opposed to seventy-five million Americans. The dovish Ottawa government of Sir Mackenzie Bowell resigned, and in January 1896 was replaced by the hawkish one led by Sir Charles Tupper, who proceeded to call up volunteers and the army reserves. Once a letter from "An American" to the London *Times* had described Canada as "a tempting prize" later that month, the already strong response from Canadian manhood became almost universal. Hastily armed militias sprang up in every town and village.

State legislatures throughout the United States soon began passing motions demanding the invasion of Canada if Britain did not accept arbitration of the boundary dispute. Senator Gray of Delaware made matters yet worse when he stated in public that "the United States cannot permit the growth of a powerful foreign nation to the north." When the American invasion came, soon after her formal declaration of war on March 1, 1896, it was stoutly resisted.

But with War Department spending of $48 million per annum being increased eightfold by Congress overnight, and 163 volunteer infantry and seven volunteer cavalry regiments being raised, the American assault on Canada, though disorganized, proved unstoppable. The forty regular army regiments formed the nucleus of the seven army corps that poured over the border as the president made a call for no fewer than 200,000 volunteers to occupy and hold Canada "forever, if need be." At the insistence of state governors, some 50,000 of these volunteers had to remain in the United States to man defensive fortifications, put down any threatened Indian revolts, and guard against the (very unlikely) possibility of any large-scale landing on American territory. Three-quarters of the volunteers nonetheless went north.

The Canadian High Command briefly considered making two surprise amphibious attacks on Baltimore and Washington, but soon opted for the fabian strategy of surrendering terrain for time and drawing the Americans farther into the limitless Canadian heartland, waiting for winter and the opportunity of repeating Kutuzov's victory over Napoléon in 1812.

The events of 1812 also guided the senior American strategists. In that year the United States had attempted but failed to seize Toronto, Montreal, and Quebec City along three wide axes, and it was an updated version of that plan that they once again put into operation in the spring of 1896, but this time with far better effect. The newly formed Army of the Great Lakes, consisting of two army corps, marched northward and then eastward from Detroit. Meanwhile the Army of the Niagara, consisting of three army corps, moved northeastward from the Niagara River. At the same time the Army of the St. Lawrence, of two corps (headed by a volunteer force raised by Roosevelt), marched northward from New York state. One advanced on Montreal, the other on Quebec City.

The Canadians were on the defensive from the beginning, but the 40,000 of them who had served in the American Civil War thirty years earlier provided a ready reserve of combat-experienced senior commanders for the large militia forces they were raising. Unfortunately, Britain's tiny standing army of only 136,000 men was stationed all over the globe, and she found it impossible to commit more than two infantry divisions and one cavalry division, an expeditionary force 20,000 strong, to the defense of her imperial cub. Most of the troops were still at sea when the war ended.

It was the fall of Montreal and Toronto on March 27 and 29 respectively that persuaded the policy makers in the British Admiralty to alter the Royal Navy's Atlantic strategy from one of blockade to one of bombardment. The battle off Long Island on April 10 (in which America lost her only first-class battleship) left New York City unprotected. There was now no reason why *Renown* and *Centurion* should not proceed to shell the city itself, starting with Manhattan. Indeed, it was the appearance of those two warships on the Hudson River on April 12, and the—perhaps in retrospect regrettable—decision by Rear Admiral Lord Charles Beresford to destroy the two-year-old Statue of Liberty with four well-aimed shells, that provided the signal for the widespread panic that gripped America's most populous and powerful metropolis.

Until the British government's papers on the crisis are finally made available under the 150-year rule, we shall never know whether Lord Salisbury would really have carried out his threatened bombardment of the unprotected civilian center of Manhattan. The prospect of such an attack, when made public by Bayard in London, certainly brought forth widespread condemnation from across the globe at the time, even from British client rulers such as the emir of Afghanistan and the sultan of Zanzibar. It was under this worldwide outcry that the Cleveland administration managed to extricate itself from a war for which it had not

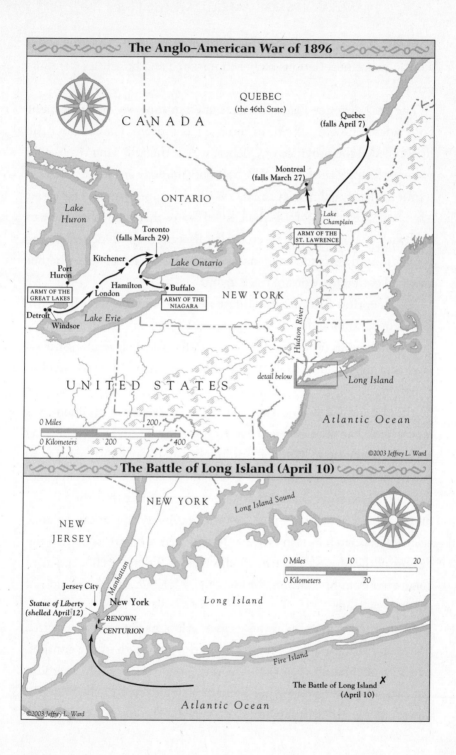

The Anglo–American War of 1896

CANADA

QUEBEC
(the 46th State)

Quebec
(falls April 7)

Montreal
(falls March 27)

Lake
Champlain

ONTARIO

ARMY OF THE
ST. LAWRENCE

Lake
Huron

Toronto
(falls March 29)

Kitchener

Lake Ontario

Port
Huron

Hamilton

Buffalo

ARMY OF THE
GREAT LAKES

London

ARMY OF THE
NIAGARA

NEW YORK

Detroit

Lake Erie

Windsor

Hudson River

detail below

Long Island

U N I T E D   S T A T E S

Atlantic Ocean

0 Miles   200

0 Kilometers   200   400

©2003 Jeffrey L. Ward

The Battle of Long Island (April 10)

NEW YORK

Long Island Sound

NEW
JERSEY

0 Miles   10   20

0 Kilometers   20

Jersey City

Manhattan

Statue of Liberty
(shelled April 12)

New York

Long Island

RENOWN

CENTURION

Fire Island

The Battle of Long Island
(April 10)   X

Atlantic Ocean

©2003 Jeffrey L. Ward

properly planned, at least in the maritime sphere. By the end of the month, peace negotiations had been initiated and hostilities were suspended.

The St. Lawrence Peace Treaty, signed in June, seemed to benefit both sides. The United States returned Toronto to Canada, but the British ceded the province of Quebec, which the following year would become the forty-sixth state. The Salisbury ministry arrived at a cynical solution that would make Canada racially homogeneous and far easier to govern. Meanwhile it was the United States that would now have to deal with the problem of an eternally discontented French-speaking population. In years to come, many Americans would wonder whether they had gotten the worst of the bargain.

By accepting Britain's "manifest destiny" on the mouth of the Orinoco, but simultaneously accepting on Venezuela's behalf a few hundred square miles of infertile but potentially gold-rich scrub nearby—land that nonetheless looked impressive on the maps reproduced in American newspapers—Olney somehow managed to keep face. But neither he nor Cleveland kept their jobs. Though the president was renominated at the Chicago Democratic convention in July, beating back the challenge of William Jennings Bryan, the populist orator from Nebraska, he lost the election to a Republican congressman from Ohio, William McKinley. Outraged Irish voters, who felt that the United States should have held on to Toronto, probably tipped the balance against Cleveland. But, in fact, hard times were a bigger issue than the defense of the Monroe Doctrine. In his famous "Front Porch" campaign, conducted from his Canton, Ohio, home, McKinley made the most of pocketbook issues.

As so often is the way in these cases, relations between the United States and Britain quickly improved in the aftermath of the conflict, especially after Salisbury supported Washington in the Spanish-American war two years later, and Arthur Balfour offered to replace the Statue of Liberty as a grand British gesture of goodwill. The wounds took longer to heal in Canada, whose insistent demands for retribution in the St. Lawrence Peace Treaty caused Lord Salisbury to lose patience with Sir Charles Tupper.

In retrospect, however, probably the most important result of the 1896 Anglo-American War was the way that it encouraged the American people to think of themselves as a global power whose fortunes were intimately bound up with events in the rest of the world. Relations with France, Germany, and of course, after 1898, with Spain were seen to matter to Americans' day-to-day lives. Once they had built the vast fleet whose keels they laid down in the immediate aftermath of the war, the United States was in a position to dictate its own terms for practical global engagement, especially once their commercial and financial power made it clear that they were likely to dominate the world economy.

It might even be that without American naval might being what it was within two decades, and without the newfound willingness of U.S. politicians to interfere in European affairs (especially the Hero of Quebec, Theodore Roosevelt), Kaiser Wilhelm II might have been allowed to unleash a general European war in August 1914, instead of meekly accepting America's demand not to support Austria-Hungary against Serbia. But here we stray into the region of counterfactual history.

JOHN LUKACS

NO PEARL HARBOR?

FDR Delays the War

Most of the what ifs of Pearl Harbor have centered around the circumstances of the day, and for Americans they run the gamut from deliverance to utter disaster. What if, for example, all three Pacific Fleet aircraft carriers had been at anchor that Sunday morning of December 7? (The Saratoga was being repaired and refitted on the Pacific coast, the Enterprise and the Lexington were delivering planes to Wake and Midway islands.) The loss of even one, or serious damage to all three, would have hampered U.S. strategy not just for the first months of 1942 but for the entire war. Without carriers, there could have been no victory at Midway, no landing at Guadalcanal. What if, too, the Japanese had not limited their attacks to a single morning but had hung around Hawaii for a day or two longer, time enough to strike the American submarine yards and to destroy the aboveground tank farm, with its 4.5 million barrels of oil? (Admiral Chester W. Nimitz, who took over command of the Pacific Fleet after Pearl Harbor, estimated that the loss of the oil would have added two years to the war.) Conversely, what would have happened if the United States had been better prepared—the Pearl Harbor commanders had received war warnings, after all. What if torpedo nets had been rigged around the battleships (they weren't) or if the Japanese attackers had met serious opposition in the skies above Oahu? The result might not have been "a day that will live in infamy."

There is another possibility, which John Lukacs brings up in the chapter that follows. What if the sneak attack of December 7 had never taken place? What if America's war with both Japan and Germany had been put on hold? The prospect was, as Lukacs maintains, not out of the question. Would it have changed the outcome of the war?

JOHN LUKACS, a professor emeritus of history at Chesnut Hill College, Philadelphia, is the author of many books, among them *The Duel: The Eighty-Day Struggle Between Churchill and Hitler, The Hitler of History, A Thread of Years, Five Days in London, May 1940,* and, most recently, *Churchill: Visionary, Statesman, Historian.* He lives in Pennsylvania.

O N NOVEMBER 21, 1941—it was the Friday after Thanksgiving Day—President Franklin Delano Roosevelt took up a pencil on his desk and wrote this memorandum:

6 MONTHS

1. U.S. to resume economic relations—some oil and rice—more later.

2. Japan to send no more troops to Indochina or Manchurian border or any place South (Dutch, Brit. or Siam).

3. Japan to agree not to invoke tripartite pact [the alliance signed in September 1940 by Japan, Germany, and Italy] even if U.S. gets into European war.

4. U.S. to introduce Japs to Chinese to talk things over but U.S. take no part in the conversations.

LATER ON PACIFIC AGREEMENTS.

He called this proposal a "modus vivendi," a term that was current in Washington during those days, meaning a temporary accommodation with Japan, in view of the accumulating news of the prospect of an imminent war between Japan and the United States. The president sent this memorandum over to the secretary of state, Cordell Hull.

Up to this point, every historian accepts the statement of these facts, but more than sixty years later there is still a roiling controversy about what happened soon afterward.

Some historians—professional as well as amateur—argue that this was Franklin Roosevelt's greatest mistake. By November 21, 1941, he knew that the Japanese were about to go to war with the United States, most probably at the end of the first week in December, including an attack as far east as Pearl Harbor. By procrastinating and in effect postponing a, by and large, inevitable war with Japan, Roosevelt contributed to the great Allied crisis in May 1942 that nearly resulted in the final victory of Hitler and of his allies in the Second World War.

Other historians do not accept this thesis: they claim that the postponement of a war with Japan in late 1941 did not essentially affect the outcome of World War II.

So let us now sum up what really happened, and what were its great and grave consequences.

Throughout November 1941 there was more and more evidence of a probable Japanese attack on American and/or British possessions in the Pacific and in the Far East as well as on the Netherlands East Indies (Indonesia now). American intelligence could read most of the Japanese codes, including their diplomatic ones. This was very important, since the Japanese government had sent two special envoys, Admiral Kichisaburo Nomura and Saburo Kurusu, to make a last attempt in Washington to negotiate a temporary settlement with the United States. They were entrusted with two Japanese overall proposals, A and B. Proposal B included at least a few Japanese concessions. It was communicated by these envoys on November 20, Thanksgiving Day 1941, to the secretary of state. Its contents were available to their recipients days before, due to the American decoding. The two Japanese envoys in Washington were honest men. They were emissaries of the emperor and of those conservative Japanese statesmen who, unlike most Japanese military leaders, wished to avoid war with the United States.

Thus the Japanese government, on top, could be described as divided, but, in a way, so was the American one. Like Nomura and Kurusu, President Roosevelt, however reluctantly, was willing to give a last try. So were some officials in the State Department who realized that there were some grounds for a possible compromise between Roosevelt's "modus vivendi" and the Japanese Proposal B. Thus on November 22 they formulated the Roosevelt memorandum into a more precise and official American modus vivendi.

The modus vivendi was then shown to America's allies and friends: the Chinese, Dutch, and British. The last two, including Winston Churchill, accepted it, though with some reluctance. The Chinese lobby argued against it vehemently. Secretary of State Hull, too, was inclined not to present the modus vivendi to the Japanese; instead he drafted a ten-point proposal requiring, among other things, a Japanese withdrawal from China, which he knew the Japanese would not accept.

There is no disagreement among historians about these events and their circumstances. However—even after a long telephone conversation with Churchill, who said, "Isn't this too thin a diet for the Chinese?"—Roosevelt overruled Hull. "It is worth a try: unless the Japs fire the first shot," he said, "and we will not maneuver them into doing so."

So it happened. He called Kurusu and Nomura to the White House on November 25. He charmed them with his customary bonhomie. He gave them the American modus vivendi proposals and said, "Let us not argue now about its details. Transmit it to your Emperor with my sincere good wishes."

So it was. The Japanese grand fleet was about to sail forth the next day from Hitokappu Bay, ready to drive east across the North Pacific, to a point about 275 miles north of Pearl Harbor. Twelve hours before sailing its mission was canceled—through the influence of the Japanese emperor and his conservative chamberlains. Thousands of Japanese officers and sailors climbed over its armaments and hawsers, clambering ashore. Their bitterness spread wide among the Japanese people, especially their high military officers, many of whom were eager and ready to go to war against the United States and Britain.

Winston Churchill, who for months had hoped that perhaps the United States would finally join in the war against Hitler by getting into a war with Japan, was disappointed but not bitter; he kept on waging his war during that dark and gloomy winter of 1941. His new ally Stalin had mixed feelings. On the one hand, he knew by early December 1941 that Moscow would not fall to the Germans—in part because of the large contingent of Russian troops that he had transferred to the central front, denuding his Siberian borders across Japanese-occupied Manchuria. On the other hand, he could not be sure that the Japanese military, frustrated because of the temporary modus vivendi with the United States, would not soon attack Russia in accord with their German ally.

Adolf Hitler, too, was of two minds. He had thought, and planned, that a Japanese war with the Americans and the British in the Pacific would tie down the bulk of the American navy there, diminishing its support of the British in the Atlantic. At the same time he was angry at the temporary ascendancy of Emperor Hirohito and of his conservative chamberlains over the militarists. "Just like the King of Italy!" he said to Ribbentrop and Goebbels. (In one of his table conversations he praised the German Social Democrats, who at least had gotten rid of the Hohenzollern monarchy in 1918.)

During the winter months of early 1942, the war in the Atlantic went on. There were a few incidents between German submarines and American ships—the latter shadowing and supporting British ones—but, still, not enough for Roosevelt to call for a declaration of war against Germany. Hitler repeatedly confirmed, ever more stringently, his June 21, 1941, directive to his naval forces: avoid any kind of incident with the Americans, even if the latter commence firing. American journalists, such as William Shirer, were permitted to stay in Germany and file their dispatches (though they were shadowed by police); the deportation of Jews eastward had begun, but those few Jews who were American citizens remained untouched; Hitler also decided to postpone the deportations of Jews from Berlin. Meanwhile, the building of the American war economy and armaments went on and on, though accompanied by increasing criticism from Republicans, some of them lamenting publicly that much of the American production of arms was going to Britain, and some of it even to the Russians.

And for Britain and Russia the skies were darkening. Both Stalin and Churchill, in their different ways, were beginning to doubt whether the United States would, or indeed could, enter the war. Hitler's armies, unlike Napoléon's, survived the cruel Russian winter after a few temporary retreats, remaining largely intact. In May 1942 they resumed their invasion of southern and central Russia, driving rapidly toward the Don and Volga, approaching the Caucasus. Stalin was deeply depressed, since the flow of equipment that was reaching him from British and American ports narrowed down to a trickle. At the same time the brilliant "Desert Fox," Field Marshal Rommel, beat the British out of Libya, corralled more than 30,000 British and Empire prisoners in Tobruk, and was about to march almost unhindered toward the Suez Canal when things were suddenly changing on the other side of the world.

On May 25, the six-month modus vivendi would expire. There were desultory negotiations about its possible prolongation in the spring. But neither the American nor Japanese negotiations were able to offer more reciprocal concessions. On the American side, President Roosevelt's situation was difficult, since the terms of the original modus vivendi, essentially a secret document, had leaked out throughout the winter. One group of Republicans, "Asia Firsters," accused the president of selling out China; another group, led by Senator Robert Taft (and supported by Charles Lindbergh), accused Roosevelt of trying to get the United States into a war with Germany "through the back door," that is, provoking war with Japan. Yet the fatal chain of events occurred not in Washington but in Tokyo.

The Japanese militarists, fretting against the modus vivendi and the conservatives of the Imperial Court, took matters into their hands. They were encouraged by the German victories. They were convinced that Japan's hour of decision must no longer be postponed. On May 20 they assassinated Kurusu, the peacemaking Japanese envoy, who had just been called back from Washington. They made the emperor move away from his chamberlains and advisers, to Sansushi Palace, where a crown council was convoked on May 25. The army chiefs argued that Japan must no longer refrain from fulfilling her commitments to the Tripartite Pact with Germany: this was a matter of Japanese honor. The alternative was going to war with the Anglo-Saxon imperialists in the Far East and western Pacific. Another alternative was (the 1941 Soviet-Japanese Neutrality Treaty notwithstanding) to attack the Soviet Union from the East, in concert with the Germans advancing across European Russia. The third alternative, that of prolonging the modus vivendi, involving more concessions to the Americans, had the fewest supporters.

The session went on into the night. In the end, the emperor felt forced to compromise. There would be no declaration of war against the United States, but one against Britain (and the Netherlands), effective at once, with coordinated invasions of Hong Kong, Malaya, Siam, and the East Indies. The militarists hoped (and many of them thought) that with the dismal situation of Britain and Russia in mind, the Americans might not choose to go to war, at least not at that time.

They were wrong. President Roosevelt immediately demanded that the Japanese halt their attacks against the British and Dutch possessions within twenty-four hours. There was no response from Tokyo, and on May 28 Japanese planes attacked and sank five ships in Hong Kong harbor, including an American passenger vessel and a destroyer. Four hundred Americans lost their lives. This melted much of congressional opposition away. Roosevelt declared May 28 "a day of infamy," and Congress declared war on Japan the next day, with only six senators and fifty congressmen abstaining (the same number as on April 6, 1917).

That same day the president authorized the transport of three hundred Sherman tanks to Africa for the beleaguered British. They would arrive there just in time. Churchill's newly appointed Field Marshal Montgomery was able to halt Rommel's advance only sixty miles west of the Nile. Three months later Montgomery felt strong enough to attack the German-Italian army at El Alamein, leading to the first considerable British victory in the field.

Churchill had planned to come to Washington at the end of May, but once he heard of the Kurusu murder and a new Japanese government and of the imminent Japanese attack on Hong Kong, Malaya, Singapore, etc., he chose to remain in London. (He also thought it best not to give any ammunition to isolationist Republicans.) He waited for a month and arrived in Washington on the last day of June. Addressing Congress, he cited Cromwell: "'The Lord hath delivered our enemies to us.'" Yet, Roosevelt told him that he was still not able to go to Congress for a declaration of war against Germany, since there were too few incidents in the Atlantic between the German and American navies. But they agreed on a master plan.

American naval forces and Marines would occupy the Azores, Madeira, and the Cape Verde Islands in October 1942. (There would be no trouble with the Portuguese: Churchill would attend to that). Then in early November American forces would invade and liberate French North Africa without officially declaring war on Germany. Churchill was elated. He and Roosevelt coordinated the American invasion of North Africa with the British offensive across Libya. And so it happened, sometime between October 24 and November 8. A week later a Russian counteroffensive encircled the German Sixth Army west of Stalingrad. The turning point of World War II had come.

During these months in the Far East the Japanese had forced the British to surrender Singapore ignominiously. But the U.S. Navy, unlike in 1941, was no longer concentrated at or near Hawaii. Two task forces had been moved to the Philippines in the spring of 1942, and in the Battle of Wake Island in October 1942 (aided by the decoding of Japanese radio signals) Admirals Spruance and Oldendorf destroyed half of Japan's aircraft carriers. Pressed by Tokyo's insistent demands, Hitler did not precisely declare war but asserted "a state of defensive warfare" with the United States on November 10, 1942, a day after Americans had landed in Morocco and Algiers. (The president proclaimed that this amounted to a German declaration of war, which even his bitterest critics found difficult to deny.) The stage was set for an invasion of Europe by the Americans and British.

The rest we know. The Japanese fought bitterly in the Far East and on the seas, on one occasion coming close to northwestern Australia, but eventually they were conquered. Hitler killed himself in his underground bunker in Berlin. After two atom bombs were cast on Japan and Stalin entered the war against the Japanese, they surrendered.

ANTONY BEEVOR

IF EISENHOWER HAD
GONE TO BERLIN

On April 12, 1945, American troops crossed the Elbe River in the heart of Germany and, at the order of their commander, Dwight D. Eisenhower, stopped. Should they, could they, have pushed on to the Nazi capital, Berlin? The controversy surrounding Eisenhower's decision has raged ever since. In the following chapter, the British military historian Antony Beevor, the author of The Fall of Berlin 1945, sheds new light on it. Eisenhower had already made up his mind and had announced to Josef Stalin his intention not to continue on to Berlin. Stalin plainly lied to Eisenhower. But Berlin may have seemed an empty military symbol to Eisenhower, and one that was not worth potentially heavy casualties at a time when the war in Europe was practically won. He was more concerned with forestalling a Soviet drive along the Baltic Sea that might envelop Denmark, and with the possibility that Hitler might make a last stand in the Alps, his so-called National Redoubt. Eisenhower's intelligence staff suggested that "here, defended both by nature and by the most efficient secret weapons yet invented, the powers that have hitherto guided Germany will survive to reorganize her resurrection: here armaments will be manufactured in bomb-proof factories, food and equipment will be stored in vast underground caverns and a specially selected corps of young men will be trained in guerilla warfare, so that a whole underground army can be fitted and directed to liberate Germany from the occupying forces." The "National Redoubt" was the stuff of Nazi dreams, but Eisenhower believed in it enough to dispatch General George Patton and his Third Army to destroy it. Patton found nothing: Hitler had chosen to make his last stand in Berlin.

The question remains: Why was Stalin so eager to get to Berlin first? As Beevor reveals, a genuine treasure lured him, one that Eisenhower knew nothing about, and the Soviet dictator was willing to sacrifice 350,000 men to secure it. But what would have happened if Eisenhower had not dawdled at the Elbe bridgehead? How easy would it have been for the Americans to reach Berlin? And what might have happened if they had done so? Might an unpleasant surprise have awaited them? There are hints that if Stalin had been frustrated in his search, the Cold War, already taking shape, would have become prematurely hot.

ANTONY BEEVOR, a former British Army officer, is the author of a number of books of military history, including *The Spanish Civil War*, *Crete: The Battle and the Resistance*, *Stalingrad*, and *The Fall of Berlin 1945*. He lives in London.

GENERAL DWIGHT EISENHOWER has often been bitterly blamed for his refusal to push on to Berlin in April 1945. His troops were in bridgeheads across the Elbe River. The capital of the Reich lay just sixty miles away and there were few German troops defending its western flank. All available Wehrmacht formations had been concentrated on the Oder, awaiting the Red Army's onslaught from the East. Yet to the dismay of Churchill and most of his own generals, Eisenhower insisted on leaving Berlin to the Red Army. He seemed more preoccupied with the idea that the Nazis might defend an Alpine Fortress, or "Final Redoubt," down in the South, despite the scepticism of his intelligence chief, General Kenneth Strong.

Like President Roosevelt and members of his administration, Eisenhower had been bending over backward to win Stalin's confidence. American leaders believed that individual friendship and frankness could win round their Russian counterparts. Eisenhower's political adviser, Robert Murphy, subsequently acknowledged that "Soviet policymakers never operate on that theory." This was putting it mildly. Eisenhower disclosed his intentions in a notorious signal to Stalin, who promptly hoodwinked him in what was perhaps the greatest April Fool in history.

On April 1, Stalin had summoned Marshals Zhukov and Konev to the Kremlin. He had made clear to them that their overriding priority was to get to Berlin before the Americans or British. "Well, then," he said looking at the two men, "who is going to take Berlin? Are we or are the Allies?"

"It is we who shall take Berlin," Marshal Konev replied immediately, "and we will take it before the Allies."

Once the meeting was over, Stalin turned his attention to formulating a reply to Eisenhower's signal. This communication, known as SCAF-252, revealed SHAEF's plans even before they had been communicated to his British allies. Churchill was appalled, if not enraged, when he heard. Stalin, with his uncanny nose for discord, may have suspected as much. In any case, he told Eisenhower in his reply that the Allied plan to meet up with the Red Army in the center of Germany, well to the south of Berlin, "completely coincided" with the plans of the Soviet leadership. Stalin then shamelessly assured the trusting Eisenhower that "Berlin has lost its former strategic importance" and that the Soviet command would send only second-rate forces against it. The Red Army would be delivering its main blow to the south to join up with the western Allies. The advance of the main forces, he claimed, would start approximately "in the second half of May." This was over a month after the real date. "However, the plan may undergo certain alterations, depending on circumstances."

But why was Stalin so desperate to deceive the Americans and seize Berlin before them? Victory was already assured and whoever captured the city was going to have to hand over the other half of it according to the agreements already made between the Allies on the occupation of a defeated Germany. Was Stalin prepared to sacrifice so many of his soldiers' lives right at the end of the war simply because Berlin was the symbol of victory that belonged by rights to the Soviet Union after all its suffering? This was undoubtedly true, but new documents from Russian archives suggest that the Soviet leaders also had a rather more material incentive to get to Berlin before the Allies. In November 1941, five months after the launch of Operation Barbarossa, Stalin was told that Britain and the United States had started work on a uranium bomb. This intelligence had come from the British communist spy John Cairncross. Stalin dismissed this information angrily as "a provocation." It was a curious repeat of his behavior when warned of the German invasion earlier in the year.

In May 1942, three months before the start of the battle of Stalingrad, Stalin summoned Beria and the leading atomic physicists to his dacha. He was furious to have heard from other communist spies in America that the United States and Britain really were working on a uranium bomb. Stalin blamed Soviet scientists for not having taken the threat seriously, yet he was the one who had rejected the first report.

Some Soviet scientists, however, soon feared that German atomic physicists, such as Werner Heisenberg, might be close to inventing a bomb. It was Heisenberg who had worked on uranium before the war at the Kaiser Wilhelm Institute in Berlin. And in late 1942, a notebook found by Red Army intelligence on the body of a German officer killed in the south of the Soviet Union showed that the Germans were looking for uranium deposits in the occupied territories. But by 1944, Soviet intelligence established that German research was not a threat. Mercifully, Hitler had failed to see the weapon's potential and Heisenberg had grossly overestimated the critical mass of uranium needed.

The real issue, as Stalin began to recognize, was a postwar world dominated by two superpowers. If the United States had a devastating strategic weapon and the Soviet Union did not, then it would be as vulnerable to attack as it had been in 1941. It is probably no exaggeration to say that the underlying cause of the Cold War was Stalin's unforgotten trauma from the shock of the German invasion.

The Soviet nuclear research program, later code-named "Operation Borodino," was accelerated in 1943 with detailed research information provided by communist sympathizers such as Klaus Fuchs, inside the Manhattan Project at Los Alamos in New Mexico. Beria himself, although suspicious of his own spies and the Soviet scientists, began to take over supervision of nuclear research from Molotov and brought Professor Igor Kurchatov's team under complete NKVD control.

The Soviet program's main handicap, however, was a lack of uranium ore. On Beria's instructions, the Soviet Purchasing Committee in the United States asked the American War Production Board to sell it uranium oxide. After consultation with Major General Groves, the head of the Manhattan Project, the U.S. government authorized purely token supplies, mainly in the hope of finding out what the Soviet Union was up to. Groves, meanwhile, was already working to ensure that the United States and Britain would have a virtual monopoly of the world uranium supply after the war, especially for the richest deposits of all in the Belgian Congo. But this plan was betrayed to the NKVD, most probably by the British traitor Donald Maclean, then working in Washington, D.C., on the Combined Policy Committee. On February 28, 1945, just as the Soviet forces earmarked for the capture of Berlin were securing their northern flank in Pomerania along the Baltic, Beria received a detailed report on every aspect of research in the United States, including the Groves plan. The idea that the western Allies wanted to deprive the Soviet Union of uranium after the war must have excited Stalin's deepest suspicions. Fresh uranium deposits in Kazakhstan were confirmed at just about that time, but still in insufficient quantities. The Soviet Union's only hope of copying the American atomic bomb lay in seizing German supplies of uranium before the western Allies got to them. Beria had discovered from Soviet scientists who had worked up to 1933 at the Kaiser Wilhelm Institute for Physics in Dahlem, a southwestern suburb of Berlin, that this was the center of German atomic research. Work was carried out there in a lead-lined bunker known as the "Virus House," a code name to discourage outside interest. Next to this bunker stood the Blitzturm, or "tower of lightning," which housed a cyclotron capable of creating 1.5 million volts. Beria, however, did not know that most of the Kaiser Wilhelm Institute's scientists, equipment, and material, including seven tons of uranium oxide, had been evacuated to Haigerloch in the Black Forest. But a German bureaucratic mix-up had led to a further large consignment of uranium oxide being sent to Dahlem instead of Haigerloch.

The main German center for processing uranium, as General Groves soon discovered, was also close to Berlin. This was the Auer plant at Oranienburg, fifteen miles north of the Reich capital. Groves, realizing that the Red Army was bound to seize it in its imminent advance on

Berlin, recommended to General George C. Marshall "that the plant be destroyed by air attack."

"On 15 March," wrote Groves later, "612 Flying Fortresses of the Eighth Air Force dropped 1,506 tons of high explosive and 178 tons of incendiary bombs on the target." Poststrike analysis of the raid claimed that all of the plant aboveground had been destroyed, but in fact some of the stores must have survived, to judge by Beria's subsequent report.

In Moscow, meanwhile, Professor Kurchatov assessed the huge volume of data provided by the Soviet spies in the United States. Estimates of the documents flown back to the Soviet Union in late 1944 and early 1945 range up to ten thousand pages. The most vital details were delivered at the beginning of April 1945, just before the great offensive toward Berlin from the river Oder involving over two million men. Continuing the policy of disinformation toward their western Allies, the Red Army high command, the Stavka, informed American liaison officers in Moscow late on April 16, the day of the general attack, that the operation was nothing more than "a large-scale reconnaissance on the central sector of the front for the purpose of finding out details of the German forces."

The following day, an American detachment led by one of Groves's officers went to a salt mine at Stassfurt, south of Magdeburg, in an area designated as part of the future Soviet zone. There they found 1,100 tons of uranium ore. This was rapidly loaded onto railway wagons and moved westward two days later. It was shipped back to the States for the Manhattan Project's development of the so-called Fat Man bomb.

Marshal Zhukov's 1st Belorussian Front, having finally broken through on the Seelow Heights just west of the Oder, advanced with all speed to encircle Berlin from the East and the North. His 47th Army reached Oranienburg on April 22. There, Beria's NKVD teams managed to recover "570 kgs. of metallic uranium in powder; also 300 kgs. of nonprocessed metallic uranium" from the Auer plant almost obliterated by American bombers just over a month before.

Stalin, meanwhile, had ordered Marshal Konev to send his two tank armies northwestward to surround Berlin from the south. It may be significant that Stalin defined his objective as Zehlendorf, the most southwestern suburb of Berlin, which lay right next to Dahlem. This was also the most likely direction of advance into the city by American troops from the U.S. First Army. Eisenhower had ordered them to halt on the Elbe, but Stalin was taking no chances. He had been forcing Zhukov to increase his rate of advance during these critical days, often with brutal threats. The pressure down the chain of command led to very high casualties. Yet, the moment Berlin was surrounded, Stalin appears to have relaxed, presumably on the assumption that the Americans would not attempt to break through the cordon.

Konev's advance troops reached Dahlem on April 24, and the Kaiser Wilhelm Institute for Physics the next day. The fighting, with Katyusha rocket batteries and tanks advancing amid the spacious villas and neat tree-lined streets, produced strange contrasts. The mechanized troops were followed by carts pulled by shaggy little ponies and even pack camels.

There is nothing to show that any commanders in General Rybalko's Third Guards Tank Army, not even Rybalko himself, had been warned of the Institute's significance. Yet they must have been aware of the large force of NKVD troops and specialists that immediately secured the nuclear physics complex off the Boltzmannstrasse and sealed it off.

Since the one thing holding up Soviet attempts to replicate the Manhattan Project's research was the shortage of uranium, the importance that Stalin and Beria attached to securing research laboratories and their supplies was evidently considerable. Beria's preparations for the Berlin operation had been enormous. Colonel General Makhnev was in charge of the "special commission." The large numbers of NKVD troops deployed to secure the laboratories and uranium stores were directly supervised by no less a personage than General Khrulev, the chief of rear area operations for the whole of the Red Army. The chief NKVD metallurgist, General Avraami Zavenyagin, had set up a base on the edge of Berlin and scientists from the main team of researchers supervised the movement of materials and the dismantling of laboratories. The NKVD commission made its report. As well as all the equipment at the Kaiser Wilhelm Institute, they found "250kgs of metallic uranium; three tons of uranium oxide; twenty litres of heavy water." The three tons of uranium oxide misdirected to Dahlem was a real windfall. There was a particular reason for speed, Beria and Malenkov reminded Stalin rather unnecessarily in a retrospective confirmation of action already carried out: the Kaiser Wilhelm Institute was "situated in the territory of the future Allied zone." "Taking into account the extreme importance for the Soviet Union of all the above-mentioned equipment and materials," they wrote, "we request your decision on disassembling and evacuating equipment and other items from these enterprises and institutes back to the USSR." The State Committee for Defense accordingly authorized the "NKVD Commission headed by Comrade Makhnev" to "evacuate to the Soviet Union to Laboratory No. 2 of the Academy of Sciences and Special Metal Department of the NKVD all the equipment and materials and archive of the Kaiser Wilhelm Institute in Berlin."

The NKVD also wanted German scientists capable of processing uranium. Makhnev's special detachments rounded up a number, including Professor Peter Thiessen and Dr. Ludwig Bewilogua, who were flown to Moscow. But the major figures of the Kaiser Wilhelm Institute— Werner Heisenberg, Max von Laue, Carl Friedrich von Weizsäcker, and Otto Hahn, who had won the Nobel Prize for chemistry only a few months before—were beyond their grasp. They had been picked up by the British and were taken back to be lodged at Farm Hall, their debriefing center for German scientists in East Anglia. Other, less important laboratories and institutes were also stripped and many more captured scientists were sent to a special holding pen in the concentration camp of Sachsenhausen. Professor Baron von Ardenne, on the other hand, volunteered to serve the Soviet Union. He was persuaded by General Zavenyagin to write "an application addressed to the Council of People's Commissars of the USSR that he wished to work with Russian physicists and place the institute and himself at the disposal of the Soviet government."

Kurchatov's scientists at last had sufficient uranium to start work in earnest, and experts to process it, but further supplies were urgently needed. General Serov, the NKVD chief of the First Belorussian Front, was ordered to concentrate on securing the uranium deposits in Czechoslovakia and above all in Saxony, south of Dresden. The presence of the uncompromising General George Patton's Third Army in the region must have caused the Soviet authorities considerable concern. It may also explain why they were so nervous about whether U.S. forces would withdraw to the previously agreed occupation zones.

Up to now, historians thought that neither Stalin nor Beria took the threat of an American atomic bomb seriously until the Potsdam Conference, but the scale of the NKVD operation in late April devoted to seizing uranium in and around Berlin certainly appears to contradict this assumption. For Stalin, the West's advance in nuclear weapons was his greatest source of fear and suspicion in 1945. His huge superiority in conventional forces was now undermined, and he was sure that the West would blackmail him.

For Churchill and President Truman, on the other hand, the Soviet Union's blatant disregard for free elections in the countries liberated and then occupied by the Red Army was the key indication that they could not trust Stalin anymore. The brutal and unscrupulous behavior of Soviet authorities in Poland was the deciding factor. This was most clearly demonstrated by the fact that while ten regiments of NKVD troops were allocated to keep order in Germany, no less than fifteen were deployed in Poland, supposedly the Soviet Union's ally. Their commander, General Selivanovsky, was ordered to "combine the duties of representing the NKVD of the USSR and councillor at the Polish Ministry of Public Security." The mutual suspicion between the Soviet Union and its western Allies fed upon itself. Berlin, the key theater in the final stage of the Second World War was soon the focal point of the nuclear-dominated Cold War.

• • •

But what of Eisenhower's much-criticized decision to leave Berlin to the Red Army? Could he have taken Berlin without heavy losses and would it have changed the course of history, as some claim? General Omar Bradley warned him that they might lose 100,000 men, and Eisenhower agreed. He was reluctant to suffer casualties for what he regarded as a meaningless objective. What they both failed to appreciate was the German Army's willingness to lose ground or surrender to the western Allies, while doing everything to hold back the Red Army. There were no major SS units left on the Elbe front to enforce resistance.

Eisenhower's reluctance to head for Berlin was supported by General George Marshall and the U.S. chiefs of staff, to the frustration of Churchill, Field Marshal Alan Brooke, and Field Marshal Montgomery. "I deem it highly important," Churchill signaled to Roosevelt, "that we should shake hands with the Russians as far east as possible." Eisenhower later commented: "Why should we endanger the life of a single American or Briton to capture areas we soon will be handing over to the Russians?" This, among other things, overlooked the rather important question of seizing German military technology and scientists before the Soviets did. If Eisenhower's idea had been followed to the letter, the huge cache of 1,100 tons of uranium ore at Stassfurt, inside the future Soviet zone, would never have been recovered.

On the evening of April 12, Eisenhower told his old friend General George Patton that he was going to halt on the Elbe. "From a tactical point of view, it is highly inadvisable for the American Army to take Berlin and I hope political influence won't cause me to take the city," he said. "It has no tactical or strategic value and would place upon the American forces the burden of caring for thousands of Germans, displaced persons and Allied prisoners of war."

"Ike, I don't see how you figure that out," Patton replied. "We had better take Berlin, and quick—and on to the Oder!"

Patton returned to the charge later that evening, arguing that the Ninth Army could be there within forty-eight hours. "Well, who would want it?" said Eisenhower, still refusing to acknowledge its importance. Patton apparently placed both hands on Eisenhower's shoulders. "I think history will answer that question for you," he said. As Patton went to bed he turned on the radio and heard of Roosevelt's death. Probably the death of Roosevelt and uncertainties over his successor, Harry Truman, confirmed Eisenhower in his decision not to risk a dash to Berlin.

General William H. Simpson knew nothing of Eisenhower's thoughts and his conversation with Patton. His Ninth Army was ready to go. The Zerbst bridgehead across the Elbe was enlarged after the counterattack of the Scharnhorst Infantry Division had been beaten back. During the night of April 14, part of the 2nd Armored Division had crossed the bridge over the Elbe constructed by the 83rd Infantry Division. If Eisenhower had given the word the next morning, General Wenck's German Twelfth Army, defending the Elbe front, could not possibly have held on for more than twenty-four hours, as both Colonel Günther Reichhelm, Wenck's chief of staff, and Colonel Baron von Humboldt, his operations officer, confirmed recently. And with sufficient air support, the American advance would indeed have been rapid. The Twelfth Army had virtually no vehicles and only a handful of tanks, while Simpson's highly mechanized divisions had less than sixty miles to go. All the main Wehrmacht formations were tied down either on the Oder front, awaiting Marshal Zhukov's massive offensive, or on the Neisse, sixty miles to the south, facing Marshal Konev's armies.

Simpson's lead units could have thrust straight up Route 246. Other detachments pushed out to the right could have taken Reichsstrasse 2, which headed northeast, straight for Potsdam and Zehlendorf, the southwestern tip of Berlin, right next to the Kaiser Wilhelm Institute. General Wenck had been told to prepare for an attack farther north "along and either side of the Hanover-Magdeburg autobahn," and his troops in front of the Zerbst bridgehead were little more than a screen. His Twelfth Army's greatest weakness was in transport. He simply did

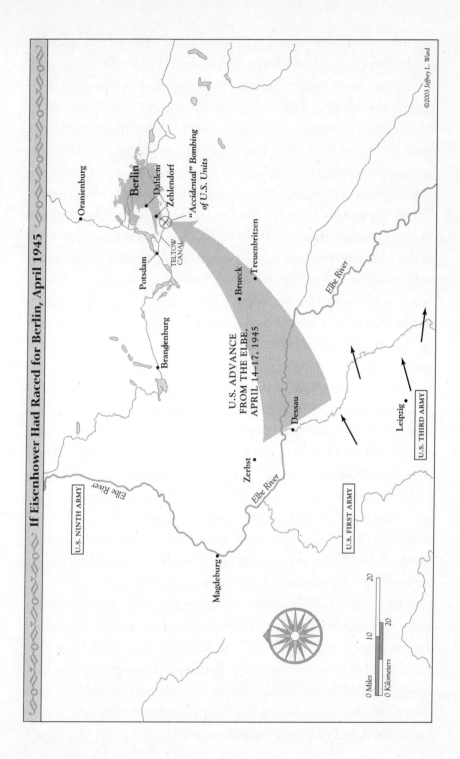

If Eisenhower Had Raced for Berlin, April 1945

©2003 Jeffrey L. Ward

Oranienburg

Berlin

Dahlem
Zehlendorf

"Accidental" Bombing
of U.S. Units

Potsdam

TELTOW
CANAL

Brueck
Treuenbritzen

Brandenburg

U.S. ADVANCE
FROM THE ELBE,
APRIL 14–17, 1945

Dessau

Elbe River

Leipzig

U.S. THIRD ARMY

Zerbst

Elbe River

U.S. FIRST ARMY

Elbe River

U.S. NINTH ARMY

Magdeburg

0 Miles   10   20
0 Kilometers   20

not have the means to redeploy his infantry units rapidly enough, pulling them back to form a new line. It would have been, in any case, little more than a line on the map, since there was no natural or pre-pared line of defense. U.S. troops therefore might well have reached Brück and Treuenbritzen on the two axes of advance by the evening of April 15. Even if word of the threat had managed to get through to the headquarters of Army Group Vistula that night, there would have been little chance of pulling back forces from the Eastern Front along the line of the Oder and the Neisse rivers. The German command knew from a captured prisoner that the Soviet onslaught was due to start at three o'clock the next morning. Every mechanized unit was needed desper-ately to face the 1.5 million–strong offensive. Hitler in his Reich Chan-cellery bunker would almost certainly have ordered some redeployment, but the Wehrmacht generals had for once a perfect excuse for ignoring his orders. And even if Hitler had ordered his own SS defense detach-ment southwestward, once again the lack of sufficient transport would have thwarted the counterattack.

The only threat to the American thrust would have been the assort-ment of Luftwaffe aircraft at Jüterbog Airfield, a dozen or so kilometers to the south of their line of advance. The main unit there was the Leonidas "self-sacrifice" squadron, essentially a kamikaze unit of aircraft loaded with explosives to attack the Red Army bridges across the Oder. Yet, the appearance of American troops so close to their base would more likely have prompted them into a premature attack on their Soviet targets. There were no significant bridges on the American line of advance until just short of Berlin itself.

If the Americans had pushed on from the line of Brück-Treuenbritzen to the southwestern outskirts of Berlin on the morning of April 16 while the city shook from the massive Soviet bombardment on the Oder, they might well have slipped through in the chaos. The attention of OKH headquarters at Zossen was so fixed on the Oder offensive that its staff officers did not realize for two days that Konev's attack to their south-east meant that they were about to be attacked.

The element of surprise when the Americans reached the Teltow Canal, Berlin's southern line of defense, would certainly have been total. When General Rybalko's 3rd Guards Tank Army reached this line on April 22, six days later, surprise was complete. One of the Soviet staff officers described their arrival as "unexpected as snow in the middle of summer." And at that stage, before General Weidling's LVI Panzer Corps pulled back into the capital, the only defenders in the southwest of Berlin were the old men and boys of the Volkssturm militia. Few people could have been more eager to surrender to the Americans at the first opportunity. Anyone in uniform had been made to dread Soviet captivity, especially after Goebbels's attempts to depict it as so terrible that death was preferable. And once word spread in the city that the Americans had arrived, even in comparatively small numbers, only the most dedicated Nazis would have fought on.

Marshal Zhukov's great onslaught from the Oder was not well handled, and German resistance was desperate enough to hold his armies on the Seelow Heights for two days. As a result, the Red Army did not manage to surround Berlin entirely until April 25. Even if one goes from the arrival of Rybalko's three tank corps at the Teltow Canal on April 22, this still would have given Simpson's forces a good week from breaking out of the Zerbst bridgehead to enter Berlin.

On the other hand, we must never forget that Stalin was determined to secure Berlin at any price. An American dash for Berlin could not have been kept secret, and Stalin would have reacted immediately. He would have had no scruples in ensuring the hostile attentions of Red Army aviation. Any "error" would have been blamed on the "criminal irresponsibility" of Allied commanders who had failed to liaise with the Stavka. And at the first hint of Soviet attacks on his troops, Eisenhower would undoubtedly have ordered an immediate withdrawal. He was greatly preoccupied by the risk of losing men in clashes with the Red Army and he had no intention of facing down the Soviets. In one way he was certainly right: American and British troops, so close to victory and heavily influenced by newspaper accounts of the Red Army's heroism, would have found it very hard to accept orders to engage Soviet formations. Even Churchill had to accept the judgment of his chiefs of staff after completing his contingency planning exercise, "Unthinkable," that the western Allies simply could not hope to push back the Red Army. On balance, therefore, we must conclude that Eisenhower probably made the right decision for the wrong reasons. The Americans could have gotten to Berlin first, but the idea that the western Allies could have seized and held the city under Stalin's nose, and thus have delayed the Soviet atomic program, is little more than a Cold War pipe dream.

TED MORGAN

JOE McCARTHY'S SECRET LIFE

The threat of worldwide Soviet domination after the Second World War was genuine enough, but the reaction to it in the United States produced some of the worst civic excesses in our history. The man most closely identified with the witch-hunts of the 1950s was Senator Joseph R. McCarthy of Wisconsin: The eponymous word "McCarthyism" has become identified with the politics of accusation and innuendo. The journalist Richard Rovere compared him to a political speculator who found his oil gusher in communism. In his heyday, there was no one McCarthy wouldn't take on, whether it was an Army dentist or the president of the United States. He claimed to have lists of Reds (the number constantly varying) in the State Department or the Army or the Voice of America (whose disruption must have brought glee to Moscow). He called Secretary of State Dean Acheson "the Great Red Dean" and denounced his "crimson crowd" at State. He accused the Democratic party of "twenty years of treason." When Dwight Eisenhower ran for president in 1952, he was so wary of McCarthy's influence that he refused to speak up in defense of his old friend George Marshall when the senator called the then–secretary of defense a traitor. Ever the Irishman, he even went after America's chief ally, demanding that all British ships trading with Red China be sunk. Each time one of his charges was proved to be bogus, he would simply produce new ones—and new headlines. Eventually he would go too far and be censured by the Senate.

The spreading influence of Moscow, McCarthy once said, "must be a product of a great conspiracy, a conspiracy on a scale so immense as to dwarf any previous such venture in the history of man." He may have been correct in that assessment, but Ted Morgan mischievously suggests that the senator himself might have been part of that conspiracy. Much of what he sets forth actually happened. Morgan, who has been working for years on a book about the antiradical hysteria of the past century, may not have his tongue entirely in his cheek.

TED MORGAN is the author of the long-awaited *Reds: McCarthyism from Woodrow Wilson to George W. Bush.* His many other books include *On Becoming American, Wilderness at Dawn: The Settling of the North American Continent,* and biographies of Churchill and FDR.

HAVING JUST FINISHED five years of research for a book on Senator Joseph R. McCarthy, I am in a position to reveal that the champion Red-hunter, whose name personified opportunistic anticommunism, was recruited by the KGB in 1950 and served the Soviet Union until his death in 1957. When President Harry S Truman said in 1951 that "the greatest asset that the Kremlin has is Senator McCarthy," he did not know how right he was. McCarthy was a Soviet agent.

The proof of McCarthy's betrayal, which was mercenary rather than ideological, is in the Venona transcripts, released in 1995. They consist of 2,900 messages between KGB Moscow and its stations in the United States, decoded over the years by the National Security Agency. I was given access to the full transcripts by Louis Benson of the NSA.

To understand McCarthy's recruitment, one must go back to his early years in the Senate. Elected in 1946, he was named to the Banking and Currency Committee. At that time, with fifteen million veterans back from the war, there was an acute housing shortage. In 1947, a fourteen-member House-Senate Committee on Housing was formed to study all aspects of the problem, from public housing to the postwar innovation of prefab houses, as answers to the shortage. The seven Senate members included three from the Banking and Currency Committee, one of them McCarthy, who was named vice chairman. The joint committee divided into a number of subcommittees, which held hearings in thirty-three cities. The junior senator from Wisconsin was active in these hearings, denouncing public housing as a "breeding ground for Communists" and backing the prefab builders.

Senator Joseph McCarthy sits at his desk behind a large pile of letters that, he claims, overwhelmingly support his crusade against American Communists. His recklessness was legendary. But if unchecked, how much more damage might he have done to his own country? © PictureHistory

One of the cities McCarthy visited on his housing rounds was Columbus, Ohio. According to the Columbus builder Robert C. Byers, McCarthy received payments and other favors to promote prefab housing. At a bankruptcy hearing on August 1, 1951, at the U.S. District Court in Columbus, Byers testified that he paid McCarthy a total of $1,500 ($15,000 in 2002 dollars).

McCarthy first came to Columbus in 1947, Byers said, to address the Association of Building Standards at a lunch at the Athletic Club. He showed up an hour late, saying he'd had "quite a night," he'd lost all his money in a crap game. He then proceeded to borrow $100 from Dale Stump, a prominent Columbus attorney.

Byers said he made a deal with McCarthy to pay him $500 for each trip to Columbus. McCarthy told him, "Charge it to advertising so my name doesn't show up on your books." On his second trip, Byers gave him another $500 in cash. McCarthy said, "Put it down as a loan and later charge it off."

Byers was planning to build ten thousand "miracle homes" and needed McCarthy to help him obtain completion bonds and loans from the Reconstruction Finance Company. But McCarthy double-crossed him, defecting to a higher bidder, another prefab builder called Lustron. "What thinking I did about this man McCarthy," Byers told the bankruptcy court, "began and ended in the fact that he was vice chairman of the House-Senate Committee on Housing. To me, anything McCarthy did was just about right. If he wanted to go to bed at night with a streetwalker or other gal that he picked up at bars or cocktail lounges, I excused him by saying, 'He's single and entitled to a little fun.' An amazing thing to me was that after a Saturday-night drunk, and having bedded with one or more 'gals,' as he called 'em, he would get up early the following morning to go to mass."

After the 1947 lunch, Byers said, McCarthy got into a crap game that evening with the Columbus businessman Denver van de Venter and others. "After losing $300," Byers said, "I got out early. At the finish, my son and the senator were shooting for a grand a roll. The last roll was for $6,000 and my son won, and of course the senator welched on his bet. It was a disgusting sight to see this great public servant down on his hands and knees, reeking of whiskey and shouting, 'Come on, babies, Papa needs a new pair of shoes.' He did stop long enough between rolls to look over the girls van de Venter brought. If one suited his fancy, he'd say, 'That's the baby, I'll take care of her just as soon as I break you guys.' The baby in question sat patiently on the bed awaiting her chances for a ten-dollar bill."

McCarthy lost tens of thousands of dollars gambling. He was a regular at the Pimlico racetrack, where he sometimes borrowed money from Carl Standlund, the president of Lustron, so that he could go on betting. His bookie, Tom Miller, who operated the Club Tavern in Washington, was arrested in August 1948. Back in Wisconsin, he was often seen at the Jack O'Lantern, an illegal gambling den in Vilas County, on the Eagle River, with tables for roulette and dice. Whenever he won, he would say, "Put it on the tab." Anyone who seemed a little interested in watching him play got the heave-ho from the bouncer.

By 1949, McCarthy was deep in debt. According to his tax return, his interest payments and stock market losses were greater than his income. He owed the Appleton State Bank more than $200,000. He owed his brothers Howard and William $50,000 and $40,000, respectively.

Once a month, in a bipartisan spirit, McCarthy went to New York to take part in an all-night poker game at the Tammany clubhouse. The Tammany boss, Carmine De Sapio, presided, and one of the regulars was State Supreme Court judge Samuel Dickstein. Even though he was a Republican, McCarthy was popular because he always lost. He was so reckless that in a game of five-card stud, he would bet the pot without looking at his hole card. Garrulous and bibulous, he drank himself into such a stupor that he would pick up the cards dealt to the person sitting next to him.

One morning in December 1949, as the game broke up at dawn, a bleary-eyed McCarthy downed his breakfast bourbon and said, "Here's to the hair of the dog. This is my last game, boys. I'm so deep in the hole I can almost see China." The others laughed and Dickstein offered him a ride to Penn Station.

Dickstein was the son of a Lithuanian rabbi who came to the United States when Sam was six. He grew up in the tenements of the Lower East Side but worked his way through law school and climbed the political ladder, from alderman to state assemblyman and finally to the House, where he served from 1923 to 1943.

Dickstein immersed himself in immigration issues. In 1934 and 1935, he was vice chairman of a House committee that exposed American Nazi groups such as the Bund and the Silver Shirts. On the side, he built up a lucrative law practice that specialized in helping immigrants become U.S. residents. He was in cahoots with an employee of the American consulate in Montreal. For $3,000, he could get an immigrant an entry visa from Canada.

Another profitable sideline was providing classified information to Washington embassies. In the thirties, Dickstein was on the payroll of the British and the Poles. In 1937, he paid a call on the Soviet ambassador, Alexander Troyanovsky, who sent the following report to Moscow: "Congressman Dickstein—chairman of the House Committee on Nazi Activities . . . came to the ambassador and let him know that his agents unmasked the liaison between Nazis and Russian fascists living in the United States." Dickstein professed "a friendly attitude toward the Soviet Union and offered to deliver information on White Russian groups collected by his investigators and for which he would need five to six thousand dollars."

Troyanovsky saw Dickstein in April 1938 and assigned him to a liaison agent code-named Igor, who was Peter Gutzeit, the NKVD station chief in New York. Gutzeit gave Dickstein the code name Crook and reported to Moscow in May that "this is an unscrupulous type, greedy for money, who consented to work because of money, a very cunning swindler."

In June 1938, when the House Un-American Activities Committee was formed under the chairmanship of Martin Dies Jr., Dickstein was conspicuously omitted and his stock plummeted. Igor reported that his information came mostly from published sources and did not justify his $1,250 monthly stipend. When he scolded Dickstein, Igor said, "He blazed up very much, claimed that if we didn't give him money he would break with us . . . That he is employing people and he must pay them, that he demands nothing for himself."

On orders from Gutzeit that September, Dickstein denounced the Dies Committee for focusing almost entirely on Communist groups. He spoke out in favor of terminating the committee, which was exposing Communists in labor and government. Eventually, however, Moscow Center became exasperated with Dickstein's unrelenting demands for money and decided that he was "a complete racketeer and blackmailer." In February 1940, the order came from Moscow to "break with Dickstein." In all, Moscow had paid Crook $12,000, or more than $120,000 in today's dollars. Dickstein left Congress and ran for the New York State Supreme Court, where he served from 1946 until his death in 1954. He was the only Soviet agent in the U.S. Congress until 1950.

On the ride to Penn Station, McCarthy said: "I don't know what to do, Sam. I'm hemorrhaging money."

"I was in the same pickle once," Dickstein said.

"How'd you get out?" McCarthy asked.

"I went to see the Russian ambassador," Dickstein said.

"I don't know if I could do that," McCarthy said.

"It's up to you," Dickstein said, dropping him off at Thirty-fourth Street.

In 1949, the Soviet ambassador to the United States was Alexander Panyushkin, who was credited with having done an outstanding job as ambassador to China from 1939 to 1944. Panyushkin was also the KGB *rezident* in Washington. That a Soviet ambassador should have to do double duty as the KGB's top spy was an indication of the disastrous state of the agent networks that had flourished during the war. Thanks to the disclosures of Whittaker Chambers and Elizabeth Bentley, many of the spies in government departments, such as Alger Hiss at State and Harry Dexter White at the Treasury, had been smoked out. Nor could the KGB count on recruitment from within the American Communist Party, which had been forced underground after the Smith Act convictions. In the fifties, the KGB had to rebuild its agent networks from scratch.

This was not an easy task, for with the onset of the Cold War, FBI surveillance had increased. Panyushkin cabled Moscow in October 1948 that the FBI was "hunting Soviet citizens (including diplomats) and establishing permanent surveillance, including bugging their apartments." In addition, Panyushkin said, the deputy station chief, Gyorgi Sokolov, spoke practically no English. Panyushkin was forced to give him a poor rating, which led Sokolov to throw a tantrum, saying he'd been called "a good-for-nothing shit."

The head of the KGB in 1949 was Lavrenty Beria, Stalin's henchman and fellow Georgian. Sly and merciless, like one of Machiavelli's condottieri, he was at Stalin's feet and at everyone else's throat. Named in 1938, Beria presided for fifteen years over the "state within a state," a conglomerate of concentration camps, secret police, and foreign espionage. In his private life, Beria was a serial rapist of underage girls. In his public life, he was a mass murderer who carried out the Katyn massacre of 1943, when fourteen thousand Polish officers were shot into ditches.

Furious at the inaction of the Washington station, Beria peppered Panyushkin with complaints: Why are you not recruiting new agents? If the FBI is watching the old ones, find some new ones. Why is it that you do not have a single agent in the State Department or any other important government institution? Panyushkin replied that "in the current fascist atmosphere" it was difficult. He was so fed up that he asked for a transfer, which was refused. In desperation, Panyushkin resorted to crude disinformation initiatives, such as the release of forged documents that would expose members of the Dies Committee as German agents.

Between Christmas and New Year's in 1949, when most Congressmen were back in their home states and the Washington papers were running "Yes, Virginia" stories, McCarthy discreetly visited the Soviet embassy. This was the "walk-in" Panyushkin was praying for. On January 2, 1950, he sent the following message to Beria:

"In an unannounced visit, Republican senator Joseph McCarthy offered to work for us. He said he badly needed money. Also, he is up for reelection in 1952 and must find what he called 'a hot-button issue.' He proposes to attack the State Department for harboring Communist spies. I told him we did not have a single agent in the State Department. He said it did not matter. He wants to show that the Truman administration is soft on communism. McCarthy is known as an intemperate and boastful person who has alienated a number of other senators. His 'anti-Red' crusade can be used for disinformation purposes. His baseless charges will make liberals skeptical about the so-called Red Menace. He will also facilitate the formation of illegal residencies, for those agents under suspicion can claim to be the object of a witch-hunt and gain the sympathy of the liberal press. His campaign will divide

America into two hostile camps. The Republican right will attack Truman and destabilize the American political scene. In a sense, McCarthy is another Dickstein. He wants money and nothing else. He feels no sympathy for our side. But he can be far more useful than Dickstein, and I have offered him $2,000 a month (he wanted $5,000). We must of course exercise caution and make sure he is not a double agent. My personal opinion is that he is driven by necessity."

Two days later, this cable arrived from Beria: "Proceed with caution on trial basis."

It should be noted that the Russians despised Truman, seeing him as an accidental president, a figurehead of Wall Street imperialism, and the instigator of the Cold War. As early as May 26, 1945, the KGB agent Vladimir Pravdin cabled Moscow from New York that there was "an organized campaign to get hold of Sailor (Truman) and bring about a change of policy toward the USSR. The most reactionary section of the press welcomes Sailor's accession to power. Sailor is friendly with such Republican reactionaries as Senator Robert Taft. He is notoriously untried and ill-informed on foreign policy. He solicits advice from [former ambassador to the Soviet Union] Averell Harriman, one of the bitterest anti-Soviet propagandists, who does not shrink from any chicanery."

Thus, any effort that McCarthy made to discredit the president fit into the Soviet Union's Cold War strategy, at a time when Truman had suffered two serious setbacks—in 1949, the Soviets exploded their first atom bomb, and Mao Tse-tung ousted Chiang Kai-shek from China.

In February 1950, McCarthy went on his five-city Lincoln Day tour, changing his figures for Communists in the State Department from 205 in Wheeling to 57 in Reno. Wallowing in headlines, McCarthy wired Truman on February 12 from Reno to "pick up your phone and ask [Secretary of State Dean] Acheson how many Communists he failed to discharge . . . Failure on your part will label the Democratic party of [sic] being the bedfellow of international Communism." Truman wrote but did not send this reply: "This is the first time I ever heard of a Senator trying to discredit his own government before the world . . . Your telegram is not only insolent, it shows conclusively that you are not even fit to have a hand in the operation of the government of the United States."

In June came the North Korean invasion, with Truman acting decisively to save South Korea by sending in American troops under a United Nations mandate. The Korean War instantly validated and magnified McCarthy's appeal. A growing number of Americans were prepared to believe him when he linked the war with the State Department whitewash. On July 2, he said that "American boys are dying in Korea" because "a group of untouchables in the State Department sabotaged the aid program." On July 12, he wrote Truman: "Today American boys lie dead in the mud of Korean valleys. Some have their hands tied behind their backs, their faces shot away by Communist machine guns . . . They are dead because the program adopted by this Congress to avoid such a war . . . was sabotaged."

On September 5, 1950, Panyushkin cabled KGB Moscow: "McCarthy's campaign has produced unexpected results. We are quite sure now that he is not a double agent and have given him the code name Adder. Thanks to Adder, the issue of corruption in the Truman government will be a major issue in the legislative elections in November. Adder is now seen as the hope of the Republican party. The front-runners for the presidential nomination in 1952 are Senator Taft and Adder. If our probationer [agent] is elected president, he will want a bonus."

In September 1950, General George C. Marshall was confirmed as secretary of defense. Marshall had grave doubts about the commander in chief in Korea, Douglas MacArthur, who reported that he could easily capture North Korea and who thought the Chinese were bluffing when they threatened to send in troops. By November, 100,000 Chinese troops had crossed the Yalu River and MacArthur had to ask for reinforcements. Marshall wanted at all costs to avoid a war with China. In January 1951, the Chinese took Seoul but were beaten back in March. When MacArthur insisted on bombing China, Truman had him recalled on April 9, 1951.

On June 1, 1951, Panyushkin arranged a meeting with McCarthy in a Soviet safe house on Decatur Place. He told Adder that MacArthur's recall upset Soviet plans. Stalin, he said, was hoping that MacArthur would bomb the Chinese, so that the United States and China would inch toward war. The Soviet Union could then act as a mediator between the two, winning international approval. Marshall had spoiled the Soviet plan by urging Truman to recall MacArthur. Stalin wanted something done to discredit Marshall. Panyushkin asked McCarthy to make an anti-Marshall speech on the floor of the Senate. When McCarthy said he would have to hire some researchers, Panyushkin gave him $5,000.

On June 15, McCarthy delivered a three-hour, 60,000-word diatribe in which Marshall was made the villain for everything from Pearl Harbor, to backing a premature second front, to the loss of China and the Korean War. Marshall, "this grim and solitary man," was accused of being behind every fiasco in American foreign policy since the war.

McCarthy outlined "a conspiracy on a scale so immense as to dwarf any previous such venture in the history of man. A conspiracy so black that . . . its principals shall be forever deserving of the maledictions of all honest men."

George Marshall retired that September, perhaps disgusted with the political climate, but this time McCarthy had gone too far even for his Republican claque. On October 22, 1951, at a press conference in Des Moines, Senator Taft said bluntly: "I don't think one who overstates his case helps his own case . . . His extreme attack against General Marshall was one of the things on which I cannot agree with McCarthy." Having earned the enmity of Marshall's fellow soldier, Dwight D. Eisenhower, now the Republican front-runner, McCarthy was no longer mentioned as a presidential hopeful. Eisenhower was nominated on the first ballot at the Republican convention in Chicago on July 7, 1952, choosing Richard Nixon as his running mate. On November 4, 1952, the Eisenhower-Nixon ticket carried thirty-nine states, and McCarthy was reelected in Wisconsin. Having won slim majorities in both houses of Congress, the GOP was in the saddle for the first time since 1932. Why should McCarthy continue his flawed crusade? Why attack a fort you occupied? Adder had his reasons and announced in December that he had only scratched the surface, placing himself on a collision course with the president of his country and the leader of his party.

Ambassador Panyushkin was recalled to Moscow in 1952. In his memoirs, Pavel Sudoplatov, the onetime head of KGB Special Tasks, said that "Panyushkin was a passive but overconfident bureaucrat who had no competence in intelligence operations but was appointed head of the First [KGB] Directorate as a result of having recruited a highly influential Washington agent code-named Adder."

Panyushkin's replacement was Georgi Zarubin, a veteran diplomat with the stern demeanor known as "school of Stalin." He did his best to conceal the fact that even though he had spent ten years as ambassador to Canada and Britain, he could hardly speak English. Perhaps for this reason, he was not given the KGB *rezidentura*, which went to one of his counselors, the veteran KGB man Vladimir Vladykin.

Stalin died in March, 1953, and in the ensuing power struggle Nikita Khrushchev was named first secretary of the party. Beria was arrested and shot. Ivan Serov, Khrushchev's hatchet man in the Ukraine in 1939, whom Beria had once called "a petty womanizer" for his affair with the Polish opera star Wanda Bandrovska, became head of the KGB.

At the time of Stalin's death, there was no American ambassador in Moscow, for George Kennan had been declared persona non grata in September 1952. Eisenhower picked the career service officer Charles E. Bohlen, who had been at Yalta with FDR and was considered one of the top experts on the Soviet Union. On March 18, the Senate Foreign Relations Committee approved Bohlen 15–0, and the confirmation went to the full Senate.

On March 19, Vladimir Vladykin, a dour, terrierlike man who was Adder's new handler, met McCarthy at the safe house on Decatur Place.

According to the report he sent to Moscow, Vladykin told Adder that the Soviets did not want Bohlen as ambassador. "He knows too much about us," Vladykin said. "He was part of the reactionary Riga group prior to recognition." Could McCarthy try to block Bohlen's confirmation?

McCarthy had become the recipient of classified information from disgruntled or dismissed State Department employees. On March 20, he announced that Eisenhower would withdraw the nomination if he saw "the entire Bohlen file." The next day, McCarthy held a press conference and told reporters: "I know what is in that file. I have known what is in his file for years."

McCarthy wasn't bluffing. He had obtained a copy of the Bohlen file as well as the security file of Bohlen's brother-in-law, which was explosive enough to scuttle the confirmation. Charles Thayer, a blue-eyed, round-faced West Point graduate, had joined the Foreign Service in 1937 and had been posted to Moscow. During the war, while in the OSS, he was assigned to the Tito partisans in Yugoslavia, and by 1945 he was chief of the U.S. military mission in Belgrade. When the OSS was disbanded, he returned to the State Department. In 1948 and 1949, D. L. Nicholson, chief of the division of security in the State Department, conducted an investigation of Thayer, which collected statements from more than a dozen informants he had worked with over the years. The report consisted of an abundance of colorful details regarding Thayer's homosexuality. He was also accused of having been pro-Tito to the detriment of American interests when he served in Belgrade, and of enriching himself through black-market activities.

When the Senate debate opened on March 24, 1953, McCarthy told Nixon that he had prepared a "real dirty" speech that would finish Bohlen. The vice president, who was under orders to shepherd the confirmation through, asked him to tone it down. Bohlen was confirmed by a healthy majority of 74 to 13. McCarthy explained to his Soviet handlers that he had made a deal with Nixon—he would refrain from exposing Thayer, and Nixon would help him open an investigation of the Army.

It was with the entire approval of his Soviet handlers that McCarthy launched his 1954 investigation of Communists in the Army. Undermining the American military at a time when a celebrated soldier was president was an extraordinary achievement for the KGB. But the hearings unraveled and led to the televised drama on the favored treatment of Roy Cohn's sidekick David Schine, which in turn led to McCarthy's censure in the Senate in December 1954. Once condemned by his fellow senators, McCarthy became a leper without a bell. When he got up on the Senate floor to speak, there was a move for the door. If senators were gathered in the cloakroom and McCarthy joined the huddle, it dispersed. At lunch in the Senate dining room, if he sat at a table, the others would hurriedly finish their bean soup and sandwiches and get up and leave.

His Soviet handlers debated whether he was worth keeping on a high retainer and decided he could still make trouble as long as he was in the Senate. After all, twenty-two Republican senators had voted against censure, which showed that the anti-Eisenhower splinter group was alive and well. As Eisenhower himself put it in a December 7 letter to his friend Clifford Roberts: "McCarthy is operating at the same old stand."

In June 1955, Eisenhower was preparing for the first summit conference since Potsdam, ten years before. The summit, to be held in mid-July in Geneva, would bring together the so-called Big Four, The United States, USSR, Britain, and France. With Stalin's death and the ascension of Khrushchev, there was a new Soviet posture of "competitive coexistence," which required some adjustment on the American side.

The Russians, however, did not want Eisenhower to bring up the captive satellite nations. What better way to prevent the issue from emerging than to have the discredited McCarthy insist on it? McCarthy went before the Senate Foreign Relations Committee on June 20 to present a resolution that the fate of the satellite nations should be a subject for discussion at the Geneva conference.

In the debate by the full Senate a few days later, majority leader Lyndon Johnson said: "The issue is very simple. It is whether the President

of the United States shall be sent to Geneva with a gun at his head."
McCarthy watched dumbfounded as his onetime allies on the Republican right jumped ship. When Senator William Knowland agreed with
Johnson, McCarthy told him he was "shocked and disappointed." An
angry Knowland replied, "I'll place my record in opposition to Communists against yours any day." McCarthy's most devoted acolytes, such as
Bourke Hickenlooper of Iowa and William Jenner of Indiana, lined up
on the side of the president. There was a decided change in climate,
with the Republican senators making a show of unity in preparation for
the 1956 presidential election. The Senate voted against the resolution
77–4, which left McCarthy virtually alone. At the Geneva conference,
the captive nations were a footnote.

At the Republican convention on August 21, 1956, Eisenhower and
Nixon rode in on a tide of "I Like Ike" banners. But on September 24,
Eisenhower suffered a moderate heart attack. A week later, McCarthy
was summoned to the safe house, where Vladimir Vladykin read him a
report on Eisenhower prepared by the Soviet Ministry of Foreign Affairs
that said: "Eisenhower has followed the principles of the most conservative elements of the American ruling circles . . . In the election campaign of 1952, Eisenhower received the support of the major financial
and industrial monopolies, including the Rockefeller, Morgan, DuPont
and Mellon monopolies . . . groups interested in intensifying the aggressive and expansionist tendencies of U.S. foreign policy. Eisenhower
himself is a stockholder in the Standard Oil Company of New Jersey
and the Aluminum Company of America. He also owns stock in the
Charm More Company, which manufactures hair cream. Eisenhower's
term in office has been marked by further suppression of the remnants of
democratic freedoms in America . . . Immediately after the Geneva
conference, Eisenhower and [Secretary of State John Foster] Dulles did
everything they could to bury 'the spirit of Geneva' . . . Intellectually,
Eisenhower is quite limited. He rarely reads the newspapers, and his
reading is limited to mysteries and Westerns. In his four years in office, he
has faithfully carried out all the wishes of the cartels . . . He is suffering

from a severe heart ailment and is for all intents and purposes a semi-invalid."

Vladykin then told McCarthy: "We would like to see Adlai Stevenson win the election. We think Stevenson is a man of peace. He has called for a nuclear test ban and an end to the draft. Since Secretary Khrushchev's speech before the Twentieth Congress [describing the crimes of Stalin], however, the Republicans seem to think that the breakup of the Soviet Union is at hand. They are calling for the liberation of the Eastern European nations under our protection. In addition, we want a free hand in the Middle East and Africa, where a number of recently de-colonized nations are friendly to us."

"So I hear," said McCarthy, according to Vladykin's report to Moscow. "The word is out that in Africa, a 'friend of the West' is a chief of state about to be assassinated."

"Spare me your humor," Vladykin said. "We would like you to prepare a speech with the most damaging material you can find about Eisenhower. Dig into his private life. Do to him what you did to Marshall. This could have an impact on the election. If it does, we will give you $10,000."

On October 2, 1956, McCarthy rose on the floor of the Senate to give the most shameful speech of his entire career, a personal attack on the president of his country and the leader of his party. Along with his diatribe that the Russians had hoodwinked Ike at Geneva, McCarthy said his health made him unfit to serve a second term.

"Here is a president," he said, "who spends more time with his doctors than he does with his cabinet. We cannot take the chance of having another Woodrow Wilson, with Sherman Adams as Edith Bolling. What if he dies in office? Can we entrust the great responsibilities of state to the vice president?"

Senator Stuart Symington: "Will the senator yield?"

McCarthy: "Wait until I finish."

Symington: "Does the junior senator from Wisconsin have a medical degree?"

McCarthy: "My old friend, Sanctimonious Stu."

Symington: "You better go see a psychiatrist."

McCarthy plunged on, waving a sheet of paper and saying: "Fortunately, there are loyal Americans in government departments who are not afraid to send McCarthy crucial information. I have here in my hand the proof that during the war, Eisenhower conducted an affair with his female driver, an Englishwoman and former model who was in Britain's Motor Transport Corps."

Cries of "Out of order!" and "This is outrageous!"

McCarthy: "Her name is Kay Summersby and she is still in England. After the war, Eisenhower wrote a letter to Chief of Staff George Marshall, saying he wanted to divorce Mrs. Ike and marry Kay. Marshall wrote him back that if he did such a thing he'd not only bust him out of the Army, he'd see to it that the rest of his life was a living hell. Here are copies of the letters, from Eisenhower's file at the Pentagon."

Various shouts and cries. The presiding officer: "Let there be order in the chamber!"

Senator Charles Potter (an Eisenhower Republican from Michigan and a World War II veteran who lost both legs in combat and was in a wheelchair): "This is odious. That a Republican senator can make such disgraceful accusations against the leader of his party one month before the election shows a complete absence of conscience. This is a senator who has already been censured. This time he should be expelled."

Cries of "Hear! Hear!"

The rest is history. Eisenhower spent the last month of the campaign defending himself against charges that he had been unfaithful to his wife during the war. In early November, following an uprising in Budapest, 200,000 Soviet troops and 4,000 tanks invaded Hungary. Eisenhower had to defend himself against complaints that Radio Free Europe had provoked the insurrection but that the United States was doing nothing to help the Hungarians. On October 29, following the nationalization of the Suez Canal, the Israelis invaded the Sinai Peninsula, and two days later French and British planes attacked Egyptian airfields. Eisenhower pressured the French and British to desist and the Israelis to withdraw.

On November 6, election night, Eisenhower was in his suite in Washington's Sheraton Park Hotel while in the ballroom the results were being posted on cards hung against a huge curtain. "It's going to be a short evening," the campaign workers were saying, but the results proved otherwise. By opposing the Suez invasion, Ike lost the Jewish vote and New York, New Jersey, and Connecticut. His fling with Kay Summersby cost him the puritan Midwest, except for his own state of Kansas. His failure to help the Hungarians cost him several industrial states with large Balkan populations, including Illinois, Stevenson's home state. It was past midnight when Ike conceded, with the final tally showing 530 electoral votes for Stevenson and 312 for Eisenhower.

McCarthy's revelations contributed to Eisenhower's defeat, and he received his bonus. The Soviets got the president they wanted. Expulsion from the Senate was a drawn-out process requiring a two-thirds vote. McCarthy beat the rap, for on May 2, 1957, he died in Bethesda Naval Hospital of "acute hepatic failure." In Moscow, Alexander Panyushkin, the chief of the First KGB Directorate, recommended McCarthy to the Central Committee for the Order of the Red Banner, in the "posthumous" category.

GEORGE FEIFER

IF THE U-2 HADN'T FLOWN

When the Big Four Paris summit was arranged in 1960, the Cold War was in its fifteenth year. As the moment in May approached, peace, however uneasy, seemed to be in the air; the nuclear minute hand had retreated a comforting distance from the midnight of destruction. Put it another way: the two sides were preparing to build a guardrail along the brink. An aboveground nuclear test ban was all but certain; President Eisenhower was preparing to visit Russia as the guest of the Soviet leader, Nikita Khrushchev. Could there be a better way to cap Eisenhower's second, and final, term?

Then, on May 1, May Day, one of the holiest of holidays in the Soviet calendar, a rocket brought down an American U-2 spy plane over the Urals. The pilot, Francis Gary Powers, was captured.

The United States had been making reconnaissance flights over the Soviet Union and along its coastline since the early 1950s and had mostly gotten away with them. In 1952, for instance, a time when war with Russia was almost as close is it would be in the Cuban Missile Crisis, overflights determined that Russian bombers were not poised to bomb Alaska and the West Coast. Later, planes photographed and mapped northern Siberia, almost to Murmansk, mainly discovering that 3,500 miles were virtually empty. One British RAF photo-taking aircraft flew all the way to Stalingrad: though

225

pursued and shot up by Soviet interceptors, it somehow made it to safety in Iran. At the end of a decade, there were twenty-three successful U-2 flights, all of them approved by the president. The twenty-fourth was Powers's flight, and it was the only one that had the ability to upset the future.

The downing of the U-2—or Puppy 68, to use its code name—was a turning point. Did it have to be?

GEORGE FEIFER is the author of eight books on Russia, including *Justice in Moscow, Moscow Farewell,* and *Red Files.* Since his first visit in 1959, he has lived there off and on extensively; he spent a year as a graduate student at Moscow University. His most recent book is *The Battle of Okinawa.* He now lives in Connecticut.

THE FREE AND COMMUNIST WORLDS were living and breathing their seemingly terminal struggle when a lone, weaponless warplane prepared to take off from a secluded field beneath the western Himalayas on May 1, 1960. Outsized wings gave the curious craft the look of a prodigious glider despite its jet engines. It was painted a special black in order to obscure it to radar. Uncluttered by markings, the sable sleekness heightened the quiet grace of design austerely serving function, in the spirit of the times. For function, primarily military, then much predominated over reflection in the formation of governmental policy.

Expectation that real war was only a matter of time darkened both worlds like winter clouds. In America, the menace from the East set the national purpose and channeled thoughts to its confines. Stop the mighty Russians, fend off the doom. Although it scarcely occurred to the builders of bomb shelters, fear gripped the Soviet Union even more tightly, and with more real cause because despite its swagger about socialism's invincibility—partly generated by apprehension of the opposite— leaders knew and people suspected the West was much stronger.

Many foreign thrusts into vulnerable Russia had had the predictable effect on the national sense of security. (Not that the invaded hadn't done the same in several directions when they felt strong enough, but the Soviet take on history resolutely avoided mention of such matters.) The current battle array of NATO bases surrounding the Soviet Union rather than the reverse, fed the inveterate anxiety which was further boosted by the threat of more than conventional war. After all, the capitalist "enemy" had the far larger arsenal of nuclear weapons, and Hiroshima and Nagasaki showed they were willing to use them. Washington gurus made no secret of the next targets, and the media of the people who were still licking their grievous World War II wounds reported and distorted every such pronouncement and heedless joke as evidence of American intentions.

Russians also had ideological reasons to fear mushroom clouds ahead. Most liked Americans, whom they saw as freewheeling cousins from that other great landmass, considerably more than the other way around. Still, even their (closet) admirers conceded the hugely rich country was run by heartless lackeys of capitalist imperialism. That wisdom, which explained the hordes of American homeless and poor, lay at the heart of the Marxist-Leninist teachings more or less believed by almost everyone. Alongside it lay the dogma that history advanced through clashes between antagonistic economic systems, victory going to the more progressive. Just as capitalism had replaced feudalism, socialism would supercede capitalism, to humanity's vast benefit. That was how the dialectic worked. It was fated—as was the clash.

If no such political ideology pervaded America, a profoundly pious temperament served to cast the adversary in an even more sinister light, and her historic near *in*vulnerability to invasion didn't alleviate the nascent national paranoia. The two peoples were indeed cousins in sanctifying pursuit of self-interest as Good's duty to defeat Evil. Russian sneers at God, from the Marxism-Leninism to which doctrinal Orthodoxy had been switched, attended a foreign policy that was as self-righteous as His holy American defense. Civilization was at stake, not mere territory or influence, let alone political philosophy. The louder the claims of a higher need for the enemy's defeat, the more similar the open and closed societies sounded. The warnings of CIA director Allen Dulles were a reverse echo of *Pravda*'s daily sermons about the other side's thirst to control the world arising *from its very nature*.

The ideological-theological brawling heated a rivalry that may well have developed even if the economic giants had had roughly the same social systems. What injected the dangerous fervor into the geopolitical combat, however, was the superpowers' anticipation, far greater than in other modern nations, of Armageddon. (At the turn of the twenty-first century, some 60 percent of Americans continued to expect the Book of Revelation's prophesies, including those about Armageddon, to come true.) None of the world's other peoples who were even more devoted to holy causes possessed nearly as much power to devastate for them.

Still, no one lived by theology alone. People also wanted to remain alive, to prosper—even, occasionally, to see some good in the adversary, who might possibly be redeemed before the shooting started. Those contradictions tugged at the pilot of the mysterious plane that was preparing to depart from the quarantined airfield beneath the snow-capped Himalayas. He was gung ho but anxious, resolved to give his all for his imperiled country but also concerned about his safety. That, for lack of a better term, was human nature.

However, categorical good-and-evil convictions, with their potential for unleashing great damage in cosmic crusades, are obviously also human, and men of the latter inclination often exercise disproportion-ate influence on national and world developments. Hitler's and Stalin's recent demonstrations of that were as convincing as any in history. The good news was that the present key players—President Dwight Eisen-hower and First Secretary Nikita Khrushchev—had no such willingness to inflict pain in messianic pursuits. Fabians rather than fanatics in their gut, they measured success much more in terms of traditional people pleasures than great causes.

Both were also a little less anxious at the moment, thanks to a slight retreat from the brink of an East-West cataclysm. It began with Stalin's death in 1953, although Washington would never fully recognize the extent of the ensuing changes in the USSR, largely because the image of the enemy under the monstrous dictator was hard to erase—and, thought many, mistaken to erase. (George Kennan's warning about "creating a Russia of our own imagination" to replace the [Stalinist] one that "did, alas, once exist but fortunately no more" went largely unheeded.) Two years later, Ike held a daring first summit with

After the shooting down of the American U-2 spy plane on May Day 1960, Soviet premier Nikita Khrushchev denounced President Dwight D. Eisenhower at the Paris summit conference that took place later in the month. Khrushchev stunned the gathering when, to emphasize his displeasure, he removed his shoe and banged it on the table, above. Had it not been for the U-2, would international tensions have escalated so dangerously? © Hulton/Archive

Khrushchev, and although they accomplished little of substance, their hours together in Geneva, *actually talking*, was itself an achievement. Many on both sides considered it dangerous and possibly traitorous for their leader to expose himself to the other's deviousness.

Nevertheless, the tenuous relationship developed. After ups and downs—*sharp* downs following the Soviet crushing of the 1956 Hungarian uprising—Khrushchev visited the United States in 1959, revealing himself as an outgoing man without horns, but intensely competitive. "It's true you're richer than we are now," he challenged in a characteristically inappropriate White House toast. "But we'll be just as rich tomorrow, and even richer the day after. And is there anything wrong with that?"

Although his mass of often contradictory bombast can support many interpretations of his goals, the "even richer" boast was a good clue to his core ones. It rephrased his 1956 "We'll bury you" prediction, for which a more accurate translation would have been "We'll beat [or trounce] you"—*you* meaning capitalism, despite the equally characteristic American misinterpretation. His preceding sentence—"Whether you like it or not, history's on our side"—was persuasive evidence that he was talking about economic systems. The toast's pivotal passage, also often repeated in various ways, called not for war but a kind of truce: "We need nothing from the United States and you need nothing of ours. *What we should do now is strengthen our relations.*"

Inflamed by his bellowing and misconstrued threats, the American public rarely read his key signals, but Eisenhower was inclined to and did. Michael Beschloss's *May Day: Eisenhower, Khrushchev and the U-2 Affair*, the fullest, most vivid popular account, records a presidential regret that no real "chip in the granite" of Soviet-American relations had been made in seven years. Talking at Camp David, the two now chiseled that chip out of compromise. The Russian withdrew an ultimatum about Berlin; the American agreed to the full-fledged summit Khrushchev had been seeking.[1]

Although the intermittent American invective against Khrushchev's 1959 visit, which included condemnation of his complicity in Stalin's heinous crimes, was rooted in conviction that Soviet rule would forever draw "rivers of blood" because it was immutable, the concept of a system forever locked into its sins by tyrants' inability to reform is better schematics than history. The still-repressive, woefully obsolete Soviet dictatorship *was* changing—unmistakably, if one cared to look.[2] The

---

[1] Having pronounced himself "delighted" with his American tour and Eisenhower's hosting, Khruschev said he was certain "our problems can be solved" if the president were elected to a second term.

[2] A Soviet joke some thirty years later would make the point that the changes were also relatively rapid. *Question:* "What's the difference between the Prague Spring [which Soviet tanks crushed in 1968] and [Mikhail Gorbachev's] *perestroika?*" *Answer:* "Nineteen years."

nightmare of the midnight knock on the door had passed. Although the cities still teemed with watchers, Westerners were being admitted, and not only fellow travelers. Eisenhower himself was anticipating an enjoyable return visit, scheduled for several months after the plane with the wings of a giant dragonfly waited for takeoff outside the Pakistani city of Peshawar.

That very May morning, new banners—supplementing the old reminders to the world proletariat to unite—were being readied for a Red Square parade. If Khrushchev's heretical posing with a Hollywood showgirl the previous year hadn't sent Stalin writhing in his grave, the new TOWARD A TOTAL END OF THE COLD WAR! slogans were more likely to. The inescapable propaganda purpose of the Party's professions of peaceful intentions didn't negate the current leader's profound desire for it.

At the same time, the *American* propaganda image of an all-powerful dictator seriously misrepresented his shaky position in the Kremlin— shaky largely just because he so itched to reduce the tensions. Khrushchev's powerful domestic opponents were as certain of capitalism's inherent evil and as distrustful of Washington's present intentions as were Eisenhower's, who were against talking with the "Communist devil." The insidious imperialists, Khrushchev's critics warned, were *using* the credulous first secretary. Peace noises from the "smash-socialism" American crusaders were a smoke screen for new intrigues.

May 1 was hot at the latitude of Peshawar. Although the curious plane's black skin reflected little of the Sunday sun beating down on it, the cockpit shimmered with heat. Sweating in his flying suit, the pilot waited for Washington's permission to take off. When it was finally signaled, the plane rose in roughly the direction of the Khyber Pass until it found the thinner air that enabled it to soar with the astonishing rate of climb characteristic of its type. Designated U-2, it had secretly set the world's altitude record.

The kit of Captain Francis Gary Powers included a pin filled with a shellfish toxin. (Days later, a dog would expire ninety seconds after being injected with it by Russian clinicians.) Half the 4,000-odd miles of his planned flight to another secluded field in Norway would put him over Soviet territory. The Ural Mountain region that would receive his greatest attention was closed to foreigners, therefore nearly impervious to espionage from the ground. His mission was to photograph its critical military and industrial installations.

What if a different day had been chosen? The parade for which the banners were being readied was for May Day—second in importance among Soviet holidays to the anniversary of the Bolshevik Revolution, but not in public affection. Celebration of the lifting of winter's siege as much as of anything political made it that much more cherished. What did such trivia matter in the Cold War's perilous scheme of things? It mattered a good deal to sentimental, sensitive Russians, who were always ready—often enough with cause—to see insults from the West mixed with relentless ridicule of their shortcomings and failures. Although State Department experts appreciated May Day's significance, their caution would have been ignored even if they'd known of the U-2 flights in general or this one in particular. Like so many current American policies and operations, they were run—in this case, with supreme secrecy—by the CIA, which had an overwhelming preference for "hard" options over kneading minds and hearts. As a result, many Russians would soon wonder whether Americans had purposely chosen May 1 in order to spoil their happy holiday and far more than that.

The cover story was that the National Aeronautics and Space Administration operated the planes. In fact, they were the CIA's, via the Lockheed Aircraft Corporation. But the ordinarily cool Gary Powers, formerly of the Air Force, still considered himself a Wild Blue Yonder man. Similar previous flights had tensed him less. Although scientific proof of a correlation between warriors' premonitions of death and their actual killing is unlikely, the living took their hunches very seriously. U-2 pilots' skepticism about their assurances of their invulnerability had been waxing. Powers, who used to like danger almost as much as flying, was increasingly apprehensive as he entered Soviet airspace from Afghanistan, still climbing at 60,000 feet.

But his intense focus on his immediate goal obscured the wider national interest that not merely lurked but positively loomed upon the horizon, and that applied also to his superiors. On that same May 1, Eisenhower and Khrushchev were preparing for a second summit, the one agreed to during their Camp David talks some six months earlier. Despite their litany of complaints about the other side's behavior, both prized the recent reduction of friction and itched to achieve more.

Khrushchev, whose praise of Eisenhower's wisdom and love of peace was unprecedented for a Soviet leader since the dissolution of the World War II alliance, appealed insistently for "peaceful coexistence" to cool, if not conclude, the conflict. Without committing himself to the language, Eisenhower too had cautious hopes for the new meetings, these to be at a four-power conference in Paris. The highest were for a limited nuclear test ban treaty, which would be the Cold War's first major agreement. Negotiators had drawn close to settling the final details, which the president was "determined" to complete. He told a friend that bringing "a ray of light" to a world weary of distrust, mutual suspicion, and the exorbitant arms race would give him "tremendous satisfaction."

In short, the ice was melted more than at any time since its forming. And so imminent were the Paris meetings, *just two weeks away*, so eager were both participants to exchange more of the old hostility for accord on "the major problems affecting the attainment of peace and stability in the world," that some observers on both sides would very soon wonder whether the real mission of Puppy 68, as Powers's flight had been code-named, was to sabotage them.

What if it hadn't been made at all? It almost wasn't. Eisenhower's approval of it, against his better instincts, had come but days earlier, after bad weather had pushed back an earlier deadline. The summit was fast approaching, and "we don't want to have that thing flying up there" while it was in progress. The new deadline was that very May

Day. Twenty-four more hours of unfavorable weather would have meant no flight, at least until after the Paris meetings. (In just a few more months, when Discovery spy satellites would be employed in August, U-2s would no longer be needed at all.) But now clear skies were forecast and "conditions at a later season," the State Department would assert, "would have prevented obtaining very important information." That peculiar explanation from the branch of government responsible for diplomacy would nourish conspiracy theorists' arguments that the flight had been organized by hawks intent on wrecking the summit. Less speculatively, the claimed importance has never been persuasively demonstrated.

The CIA had designed and commissioned the U-2 with unprecedented speed. Eisenhower authorized the reconnaissance harvester's use in 1956, after Moscow rejected his Open Skies proposal the previous year. Soon "one of America's most remarkable intelligence achievements . . . beguiling in its simplicity and breathtaking in its boldness," as the agency would later describe it—a "masterpiece of aviation technology," Russians agreed—was providing most hard intelligence about the Soviet Union. Superb photographic equipment enabled inspection of its "every blade of grass," as the same Allen Dulles, the CIA's now delighted director, put it. (To convince Ike of the U-2's value, he was shown a photograph of himself taken from the full spy altitude. He could make out the ball with which he was playing golf.)

To top it off, literally, the craft's ability to cruise at an unprecedented 70,000 feet made it unreachable by interceptors, missiles, and antiaircraft fire. Richard Bissell, Dulles's deputy who directly ran the program, exulted that the Soviets "can't lay a hand on" his planes that were taking detailed photographs of virtually all their cities and military installations. Thirty years later, the still-enamored agency would gloat about obtaining "precious data that unmasked the nature of Soviet deployments and may have saved America billions of dollars in unneeded defense expenditures."

Yes, but what did it cost? What if the CIA's calculations—not to speak of its vision—had been broader, or its influence smaller? In financial expenditure alone, the loss dwarfed the savings. Only a third of the Cold War had been waged when Powers's Puppy 68 passed its first major Soviet city at its so far untouchable 70,000 feet. Its fifteen grim years would be followed by thirty more, some even grimmer, with both sides' spending vastly increased, together with the risk of calamity.

From that first Soviet city—Dushanbe, capital of the Tajik Republic—Powers headed for the Tyura-Tam Cosmodrome, from which satellites were launched, including the pioneering Sputnik in 1957. Photographing military airfields en route, he flew on toward the Urals' most important industrial center, some eight hundred miles north: "Russia's Pittsburgh," as some called the city of Sverdlovsk—which is now, again, Yekaterinburg, its pre-Soviet name. His primary target was a nearby center of nuclear industry called Chelyabinsk-40.

The U-2's inaugural violation of Soviet airspace and international law had taken place on another national holiday, this one in 1956. Informed of the radar contact, Khrushchev concealed his anger to play the genial guest at a July 4 reception by the American ambassador in Moscow. He proposed a toast to Eisenhower's health.

Powers's mission those near four years later was the twenty-fourth in the series. The small number was due to Eisenhower's caution, which always far exceeded his advisers'—just as his successor John Kennedy's would exceed *his* experts' during the forthcoming Cuban Missile Crisis. Eisenhower appreciated that overwhelming American professional and public opinion would regard any such intrusion by a *Soviet* plane into *U.S.* airspace as an attack—which was precisely how the U-2 was regarded by many Soviet officials, including Khrushchev, whose initial alarm was heightened by fear the planes might be carrying nuclear weapons. From the first, Ike worried and warned about the gloomy consequences if something went wrong with one of the flights. Again and again, he placed constraints on the program he'd authorized.

He went so far as to assume personal control, reserving final approval or rejection of flights proposed by the CIA according to his judgment of whether the wanted information justified the risk of possible disaster if a plane was downed. The upping of that risk, manifested by the pilots' observations of interceptors approaching more closely, heightened his uncertainty during 1959 and 1960. He put the program on hold.

That distressed Allen Dulles, whose larger concern was Eisenhower's softness on communism. Before the Geneva summit in 1955, the coiner of the term "brinkmanship" feared the commander in chief's inclination "to be humanly generous." The President's liking for "things to be right and pleasant between people" opened him to ". . . appeasement is too strong a word, but you know what I mean." Now the CIA director suspected the enemy was taking advantage of the suspension to construct, move, and/or conceal new installations. Warning of great menace, he and Richard Bissell pleaded for its lifting. That came on April 9, 1960, when Eisenhower sanctioned the twenty-third overflight for photographing a nuclear testing ground in Kazakhstan and an air defense missile site near Lake Baikal. Then Dulles requested permission for the twenty-fourth mission, which would be assigned to Powers, and the president's reluctant approval came with that first deadline—of April 25, two weeks hence. But when the bad weather persisted throughout that window, Bissell pressed for an extension. Granting it, Eisenhower imposed the final May 1 deadline.

As with most military and intelligence projects, the audacious U-2 had stumbled through enough mistakes and missteps to give participants looking back on the eventual success—apart from the commanders and their public relations officers—reason to wonder how on earth it was achieved. For example, Eisenhower was originally assured Soviet radar was much too weak to reach the plane's operational altitude. It wasn't, from the first flight to the last.

That last was also victim to curious lapses. In order to minimize the possibility of attribution in case of mishap, the planes and pilots were sanitized before takeoff to remove all identifying personal effects. But not Puppy 68. Powers's pistol was marked U.S.A. His wallet contained a driver's license, a Social Security card, and a second card identifying him as a civilian pilot of the Air Force. (Soviet authorities would also list "erotic literature" among his effects.)

But whatever flaws dulled the CIA's self-polished shine, Soviet ones far surpassed them in variety and persistence on that fateful morning. Despite the grim resolve and the condition of readiness supposedly prompted by the previous twenty-three incursions, frantic efforts on the ground as radar scopes found and tracked the hated new trespasser were plagued by missed signals, fear, fury, faked reports, and other dissembling to superiors. (Little of the confusion would have been remedied by 1983, when Korean Airlines Flight 007 was downed.) By the time the local air defense command center, badgered by storming marshals in Moscow, finally got its act together, it was almost too late to attempt an interception. Finally, however, the antiaircraft batteries were readied, a squadron of MiG-19 planes was scrambled, and no less than fourteen new V-750 "Guideline" missiles—known in America as the SA-Z or SA-2 or the generic SAM—were fired. Twelve went astray. The thirteenth shot down one of the MiGs. The air defense commander crowned a pack of half-truths told him by wincing subordinates with one of his own, proclaiming the mistakenly downed pilot had "died a hero, and that's the end of the story."

It was far from the end of the Soviet cover-your-ass story, let alone the larger ones. The commander also contrived to report that two new Su-9s had joined the scrambled MiG-19s. The actual number was one, which took off only after frenzied ground personnel managed, at the very last moment, to locate its pilot at a municipal bus stop. The startled captain was ordered aloft immediately, without taking time to change into his flight suit. The more significant impediment of his plane's unarmed state was also dismissed. Hurrying to obey his order to ram the bogey, he appealed for care of his pregnant wife and mother—and was saved from a genuine hero's death only by his inability to locate

Powers's plane as they approached each other at a combined speed of 2,000 odd miles an hour.

If Russian sloppiness was nothing new, however, neither were Russian scientific distinction and technological ingenuity. In appraising the pursuit of Puppy 68, the enemy's May Day failures were much less significant than the successes. For one thing, the solo Su-9 achieved the U-2's supposedly prohibitive altitude. In fact, the ramming was missed because it actually overflew the intruder, neither pilot catching a glimpse of the other.

And one missile—of the dozen more than the regulation *two* supposed to be employed in such actions—was yet to be accounted for. Actually, that one was the very first of the barrage. The thirteen others would follow, partly in desperation because so few left their pads when the buttons were nervously pushed. Still, the one was enough. Precisely why remains disputed. Allen Dulles would testify to the Senate Foreign Relations Committee that the plane hadn't been shot down. Still, most experts agree the missile exploded near enough to the target—probably slightly behind—to disable it. Contrary to Soviet propaganda, Powers's parachute drifting down caused no smoldering indignation on the good earth below. Local farmers all but poured the handsome stranger some holiday vodka before military and KGB officers appeared to take him away. Nor is the rest history because too many unanswered questions remain.

Didn't the CIA know about the Soviet weapons' increased capabilities? Or at least suspect enough not to press for the twenty-fourth flight, all the more because it did know perfectly well that one of Eisenhower's greatest concerns—no apology will be made for repeating this because he so often did—was evidence of the program becoming available in a form Moscow could use to discredit America? The former supreme commander of the Allied Forces in Europe had never been shy about making that clear. Michael Beschloss would stress, also repetitively, that a downing was what "Eisenhower had feared since the start of the U-2 program." He feared it even more as the Paris summit approached, not only for what it would do to world opinion but also his hopes for cooperating with Khrushchev.

The CIA's ignorance or recklessness is hard to comprehend. Allen Dulles knew it was scarcely possible to keep the U-2 secret. "Sooner or later, this would have leaked out," he acknowledged in his *The Craft of Intelligence*. (Perhaps *The New York Times* and *The Washington Post*, which learned of it fairly soon, would have done more for their country by running at least part of the story than suppressing it, in deference to the CIA's definition of their patriotic duty.) The Su-9s and V-750s had entered service in 1959. On top of whatever other information the agency previously or subsequently acquired about them, the evidence of the eyes—the red stars on the wings approaching the U-2s ever more closely over the years—was blatant.

But there were trump cards. One was the Soviet silence. Khrushchev had sent but a single note of complaint to Washington after the earliest overflights, which, more than anything, was probably to signal the plane wasn't invisible to Soviet radar. (That note was what prompted Eisenhower to take personal control, forbidding further flights without his explicit permission—while Khrushchev, for his part, personally managed the radar trackings.) The CIA interpreted the absence of later protest, even during meetings of high officials, as indication the penetrations weren't much resented. The president allowed himself to be persuaded of that, although without accepting the argument that the U-2 was no different in spirit than the ground-level espionage in which Soviet agents excelled because, he felt, violation in the skies carried much greater provocation of war.

What if the CIA's intelligence had been better? What if it were more skeptical of its rhetoric about the totalitarian nature of Soviet society, which was useful for boosting its own funding and prestige but not for choosing the cards to play against the quarreling Politburo? What if its interpretations reflected less its own view of the world—and its wishful thinking—than the Russians'? Khrushchev's principal reason for rejecting Eisenhower's Open Skies proposal had been essentially opposite to the one Langley attributed to him. It was less to protect the secret of some supremely dangerous weapon development than of the country's weakness in nonconventional forces. The first secretary feared a Washington that discovered how far Soviet missiles lagged behind—by nearly twenty times, during the period—might be tempted to launch a nuclear strike. Nor was it resignation, let alone acceptance, that explained his failure to decry the specter of the U-2 overhead—which, when you think of it, had to be profoundly humiliating even to anyone who swallowed the argument that no form of espionage is more provocative than others. In fact, he who never ranted louder than when he felt misused throttled internal rage about what he called the "spit" in the Soviet people's face. "'Americans must be chortling over our impotence,'" his son Sergei, who now teaches at Brown University, would report his feelings. Cries of protest would have only increased their pleasure.

Eisenhower valued another trump card more. As often as he'd voiced his chief worry to the CIA, its captains repeated their assuances that even if the plane *were* somehow downed, nothing would be left of it to embarrass him or the United States. The U-2 had been designed to fall apart if hit or forced into a step dive. The president was virtually guaranteed that retrieving the equipment—and "unfortunately," he'd write, also a pilot—would be impossible. Richard Bissell put the chances of pilot survival at less than one in a million. John Eisenhower repeatedly heard Allen Dulles offer the same "absolutely categorical" undertaking. Dulles "lied to Dad," and even years later, the president's memory of the fiasco boiled his blood.

Long, thin wings that easily snapped off did give reason to hope that the pilot of a hit U-2 would indeed be very unlikely to live, but controversy also persists about whether the CIA really wanted to make certain of that. After all, it provided a parachute together with the shellfish toxin—and also an ejection seat (which, to complicate matters, pilots feared might be timed to kill rather than eject them). There were also somewhat ambiguous instructions not to play hero in case of capture.

Still, Powers did have his lethal pin, and during his ride down in the parachute, he removed it from its concealment inside a silver dollar that screwed apart.

What if he'd used it? That would have made little difference because he hadn't pushed the plane's destructor switches. Consequent recovery of the downed espionage equipment in largely workable condition nullified the possibility of ever-so-thin plausible denial by Eisenhower.

But something far less technological would almost surely have made a great difference: an apology from Eisenhower. It wasn't too late.

It wasn't too late even a week later, after Khrushchev had used a different kind of concealment to play him the fool. Not revealing that Powers was alive, he led Eisenhower, so often promised of the impossibility, into a trap. The president humiliated himself before the world by (reluctantly) following a sickly CIA script about Puppy 68 being a NASA weather reconnaissance plane that lost its way. With the fall-guy line delivered, Khrushchev proceeded to relish his triumph by revealing the truth about the "bandit flight" to a hooting session of the Supreme Soviet:

> Comrades, I must let you in on a secret. When I made my report two days ago, I refrained from mentioning we have the remnants of the plane—*and we also have the pilot, who is quite alive and kicking.* We did that deliberately because if we'd released the whole story, the Americans would have concocted still another fable. Even now, just look how many silly things they've said.

He waved copies of Powers's photographs of military airfields.

> *Here, look at this!* . . . Also a tape recording of the signals of some of our ground radar stations—incontestable evidence of spying. And [they] couldn't think up anything better than the stupid story

that this was a weather plane, and when the pilot lost conscious-ness, his plane . . . dragged him against his will into Soviet terri-tory. *What innocence!*

The hall resounded with cries of "Shame, shame!" The speaker's delight was as rich as he'd envisioned. But it wasn't too late because, despite his mockery and sense of affront, the first secretary still wanted to negotiate. In fact, he wanted that more than ever and took pains to blame the U-2s not on Eisenhower but his subordinates:

> Even now, I profoundly believe the American people—except for certain imperialist and monopolistic circles—want peace and friendship with the Soviet Union . . . I don't doubt President Eisenhower's sincere desire for peace . . . We are so close to the summit and to peace. I'm ready to accept this was a cruel and ter-rible provocation by others, without the American president's knowledge.

In fact, Puppy 68 cornered Khrushchev in ambivalence. Pleased as he was by the feat of its downing, the tangible confirmation of the insult-ing overflights, now even to the Soviet public, lent ammunition to his domestic adversaries who opposed talks with perfidious Washington that had again betrayed its real colors. That made progress with Eisen-hower—concrete results with which he could counter his detractors—all the more important, and he was prepared to be accommodating in Paris, after accepting the president's apology. At that point, he had little doubt that the apology would be given in the French capital. Of course he'd made good propaganda of the U-2 business, but together with bending over backward to exculpate the president, he made his desire for a successful summit perfectly clear.

Wanting the same, also probably more than before, Ike's instinct was to straighten things out with Khrushchev at a private talk before the formal ones. However, his advisers persuaded him that an invitation to an earlier meeting would be interpreted as "a gesture of weakness." And the chief himself felt that American honor, together with the Soviets' own relentless espionage, precluded a presidential apology or promise of no further spy flights.

Thus the hopes for Paris vaporized. But why wasn't fully portrayed because the cameras trained on Khrushchev's surly exit from the conference registered no thoughts or emotions. At Camp David the year before, he—like one war veteran trusting another, as the Soviet ambassador saw it—came to accept that Ike loathed military confrontation. He even learned enough English to call the president "my friend." That courageous word from a Communist first secretary was prompted partly by private walks in the woods during which the two agreed that nothing was worse than war. How could the *friend* have deceived him? He *knew*, didn't he, how much opposition he faced from his hard-liners at home? How could a genuine lover of peace refuse to give the gesture for which he all but pleaded?

What if Ike had accommodated him? What if he'd followed the secret warning of Llewelyn Thompson, the American ambassador in Moscow, not to admit he'd known of Powers's flight? An apology, followed by significant progress in Paris and at later summits—whose number and achievements would have no doubt increased—couldn't have healed the sundered planet. To resolve its multiple problems, to loosen Moscow's nervous oppression of Eastern Europe in particular, would have taken more than even total trust between the leaders, especially because their influence on their countries was limited. One way or another, both would soon name their respective military-industrial complexes—shorthand for the people and institutions that profited from continued tension, apart from or blended with their political inclinations—as hulking obstacles to progress.

Besides, the global rivalry had deeper causes. Perhaps the major one, or at least the instigating one, was the communist belief that for the sake of a better world, capitalism and the more or less democratic institutions that went with it in the West—immeasurably more democratic as well as more efficient than anything in the East—had to be helped to fall. Surrendering that canon would have required the same for the sister one that the supposedly historical process had to be led by the Party, something hard to imagine from its first secretary because that leadership was the principal justification for the Party's swollen powers. (All his attempts to use the Party to solve the country's economic and other problems never awakened him to see that the largest problem was that bloated, benighted, self-serving organization itself.) Besides, Khrushchev's clumsy bluster seemed too inherent to him to picture without it. *But what if he hadn't frightened the world with his claims of military as well as ideological superiority? What if he had been wiser?*

Those questions point to Puppy 68's greatest effect, since the bluster fed mostly on fear. Jumpy about the weak Soviet bomber force, the pitchman crowed about producing missiles "like sausages"—another boisterous bumble—because, he explained in confidence, "the main thing is that Americans think we have enough for a powerful strike in response. So they'll be wary of attacking us."

That was the largest loss—of the opportunity, during that time of dogged misunderstanding of enemies largely known as cartoon characters of evil, to temper the fear that underlay the ideology and stratagems. The scholar Adam Ulam, no apologist for Soviet oppression, saw the chief source of the huge world threat in the "irrational premises and impulses" that underlay both superpowers' policies. Rendered into support of militancy, the Soviet illusion about the Communist unlocking of the meaning of history and existence and the American one about the special virtue and universal desirability of the American way of life were especially dangerous. They made personal contact extremely important for Americans and even more so for Russians raised in their deeper isolation and indoctrination. While more Khrushchev-Eisenhower dialogue couldn't have erased the conflict's history, legacy, and habits, it would have moved in that direction by further diminishing Khrushchev's propensity for bluff and intimidation, so much of which was driven by apprehension, suspicion, and wounded pride. The 1955 Geneva summit had made some dents in the myths by tapping in a touch of the trust most needed for their deflation, and it's hard to imagine a real one in Paris not making more.

The president and first secretary were well suited for that tapping. Eisenhower had much more affection than most Americans for Russians, no doubt thanks partly to memories of salutes to him at Moscow ceremonies marking the defeat of Nazism and his knowledge that the Red Army took down four in five of the German soldiers who fell in the struggle. The former supreme commander also had the domestic advantage of relative protection against charges of treason when he chose to negotiate with rather than challenge the "godless Communists." For his part, Khrushchev, beneath his political persona, shared some of the awe and admiration for Americans of almost every Russian of his generation. (Paradoxically, that reservoir of good feelings largely evaporated after communism's collapse in 1991.)

More significantly, both leaders had seen enough real war to dislike preparation for it. More interested in practical than philosophical issues, they especially disliked the waste.

Ike, too, said so many occasionally contradictory things in various settings—including political rallies, where even prudent statesmen sometimes hurl slogans at complicated issues—that his speeches can support many interpretations of his inclinations. Still, one of the most constant—soon to be memorably expressed in his farewell speech that coined the term "military-industrial complex"—was resentment of the cost of the arms race. "Every gun that is fired," he deplored two weeks before leaving for Paris, "every warship launched, every rocket fired signifies, in the final sense, a *theft* from those who hunger and are not fed, who are old and not clothed." Together with money, "the world in arms" was wasting its laborers' sweat, scientists' genius, and children's hopes. "This is not a way of life at all . . . it is humanity hanging from a cross of iron."

As for Khrushchev, his determination to reduce costs, except for special programs, put him in permanent struggle with his own military establishment. The passionate apostle of American corn cared much more for the food and housing races than the arms or space ones—and no wonder, he himself having launched the former, his noisy competition with capitalism nourished by shabby Russia's urgent consumer needs. Since establishing his reign's tone and direction with his celebrated de-Stalinization speech four years earlier, he reduced his armed forces from 5.8 to 2.4 million men, the most recent cut, of a whopping 1.2 million, coming in January 1960. Those slashes, scarcely mentioned in the CIA's public alarms about the threat from Moscow, provoked wrath from his industrial chiefs as well as military and civilian hardliners. (Memory of relatively recent American resistance to closings of the smallest bases might help picture the Soviet ire and also rectify the image of a totalitarian dictator whose word was law.) For all his spirited participation in the murderous collectivization of agriculture and purges of the 1920s and 1930s, the first secretary's present vision of communism was more butter—or, for millions of Soviet citizens, *some* butter—on the bread. *We'll be just as rich [as you Americans] tomorrow—and even richer the day after.* That consumerism, mutated as it may have been, was what really excited the ebullient man who bragged of his peasant origin, and although it too posed a threat, it wasn't the kind that required schoolchildren to duck under their desks. Better to have encouraged his preferred form of rivalry than the incomparably more dangerous other.

It would defy logic, psychology, and much historical precedent to argue the leaders' primary instincts wouldn't have further melted the Cold War with more mutual confidence-generating dialogue, despite the limits on both imposed by their respective establishments. To contend not launching Puppy 68 would have had no substantial effect on the superpower struggle would require supplying another explanation of why it in fact plunged the relationship back to icy, starting with the shelving the nuclear test ban treaty, Soviet departure from disarmament talks in Geneva, and the cancellation of Ike's summer Moscow visit, which would have made a large puncture in the Soviet presentation of American leaders as servants of capitalist exploitation.

So although the CIA still loves the U-2—about whose "great legacy" and "triumph" that must be "replicated again and again if we are to protect our country," Director George Tenet rhapsodized in 1998—the triumph was disastrous for the two countries, not to mention the planet, as a whole. Khrushchev never stopped regretting the erasure of "the spirit of Camp David" and all he and Eisenhower had previously worked for. Ike, always more reserved in public commentary as in statesmanship, limited himself to complaining that all his advisers "missed badly" about the U-2, but persistent rumor had him long and deeply angry.

As for the larger costs, they soared after May 1960. The Cold War's final two-thirds begat the greatest squandering, narrowing of national purposes, and dangers, especially during the Cuban Missile Crisis, when the antagonists came closer to nuclear war than even the terrified then suspected. As son Sergei recently lamented anew, fear and frustration sired his father's reckless schemes.

Pace the Marxist premise that bad prompts good, as with revolution, bad usually provokes bad in world politics, as when Khrushchev was jarred back into defensive snarls and swipes. Without Puppy 68, it's extremely unlikely he'd have sent missiles to Cuba—or that America, secretly pushed by the same CIA, would have become obsessive about Fidel Castro. Without those goads—the return to the pattern of fear-provoking threats of reprisal that in turn provoked more fear—the missiles wouldn't have proliferated and the immensely destructive proxy wars in Asia and Africa might have been avoided, with incalculable savings.

Instead, the immense costs will continue well beyond the twenty-first century, thanks not only to the natural and human resources—including thought patterns—diverted from socially valuable to socially destructive use. Although the full extent of the earth's poisoning remains secret, the United States is known to have conducted more than nine hundred tests of nuclear weaponry, including two hundred aboveground. The Soviet Union caused much worse environmental and economic damage to itself in every way. The scars are appalling. Mental and physical deprivation will continue for generations.

Eisenhower's presidency ended eight months after the Paris conference. Instead of the "splendid exit" of a peace-building agreement for which he'd hoped, he left in a whirl of anger against Moscow.[3] His successor took office, as did most of the era's, as a strident anti-Communist. Before reality diminished the warrior whooping, one had to get himself elected, which meant proving his toughness by accusing the rival candidate of being soft. John Kennedy did that with deceitful exaggeration of the threat from Soviet missiles.

Soon enough, Khrushchev, too, was gone. Many factors contributed to his overthrow, including "harebrained" agricultural schemes born of his fervor for more food, and the Party apparat's fear of a threat to its control from his cultural and political liberalization. But resentment of his continued cuts of military spending remained paramount.

As for prisoner Gary Powers, he was exchanged for the Soviet spy Rudolf Abel in 1962. Some fifteen years later, after the crash of the helicopter from which Powers was reporting on traffic for a Los Angeles television station, disgraced Khrushchev sent Powers's father a telegram of condolence. By that time, the CIA had become devoted to more Soviet-style methods, such as one revealed the day the pilot died: secret use of private medical institutes for developing mind-control techniques. The arms race had ballooned enormously. Cold War was ingrained enough for compromise to be perceived as all but impossible. The missed opportunity of 1960, the moment that had come and gone, was scarcely remembered.

---

[3] Shortly before his death in 1969, Ike lamented to a friend that he'd been able only to contribute to a Cold War stalemate instead of to the lasting peace he'd "longed to give the United States and the world."

ROBERT L. O'CONNELL

THE CUBAN MISSILE CRISIS:

Second Holocaust

Had it not been for the downing of the U-2, the Cuban Missile Crisis of October 1962 might never have come about: Eisenhower's reluctant adventurism (to use a favorite Marxist word) plunged us into the most dangerous period of the Cold War. Indeed, on the fever chart of these forty-five years, the Cuban confrontation gives off the highest reading, signaling a near-terminal breakdown.

Conventional interpretations and reconstructions of the crisis that followed the discovery of Soviet intermediate-range missiles in Pinar del Río Province, the region of Cuba closest to the United States, tell us that the shooting down of another U-2, Major Rudolf Anderson's, presented the moment of utmost peril. That was October 27, the day that came to be known as "Black Saturday," when Khrushchev remarked that "a smell of burning hung in the air." But perhaps the most serious threats, as Robert L. O'Connell makes clear in this chapter, may have lurked under the water, in the form of Soviet submarines armed with tactical nuclear torpedoes. Their commanders were prepared to use them on the spot, and there would be no waiting on Moscow's word—just as the Soviet general who ordered the firing of the SA-2 surface-to-air missile at Anderson's plane did so on his own initiative. And if the American invasion of Cuba had taken place, probably the following Tuesday,

October 30, *local Soviet commanders also had the authority to fire tactical nuclear weapons, without prior approval. President John F. Kennedy may have been ready to risk not going to war, and so, as the crisis deepened, was the man who had initiated it, Khrushchev. But as O'Connell points out, other factors might have led the two antagonists over the brink. History is too often determined not by its obvious movers and shakers but by its loose cannons.*

On Black Saturday, the former secretary of state, Dean Acheson, who was one of Kennedy's advisers, advocated a strike against the missiles. "I know the Soviets well," he began:

> *"I know what they are required to do in the light of their history and their posture around the world. I think they will knock out our missiles in Turkey," Acheson said.*
>
> *"What do we do then?" he was asked.*
>
> *"I believe that under the NATO treaty, with which I was associated, we would be required to respond by knocking out a missile base inside the Soviet Union," Acheson went on.*
>
> *"Then what do they do?"*
>
> *"That is when we hope," Acheson replied, "that cooler heads will prevail, and they will stop and talk."*

It might not have been that simple.

ROBERT L. O'CONNELL is a former member of the U.S. Delegation to the Conference on Disarmament in Geneva. His books include *Of Arms and Men: A History of War, Weapons, and Aggression; The Ride of the Second Horsemen: The Birth and Death of War; Sacred Vessels: The Cult of the Battleship and the Rise of the U.S. Navy; Soul of the Sword;* and a novel, *Fast Eddie,* based on the life of Edward Vernon Rickenbacker. O'Connell lives in Charlottesville, Virginia.

October 27, 2002

Archivist of the United States
Room 1200
John Fitzgerald Kennedy Memorial Records Center
New Capital District
Cheyenne Mountain 80903-2000

The Honorable Ted Stevens
Chairman
Senate Select Committee on Intelligence
The Congress of the United States

Dear Mr. Chairman:

On this day, the fortieth anniversary of the commencement of the Two Days' War, I am forwarding to you for final clearance and publication the narrative summary of the findings of the Danforth Commission. As you know this document has remained classified since its completion in 1972, and is only now being released as the result of a long judicial process, culminating in a ruling by the U.S. Supreme Court.

Following the mandate of the court, my staff has made every effort to preserve the details of the original narrative summary, without compromising the relatively small amount of information still classified after forty years. I believe we have succeeded. However, our accomplishments pale before those of the Danforth Commission—the historians, members of the military, archaeologists, cryptanalysts, climatologists, physicists, physicians, and the host of other specialists—who worked continuously for three years to reconstruct the events of October 27–8, 1962 and their aftermath. In doing so they overcame enormous gaps . . . hiatuses literally burned in the fabric of the evidence, pursuing clues at times at the risk to their own health and longevity. We owe them a profound debt of gratitude. Together they produced a document that I believe will explain to the American people how and why history took such a tragic turn, and help remove the remaining veil of guilt and suspicion that continues to hang over our beloved nation.

I remain, respectfully,
Newton Leroy Gingrich, Ph.D.

SUMMARY AND ANALYSIS

Introduction

Far more than any of the other momentous occurrences of the twentieth century, the events surrounding the Two Days' War remain shrouded in uncertainty. It was the charter of the Danforth Commission, directed by the president and confirmed by a Joint Resolution of Congress, to gather and analyze all available evidence with the aim of clarifying the causes of the war, its course, and the subsequent response on the part of the world community. In this we have only partially succeeded. The near-simultaneous demise of virtually all the key decision makers on both sides left gaps in the record that simply could not be overcome. This remained a particular handicap in interpreting motivation and causation. With two important exceptions on the U.S. side (Ambassadors Bohlen and Stevenson) and one on the Soviet (Captain Dubivko), we were forced to fall back on what amounted to secondary sources—comments made by principals to subordinates and foreign diplomats, a limited amount of message traffic, and data gleaned from patterns of nuclear release authority, launch procedures, and subsequent weapons effects. Despite these impediments, we believe that the passage of time, unprecedented access to those sources that do exist, along with the talent and dedication of our professional staff, has allowed for a reasonably accurate profile of this tragic war and its aftermath. Subsequent historical research will undoubtedly alter the facade, but the underlying frame of events should continue to stand.

Causation

The understanding of Nikita S. Khrushchev's motives for deploying nuclear forces to Cuba has undergone a fundamental shift. At the time of the missile crisis it was understood by the United States and its allies as an offensive move aimed at threatening the American people and laying the foundation for the eventual Soviet dominance of the Western Hemisphere. In large part, the USSR was viewed as an aggressive power intent on world hegemony, disdainful of U.S. political will, and recklessly determined to gain a fundamental psychological advantage over its chief adversary. However, subsequent revelations, particularly those of the Chinese and Indians, point to this as a basic misinterpretation.

The weight of evidence now indicates that Khrushchev's motives, though profoundly misguided, were defensive and centered on two separate sets of concerns. First, reporting indicates that the Soviet leadership prized the Cuban revolution as the first example of a people willingly embracing communism and were apparently determined to protect it from what was perceived as an almost inevitable invasion on the part of the United States (a conclusion made all the more plausible by two very large amphibious maneuvers held in the spring and fall of 1962 off nearby Vieques Island). Secondly, it was apparent to Khrushchev and his colleagues that not only was the United States far ahead of the Soviet Union in the race to build a ballistic-missile–based nuclear strike force, but that the Americans were perfectly aware of their lead, a fact made painfully obvious in October 1961 during a speech by Deputy Secretary of Defense Roswell Gilpatric, a known Kennedy confidant.

It is estimated that by the spring of 1962 the Soviets had less than 25 operational intercontinental ballistic missiles (ICBMs) and fewer than 500 strategic nuclear weapons, the great majority dedicated to ballistic missiles and bombers without the range to reach the continental United States. In comparison, the U.S. strategic force was huge: 174 deployed Atlas and Titan 1 ICBMs; 105 Jupiter and Thor intermediate-range ballistic missiles (IRBMs); 8 Ethan Allen– and George Washington-class ballistic missile submarines mounting a combined 128 Polaris IRBMs; along with a fleet of over 1,500 B-47, B-52, and B-58 jet bombers each carrying multiple bombs in the 1-to-24-megaton range—a grand total of over 3,500 nuclear weapons, all of them deliverable to within the borders of the USSR. Since much of this information was available in the open press, it can be assumed that the Soviets fully understood the magnitude of their disadvantage.

It was in this context that Khrushchev decided, probably in the spring of 1962, to surreptitiously deploy forty-two SS-4 medium-range ballistic missiles (MRBMs) with a range of 1,200 miles and quite possibly a dozen or more SS-5 IRBMs with significantly longer ranges. (These never reached Cuba, and the ships transporting them were subsequently sunk at sea before a positive identification could be made.) From a Soviet perspective, this must have been a highly attractive though risky option. In one quick move they would have not only moved decisively to protect the Cuban revolution but also significantly redressed the strategic imbalance by more than doubling the number of their ballistic-missile–mounted nuclear warheads capable of reaching the United States.[1] Of course, the Soviet leader and his colleagues must have realized that the introduction of these missiles into Cuba would be inter-

---

[1] The central attraction of all ballistic missiles was their speed, which at this time rendered them invulnerable to interception once successfully launched.

preted by Americans as a direct challenge to their strategic preeminence in the Western Hemisphere, but this apprehension was likely balanced by the fact that the United States had already deployed Jupiter IRBMs along the Soviet border in Turkey, thereby posing a similar threat to the Eastern power. Also, the Soviets plainly hoped to keep the true nature of the scheme secret from U.S. Intelligence until the missiles were fully operational, thereby presenting their adversary with an irreversible reality. However misguided this reasoning may have been, it does at least give the impression of having been thought through. The true devil was to be found in the operational details of the Soviet deployment; this in the end was what led them to disaster.

The Soviet MRBMs arrived in Cuba with a massive support structure: a cadre of ground forces troops to defend the island and construct the required missile bases and infrastructure (estimated at the time at around 16,000, but now thought to have been much larger); multiple SA-2 surface-to-air missile (SAM) units; a variety of frontline Soviet combat aircraft including IL-28 light bombers, approximately one hundred tactical cruise missiles along with six unguided Frog rockets; and a naval contingent consisting of a number of small patrol boats and at least four 641-class diesel-electric submarines. While U.S. Intelligence would assume that the Soviets had delivered nuclear warheads for their strategic SS-4s, they had no idea that their adversaries, apparently as a matter of course, also brought along approximately one hundred nuclear weapons for their Frogs, cruise missiles, and IL-28s, and, fatally, one nuclear torpedo for each of the submarines. Compounding matters, Soviet nuclear release authority was profoundly faulted. Control by Moscow of the SS-4 warheads was likely provided through KGB elements in Cuba, a procedure, though it ultimately failed, that was at least credible. Unfortunately, no parallel regulation was extended to the tactical weapons, which might be activated by the commander on the ground or at sea by his own authority. More than any other single factor it was the failure of these procedures that brought about the terrible consequences of the Two Days' War.

Road to War

Shortly after an American U-2 reconnaissance aircraft first photographed MRBM sites being readied at San Cristóbal on October 14, 1962, President John F. Kennedy assembled a body of advisers to aid him in dealing with the impending crisis. The key members of this group were Vice President Lyndon B. Johnson; the president's brother and attorney general, Robert Kennedy; the secretary of state, Dean Rusk; Undersecretary of State George Ball; Llwellyn Thompson, recently U.S. ambassador to Moscow; Secretary of Defense Robert McNamara; Roswell Gilpatric; Chairman of the Joint Chiefs of Staff Maxwell Taylor; Assistant Secretary of Defense Paul Nitze; Secretary of the Treasury Douglas Dillon; National Security Assistant McGeorge Bundy; Theodore Sorensen, the president's speechwriter and factotum; former secretary of state Dean Acheson; the director of Central Intelligence, John McCone; soon-to-be ambassador to France Charles Bohlen; and Ambassador to the United Nations Adlai Stevenson. The group was all male, included not a single member of Congress, and was notably hostile toward the Soviet Union (two members, Acheson and Nitze, were virtually the architects of America's Cold War security structure). Tragically, the entire membership, with the exception of Bohlen and Stevenson, would be dead within two weeks. It is upon the testimonies of these two men alone that our knowledge of this body's deliberations and even its existence rests. Unfortunately, the reporting of each was circumscribed by time and circumstances. Ambassador Bohlen was available to be interviewed by the Danforth Commission staff, but he had attended only one meeting before leaving to assume his duties in Paris and therefore was familiar with only the opening circumstances. Ambassador Stevenson, shuttling between Washington and the United Nations' former headquarters in New York, was knowledgeable of the group's activities. Unfortunately, he died in 1965. Before his death, however, he did produce a long manuscript on his recollection of the events leading up to the Two Days' War. Stevenson was plainly dismayed by the outlook and conduct of the president's advisers, complaining bitterly that when he proposed giving up our base in Guantanamo and withdrawing the IRBMs in Turkey in exchange for the Soviet removal of their missiles from Cuba, he was reviled as an appeaser. "This was a group," he concluded, "more determined to make a point than to avoid a nuclear war."[2]

Yet, the evidence indicates that it would hardly be fair to characterize the group's behavior as reckless. So far as is known, the general outlook of the participants became increasingly less aggressive as the crisis transpired. Three basic options were considered: air strikes to destroy the missiles, an invasion of Cuba, and a naval "quarantine" (actually an embargo, but since embargoes constituted an act of war under international law, this euphemism was employed). It is known that these policy choices were thoroughly debated, and the one perceived the least dangerous of the three, the "quarantine," was chosen. Planning for all was nonetheless continued, bringing forth from the Joint Chiefs of Staff Operational Plans 312 (air campaign), 314 (embargo), 316 (incursion). But when President Kennedy delivered his famous televised speech on the evening of October 22, informing the American people of the presence of the Soviet missiles, it was naval interdiction that served as the keystone of his plan to halt and reverse the offensive buildup.

The next several days seemed to point toward a peaceful resolution of the crisis. The USSR found little support for its actions. An intensive U.S. diplomatic campaign brought our European allies and the Organization of American States solidly behind the Kennedy administration's position. Then, at a meeting of the UN Security Council on October 25, Ambassador Stevenson publicly confronted doubters around the world and, in particular, the Soviet delegation with photographic evidence of the offensive missiles in Cuba, a presence they had heretofore denied. This appears to have thrown the USSR on the diplomatic defensive,

---

[2] Adlai E. Stevenson, "My Memories of October's Path to Apocalypse," The Papers of Adlai E. Stevenson, University of Illinois, p. 547. Subsequently published as *A Man of Peace in a Nest of Hawks* (New York: 1971).

and it is believed that Khrushchev was ready to defuse the crisis. Yet, the most dramatic and positive indication of Soviet intentions occurred the day before, when two Soviet transports, *Gagarin* and *Komiles*, stopped dead in the water just before approaching U.S. Navy Task Force 136 led by the aircraft carrier *Randolph*. Shortly after, it was reported that the twenty Soviet ships closest to the blocking force had either stopped or reversed their course. Collectively, America and the rest of the world breathed a sigh of relief. But the vision of peace proved to be a mirage.

On October 26, the White House announced, on the basis of U-2 overflights, that rather than signs of dismantlement "the development of ballistic missile sites continues at a rapid pace, . . . apparently directed at achieving a full operational capability as soon as possible."[3] Yet, it is also apparent that intense diplomatic efforts were being made through official and unofficial channels to head off a confrontation. On the same day as the White House announcement, Khrushchev had written a public letter to Kennedy offering to withdraw the missiles from Cuba in exchange for an American removal of the Jupiter IRBMs from Turkey, along with a formal pledge not to invade the island. Ambassador Stevenson's manuscript, however, refers to "a much better offer."[4]

Apparently, the Soviet leader had written Kennedy a private communication the same day. Stevenson, who was in New York, never saw the letter, but it was authoritatively described to him as long, rambling, and highly emotional, but nonetheless clearly stating a willingness to eliminate the missiles from the island for a simple promise not to invade. Whether the proposals would have allowed the U.S. and Soviet leadership to steer away from impending catastrophe remains today a matter of speculation, since the miscalculations of subordinates and disastrous operational procedures almost immediately seized the initiative.

---

[3] White House statement on continuation of missile buildup in Cuba, October 26, 1962.

[4] *Op. cit.*, "My Memories of October's Path to Apocalypse," p. 372.

And in this regard, the record is clear: it was Soviet subordinates and Soviet operational procedures that led the two antagonists over the brink.

The Two Days' War

Saturday, October 27, 1962, began inauspiciously and ended far worse. Bad news came in an avalanche. First, it was learned that a U-2 gathering data on nuclear testing near the North Pole had strayed into Soviet airspace and was unaccounted for. Far more serious was the news that around noon a Soviet SAM battery had shot down a U-2 on a reconnaissance mission over Cuba, killing its pilot, Major Rudolf Anderson. Why this was done and exactly who was responsible has never been resolved. But it was plainly part of a pattern of local Soviet commanders taking matters into their hands.

At 1343 hours, two destroyers of Task Force 136, *Blandy* and *Domado*, picked up on their sonars a Soviet submarine approximately twelve miles south of the island of Andros, moving in the general direction of the aircraft carrier *Randolph*. We know from Captain Lev Dubivko, who survived the sinking of his own submarine later that day in the waters south of Cuba, that the boat in question was a B-130, a member of the 641 class and commanded by Captain Anatoli Shumkov. When the B-130 moved to within 12,000 yards of the *Randolph*, *Blandy* and *Domado* maneuvered to intercept, the former firing two depth charges, "solely as a warning," it was later maintained by the ship's commanding officer, James O. Robinson.[5] Whatever the intent, the B-130 surfaced shortly thereafter. Then, at 1412, a huge explosion engulfed the *Randolph* and within minutes formed a characteristic mushroom cloud. Since *Randolph* was conventionally powered, it was clear that the explosion was a result of hostile action. Captain Shumkov had fired his 53-58 nuclear torpedo. It was learned from Captain

---

[5] Deposition of Lt. Cmdr. James O. Robinson, Portsmouth Naval Prison, December 14, 1962, p. 341.

Dubivko that Soviet submarine commanders off Cuba had the authority to employ nuclear torpedoes if their hulls were breached. Whether this was the case with the B-130 will never be known, since it was immediately sunk by the combined fire of the two U.S. destroyers.

The reaction in Washington was almost immediate. At 1426, the order went out from the National Command Authority (NCA) to "Execute Op Plan 312 followed by 316."[6] In practice, this meant immediate air strikes on Soviet offensive missile bases at San Cristóbal, Sagua la Grande, and Remedios, along with a variety of air defense sites. Meanwhile, because preparations for a full-scale invasion were not yet complete, Plan 316 would be limited to paradrops of the 82nd and 101st Airborne Divisions along with amphibious landings by ten battalions of Marines in ships hovering off the northwest coast of Cuba, operations that were shortly overtaken by events.

Again, one or several local Soviet commanders (extensive research of Red Army command-and-control patterns points to either General Issa Pliyev or General Igor Statsenko as the key initiator[7]) chose on his own authority to employ nuclear weapons. As the first U.S. F-100 and F-101B fighter bombers swept in from the north, a barrage of four Soviet nuclear-armed Frogs was fired at Guantanamo, obliterating the base and wiping out the Second Marine Division. This was shortly followed by the launch of two nuclear-tipped cruise missiles in the general direction of the Marine ships offshore, which, though they each missed by over a mile, set off explosions that nearly swamped several ships.

Much worse would follow. The initial U.S. tactical air strikes were highly destructive, but several of the bombs released over San Cristóbal failed to detonate, leaving two SS-4s and their launch sites completely

---

[6] Records of the Joint Congressional Panel to Investigate the Conduct of the Two Days' War (JFK Memorial Records Center), vol. 26, p. 2457.

[7] Ibid., vol. 30, pp. 301–367; see also Seymour Hersh, Who Fired First in Cuba? (New York, 1970), Gerhardt Weinberg, The Broken Tripwire: An Inquiry into the Release of Nuclear Weapons in Cuba (Chapel Hill, 1973).

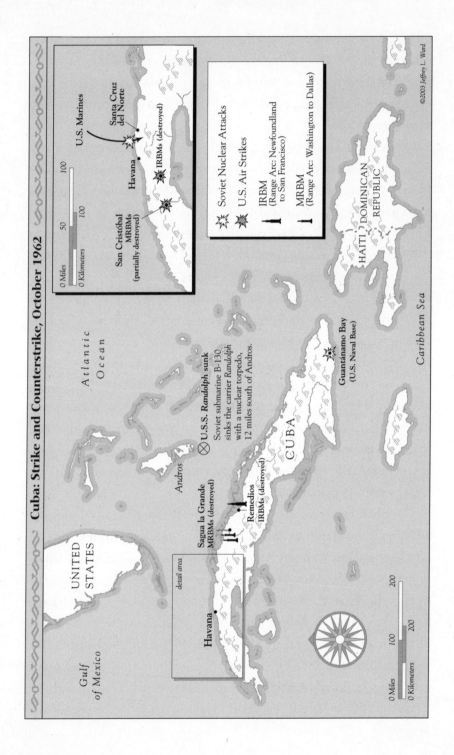

Cuba: Strike and Counterstrike, October 1962

UNITED
STATES

Gulf
of Mexico

Havana

detail area

Atlantic
Ocean

Andros

⊗ U.S.S. *Randolph* sunk
Soviet submarine B-130
sinks the carrier *Randolph*
with a nuclear torpedo,
12 miles south of Andros.

Sagua la Grande
MRBMs (destroyed)

Remedios
IRBMs (destroyed)

CUBA

Guantánamo Bay
(U.S. Naval Base)

HAITI DOMINICAN
REPUBLIC

Caribbean Sea

0 Miles   100   200
0 Kilometers   200

Detail inset:

0 Miles   50   100
0 Kilometers   100

San Cristóbal
MRBMs
(partially destroyed)

U.S. Marines

Santa Cruz
del Norte

Havana

IRBMs (destroyed)

Legend:

☆ Soviet Nuclear Attacks

✶ U.S. Air Strikes

IRBM
(Range Arc: Newfoundland
to San Francisco)

MRBM
(Range Arc: Washington to Dallas)

©2003 Jeffrey L. Ward

undamaged. Once again, Soviet procedures for nuclear release proved tragically inadequate. During the lull, Soviet personnel not only managed to prepare the two rockets for launch but also obtained their associated nuclear warheads, mated them to the missiles, and completed the arming procedures.

On or about 1610, the first missile was launched. It impacted about eight minutes later in a field in rural northern Kentucky, forty-two miles short of Cincinnati, but its warhead malfunctioned and did not produce a nuclear event. Unfortunately, this was not the case with the second SS-4, which was fired approximately eight minutes after the first and detonated at 1625 hours and 31 seconds, approximately 2,000 feet above the Lincoln Memorial. The resulting thermonuclear blast, conservatively estimated at 640 kilotons, leveled everything within a radius of 1.5 miles, including the White House, the State Department, and the Pentagon, killing in the process the entire National Command Authority. Strategically, this unsanctioned act of preemption may have decapitated the U.S. government and military, but it sealed the doom of the USSR. Had President Kennedy and his key advisers remained alive and in control, it is likely that they would have responded in a measured and judicious manner. Now, instead, the entire Single Integrated Operations Plan (SIOP) would be executed against the Soviet Union without regard for the consequences.

The SIOP had evolved gradually and in relative obscurity during the 1950s and early sixties, driven almost exclusively by targeting policy. As new U.S. nuclear weapons and delivery systems were deployed, Soviet targets were found for them, until they numbered literally in the thousands. When the Kennedy administration assumed power, Defense Secretary Robert McNamara expressed something close to horror at its implications. On June 16, 1962, during a speech, McNamara first publicly articulated the need for a "damage limitation" strategy. Yet, by autumn nothing tangible had been accomplished. Thus on October 27 the full-blown SIOP remained in place, a terrible instrument of retribution.

There ensued a lull of approximately twenty-five minutes, during which time General Thomas Powers, head of the Strategic Air Command (SAC), struggled to learn what had happened in Washington, and if in fact the National Command Authority was defunct. At 1652, after being assured that a nuclear blast had gone off directly above the District of Columbia and having failed to reestablish contact with any elements of the NCA, Powers, on his own authority, sent out orders to SAC elements around the world to initiate the SIOP. Twenty-two minutes later, the general was put in touch telephonically with John W. McCormack. The speaker of the House of Representatives, at home for the weekend in the Boston area, had been located and already sworn in as president. When Powers informed him of his order, McCormack replied: "Johnny and Lyndon are dead. You only did what you had to."[8]

Meanwhile, the Soviets had failed to initiate further attacks. The status of communications between the leadership in Moscow and their forces in Cuba remained very much in doubt. It is unlikely they were made aware of Captain Shumkov's actions, since his submarine was sunk so quickly. It is also open to question whether they were promptly informed of tactical nuclear weapons use in Cuba. Even the nature of the attack on Washington may have remained obscure to them, since their own embassy and its communications gear was completely destroyed in the blast. At any rate they had very little time left.

Within minutes of the Powers order, thirty-five of the forty-two prefueled Atlases and Titans along with fourteen Jupiters and Thors had been successfully launched. Approximately eight minutes later the first of the IRBMs, each armed with a four-megaton W-49 warhead, began impacting in and around Moscow, Leningrad, and several specifically military targets, paralyzing the national command-and-control system

---

[8] Testimony of Gen. Thomas Powers, December 11, 1962, before the House Armed Services Committee, St. Louis, MO. Records of the Joint Congressional Panel to Investigate the Conduct of the Two Days' War, vol. 4, p. 12: written deposition, Pres. John W. McCormack, Jan. 4, 1963.

and its ability to coordinate a response. Strategically, the war had already been won, but the punishment had just begun.

About twenty-five minutes after the IRBMs, the first of the Atlas and Titan ICBMs, also armed with W-49 warheads, began hitting a broad range of civilian and military targets. Over the next 1.5 hours, sixty-three more ICBMs and seventy Thors and Jupiters arrived and detonated over their targets. (Of the total number of ballistic missiles launched during this period, seven malfunctioned catastrophically at or near their points of departure, creating serious nuclear contamination problems, particularly at IRBM bases in Italy and England, which were close to population centers.)

Next in order of appearance were the manned bombers of the Strategic Air Command, an eighth of which had been kept airborne in rotating cycles to avoid preemption and shorten the time and distance to their targets. Approximately half an hour after the initiation of the SIOP, a flight of B-47E Stratojets, each armed with multiple nine-megaton Mk-53 gravity bombs, crossed over into Cuban airspace and laid down a radioactive path of destruction. (Before the Two Days' War had played itself out, a total of forty-one nuclear weapons would be detonated over Cuba, ultimately killing 95 percent of the population and creating serious fallout problems in southern Florida, the Bahamas, Hispaniola, Puerto Rico, and the Leeward Islands.) In return, Soviet-manned Cuban air defenses managed to shoot down just four B-47s before collapsing in the general devastation.

Nor were the PVO Strany elements charged with protecting the skies over the Soviet Union any more successful in thwarting the SAC bombers that began arriving about 2.5 hours after the ICBMs in the form of sixty-three supersonic B-58 Hustlers. Their command-and-control already shattered and their SAMs designed for much slower targets, Soviet air defense troops were virtually helpless in the face of the Mach 2 Hustlers, flying at 70,000 feet and carrying either a single Mk-53 or up to five single-megaton B-43s. "Redundant target servicing," or simply overkill, only grew more horrific with the arrival of 242

B-52G and H-model heavy bombers. After releasing their two AGM-28 Hound Dog supersonic cruise missiles against preprogrammed locations, many spent the next several hours wandering the Russian heartland in fruitless search of viable remaining targets for their Mk-41 and B-53 gravity bombs. To their credit, numerous crews returned home with their weapons bays full, but in all too many instances thermonuclear fuel was added to the fire in the form of bombs dropped on locations devoid of strategic significance.

The situation was much the same along the periphery. Over a period of thirteen hours after the initiation of hostilities, five members of the U.S. Navy's ballistic missile submarine fleet launched their Polaris A-1s and A-2s against Soviet targets along the littoral. Many malfunctioned—the USS *Patrick Henry* was lost with all hands due to an explosion of a missile prior to ejection—but over fifty detonated at or near their targets, obliterating coastal assets along the Baltic and Barents seas, the Black Sea, and in the Pacific. Meanwhile, an armada of B-47s and tactical-attack aircraft went after Soviet ground force concentrations in East Germany, Poland, Czechoslovakia, and Romania. Among the members of the Warsaw Pact, only Hungary was spared some measure of nuclear consequences.[9]

By the end of what in all probability should have been the only day of the war, the Soviet Union and its allies had been subjected to over 950 nuclear blasts—damage incomparably greater than what was necessary to pound them below the threshold of functioning opponents. In response, the USSR managed to deliver precisely two more glancing but still nuclear blows to the continental United States. Yet, they were sufficient to ensure another measure of gratuitous retribution.

At approximately 2200 hours a 611AV-class Soviet ballistic missile submarine (probably B-67) surfaced fifty-five miles west of Virginia

---

[9] There remains some dispute as to exactly why, but most authorities agree that this was primarily due to Hungary's revolt against communism and Soviet occupation in 1956.

Beach and over the course of the next fifteen to twenty minutes launched two R-11FM missiles (the naval equivalent of a Scud) in the direction of the Norfolk naval complex. Both overshot the mark—one detonated in open country north of Fort Pickett, the other hitting Sussex, Virginia. The submarine's captain probably received word of hostilities and was carrying out an assigned mission, but this remains uncertain since the boat was sunk within minutes after the missiles were fired. Together, both blasts killed less than 6,000 people, but they led U.S. military authorities to conclude the USSR was still dangerous.

Thus the stage was set for the secondary strikes of October 28 and the delivery of another 370 nuclear weapons, all but a few into Russia. Many targets were simply "reserviced," but there also appeared an entirely new and ominous tactic. A substantial number of nuclear weapons were detonated in the heavily timbered areas of central and western Siberia with the intention of setting huge forest firestorms across the taiga. Of all the excesses committed by U.S. forces during the two days, this was its most inexcusable, and one that would have dire consequences for the postconflict environment. If anything can be said for this wanton act of mega-arson, it is that it marked the final act of the terrible drama. All U.S. Intelligence sources pointed to the complete destruction of the USSR. There had been no signs of resistance for many hours and precious little signs of life. At last the generals sheathed their nuclear swords. The Two Days' War was over; now it was necessary to come to terms with its consequences.

Aftermath

For those who survived, the initial response was largely one of relief that the conflict was over so quickly and that it had not spread worldwide. The United States had lost over a quarter-million people but was basically intact, and the magnitude of the damage suffered by the USSR and its allies was understood by only a very few. Otherwise, the rest of the globe appeared to have escaped basically unscathed. Unfortunately, this initial judgment was based almost entirely on ignorance and was utterly contradicted within weeks by the harsh reality of what nuclear warfare really meant.

While the costs of the Two Days' War are common knowledge, they bear repeating in light of the blame assigned to the United States and the resulting consequences.

The first to suffer were the Japanese, who for the second time in just seventeen years were victimized by severe nuclear effects, when prevailing southwesterly winds delivered a cloud of very heavy radiation directly from the Vladivostok area. Europe, due to generally easterly winds, escaped this initial fate, but dramatically elevated radiation levels were soon reported in China, the Indian subcontinent, across the Middle East, and into eastern Africa. Of course, this was only the preface.

The near-simultaneous explosion of more than 1,300 nuclear devices had already lofted approximately 100 million tons of fine radioactive dust into the upper atmosphere. This mass, when combined with the pall of smoke from urban and forest firestorms, spread a cloud that, within a month, girdled the entire Northern Hemisphere, particularly the areas between 30 and 60 degrees latitude. By January 1, 1963, sunlight had been reduced in this band by up to 50 percent, resulting in by far the coldest winter ever recorded. The so-called nuclear twilight caused widespread public fear that the condition was permanent and even predictions by respected scientists that a new Ice Age was inevitable. Fortunately, these fears were dispelled when the dust settled during the next year, though at the cost of greatly increased radiation levels. In the end, however, the most serious consequences of nuclear twilight was the virtual absence of spring in the Northern Hemisphere and the resultant drop in food production, setting off severe famines in India and China and very serious food shortages across Europe and North America.

By the late summer the return from Russia of Chinese and European reconnaissance parties confirmed what had become increasingly apparent during the previous year: the Soviet Union had not just been crushed militarily, it had suffered something close to extermination. Even the states of Eastern Europe, whose urban centers had been spared, suffered immediate casualties ranging from 15 to 30 percent. Death and destruction in the USSR was far worse, akin to Cuba's. Of the initial population of 233 million, it was estimated that only around 80 million were alive a month after the war. Roughly two-thirds of this number would succumb to starvation and the effects of radiation during the following year, leaving the population only a little more than a tenth of what it had been. It was during the fall of 1963 that the term Second Holocaust was first applied to the conflict, and the United States began to be viewed increasingly as malefactor, not victim, by people around the globe. The trend would only gain momentum until the United States was virtually ostracized from the world community.

During the early stages, Americans were thoroughly preoccupied with their own misfortune. The seat of national government and many of its functions had been shattered, and reestablishing order and coherence in the face of a collapsing food supply proved a Herculean task. Elsewhere, Americans may have been seen as callous and self-absorbed, but in their own eyes they were struggling for survival as a nation.

To his everlasting credit, President McCormack rose to the emergency, discharging his duties with a wisdom and dignity that earned him the nearly universal sobriquet Grandfather John. Yet, at age seventy-two, he had easily been the oldest man every to assume the presidency, and the unrelenting series of crises he faced left him in ill health and without the slightest desire to contest the office as his term wound down.

The campaign of 1964, waged in the shadow of growing world hostility against the United States, pitted two veterans of the Cold War, Senator Henry M. Jackson and ex–vice president Richard M. Nixon, against each other. While neither candidate was inclined to concede any measure of war guilt, it was Nixon who seized the initiative and ultimately the election with his famous "nothing to be ashamed of" speech.

Although the passage of time may partially rehabilitate the image of the Nixon administration, at present little has emerged that is positive. In essence, Nixon and his advisers were guided by political expediency—choosing a path aimed at satisfying a short-term domestic agenda over one that sought to accommodate at least some of the desires and aspirations of the world community. This choice led inexorably toward isolation. Most notable was the administration's scarcely concealed contempt for the global disarmament movement and its refusal to participate in the 1966 Geneva Convention for the Abolition of Nuclear Armaments, a decision that left the United States in a minority of one. This status was confirmed by Nixon's decisions to rebuild the war-depleted nuclear stockpile, continue the deployment of solid-fueled Minuteman ICBMs, and prioritize the development of a ballistic missile defense. While these moves were plainly aimed at reassuring the American public, which undeniably had been the target of a recent nuclear attack, they galvanized worldwide opinion. Anti-American demonstrations of unprecedented size became virtually a daily occurrence; NATO collapsed in early 1967 when the entire European membership withdrew, and a movement to expel the United States swept the UN General Assembly later that year. Once again attempting to play on domestic outrage, Nixon, in a nationally televised address on January 23, 1968, renounced membership and ordered all UN functions and functionaries out of New York.

By declaring the 1968 presidential election a "referendum on national security" Nixon plainly drew a line in the sand, a challenge taken up by the Democratic party with the nomination of Eugene J. McCarthy, an advocate of what he termed "global reconciliation and healing." McCarthy's victory, by an unprecedented 76 percent of the popular vote, made it clear that the American people believed that Nixon had taken the wrong turn and that isolation amounted to national exile.

Now, on the eve of the 1972 elections, President McCarthy's record remains a mixed one. The United States has reestablished diplomatic relations with twenty-four states and also assumed an "observational" status in the UN, offering to take up full membership if and when those resolutions dealing with war guilt and reparations are dropped. The

American scientific community, with massive support from the U.S. government, has assumed a leading role in the global nuclear decontamination effort. American agriculture is once again producing bountiful harvests, which are being systematically distributed to what are now termed the Victim States. U.S. international trade is once again growing, and we are now participating in the deliberations of the General Agreement on Tariffs and Trade.

Nonetheless, President McCarthy's record is less positive on the core issue of nuclear disarmament. Unilateral reductions of the American strategic arsenal and offers to enter negotiations aimed at an eventual "zero option" have plainly fallen on deaf ears, especially among the signatories to the Geneva Convention. Among state parties there is no option but the treaty itself and the immediate renunciation and disarmament it entails. This position is unquestionably founded on a continuing belief that the United States was primarily responsible for the outbreak and consequences of the Two Days' War.

After viewing the evidence in the greatest possible detail, it is the opinion of the Danforth Commission staff that this is far from the case. The United States only responded after suffering nuclear attacks by Soviet forces in three separate venues: the sinking of the *Randolph*, the use of tactical nuclear weapons in Cuba, and the destruction of its national government in Washington. It is true, however, for reasons having to do more with planning and accident than intent, that the U.S. response greatly exceeded that which was necessary to militarily defeat the Soviet Union. It must be admitted that we did, in this process, commit something close to genocide, and that the use of the term "The Second Holocaust" is not inappropriate. Plainly and undeniably, this tragic consequence was the direct result of the accumulation of nuclear weapons and their delivery vehicles. Nuclear war in any form is unsustainable. Yet, the only way to ensure its end is to ensure the elimination of the means by which it is waged. We, therefore, believe that the United States has no choice but to become a state party to the Geneva Convention on the Abolition of Nuclear Armaments at the earliest possible date.

ROBERT DALLEK

JFK LIVES

Probably no question in recent history is more poignant than what would have happened if John F. Kennedy had not chosen to visit Dallas on November 22, 1963. Barely more than a year had passed since his most memorable success, the resolution of the missile crisis. What would the forty-six-year-old president have achieved if he had lived? How would the world have been different? In the chapter that follows, Kennedy's biographer Robert Dallek reflects on some of the possible might-have-beens of a lengthened public career. Domestic reforms, especially in civil rights, are probably a given. But what about Cuba and our ever-expanding Vietnam ulcer? Or would his relentless womanizing or his fragile health have derailed his progress toward greatness?

Kennedy was the youthful symbol of youthful age. Rarely in history has the death of one individual so tainted the future. Would the sixties have turned quite so sour if the nation, and the world, had continued to depend on, and take nurture from, his special grace under pressure? We still would have had the Beatles and Woodstock, the miniskirt, women's liberation, Twiggy, the Twist, the Prague Spring, and Swinging London. But would our energies have been diverted to outlets more creative, more fruitful, than protesting a war in Vietnam that he might have terminated? Would we have been spared the Chicago riots at the 1968 Democratic convention, the SDS occupations of

Columbia and Harvard, Watts, Charles Manson, LBJ and Richard M. Nixon, and the assassinations not only of JFK but of his brother and Martin Luther King? And Watergate?

ROBERT DALLEK is a professor of history at Boston University and the author of numerous books, including *The American Style of Foreign Policy*; *Lone Star Rising: Lyndon Johnson and His Times, 1908–1960*; *Flawed Giant: Lyndon Johnson and His Times, 1961–1973*, and, most recently, *An Unfinished Life: John F. Kennedy, 1917–1963*, which spent weeks atop numerous nonfiction bestseller lists.

JOHN F. KENNEDY'S assassination on November 22, 1963, shocked the world. Theodore Sorensen, his White House counsel and speechwriter, said, "Countless individuals have noted that the President's death affected them even more deeply than the death of their own parents." The reason for this was that "the latter situation most often represented a loss of the past—while the assassination of President Kennedy represented an incalculable loss of the future."

But what if Kennedy had decided against going to Dallas? There had been expressions of concern about visiting a city where right-wing fanatics had publicly attacked Lyndon Johnson during the 1960 campaign and Adlai Stevenson in October 1963 during an appearance celebrating United Nations Day. On November 4, Texas Democratic National Committeeman Byron Skelton sent Attorney General Bobby Kennedy, Jack's brother, a newspaper story about retired General Edwin Walker, a supporter of the radical right John Birch Society, who said that "Kennedy is a liability to the free world." "A man who would make that kind of statement is capable of doing harm to the President," Skelton advised. "I would feel better if the President's itinerary did not include Dallas. Please give this your earnest consideration." Bobby had passed the letter along to JFK aide Kenneth O'Donnell, who had concluded that "showing the letter to the President would have been a waste of his time." Kennedy would have dismissed him as mad if he had suggested "cutting such a large and important city as Dallas from the itinerary because of Skelton's letter."

But Kennedy's decision to visit Dallas does not foreclose the possibility that he could have survived the trip. If his motorcade had taken a

A shot that changed the world: President John F. Kennedy (left, with his wife, Jacqueline) waves to a Dallas crowd moments before a sniper's bullet cut him down. © Hulton/Archive

different route in the city on the morning of November 22, it would have taken the president out of Lee Harvey Oswald's line of fire. And what if Kennedy's route had been unpublished and Oswald could not prepare his assassination plan or if the president's limo had included a bubble top to shield him from inclement weather? Any of these changes could have averted Kennedy's death and avoided that "loss of the future."

Speculation on the "might-have-beens" about a president who died before completing his term is transparently risky business. However confident the historian may be about judging a biographical figure he has studied closely, there are so many imponderables no one can say with much certainty what his continuing presence in the Oval Office might have meant.

Yet, for all this, some of Kennedy's political future seemed readily predictable. Given his consistently strong public approval ratings between January 1961 and November 1963, there is every reason to believe that he would have been elected to a second term, especially if Arizona senator Barry Goldwater were his Republican opponent. Goldwater's ultra-conservative stand on domestic programs such as Social Security, the Tennessee Valley Authority, and civil rights, coupled with what most Americans saw as his intemperate statements on foreign affairs ("We should think about lobbing one into the men's room of the Kremlin," he said), suggests that he would have had no more chance of beating Kennedy than he did of defeating Lyndon Johnson, who in fact won by a landslide in 1964.

Like Johnson, Kennedy would likely have had big Democratic majorities in the House and the Senate in 1965–1966. As a consequence, Kennedy almost certainly would have passed all his major pending domestic reforms—an $11 billion tax cut aimed at expanding the economy; civil rights ending discrimination in places of public accommodation; federal aid to elementary, secondary, and higher education; and Medicare-Medicaid insurance for the elderly and the poor.

Less certain is what Kennedy's response might have been to the pressures generated by Martin Luther King's Southern Christian Leadership Conference for a voting rights act in 1965 and the inner-city riots that roiled America between 1964 and 1968. A plausible case can be made for a JFK voting rights initiative. Like his response to events in Alabama in the spring of 1963 that had produced his call for a major civil rights law, the violence against blacks in 1965 protesting their exclusion from the polls would have persuaded Kennedy to ask for a voting rights statute similar to the one Johnson requested and passed.

By contrast, however, it is conceivable that ghetto uprisings in Los Angeles, Detroit, Newark, Washington, D.C., and elsewhere between 1965 and 1968 could have provoked the Kennedy administration into repressive measures that undermined the president's popularity in a second term and his historical reputation for effective civil rights leadership. It is also conceivable that Kennedy's notorious womanizing might have become public knowledge and that he could have faced impeachment and even ouster from office, as some biographers believe. But given the reluctance of the mainstream media in the sixties to discuss a president's private life so openly (American journalists at the time did not make their knowledge of any politician's philandering public), it seems likely that Kennedy would have averted such an outcome.

It is also possible that health problems could have undermined Kennedy's capacity to govern between 1963 and 1969. As we now know, irritable bowel syndrome, Addison's disease, the malfunctioning of his adrenal glands, osteoporosis of the lumbar spine, prostatitis and urethritis, sinusitis, food allergies, and cholesterol levels in the three hundreds compelled Kennedy's dependence on antispasmotics, testosterone to keep up his weight, cortisone and salt tablets to manage stress, painkillers to relieve backaches, antibiotics to control infections, antihistamines to reduce allergic reactions, and sleeping pills to function effectively as president. Judging from his responses to the various crises he faced at home and abroad, especially the Cuban Missile Crisis of October 1962, the medicines allowed him to meet his responsibilities at a high level. It is of course possible that any of these conditions could have worsened over the five years after 1963 and undermined his ability to walk and/or deal with the sort of stress presidents constantly face. But even if his health did not deteriorate in a second term, the likelihood that he would have lived to a ripe old age seems open to question. His high cholesterol levels and the long-term side effects of his various medications make it possible that he would not have lived much beyond his fifties. How different the view of him as a historical figure would likely be if he had not been martyred at the age of forty-six!

As intriguing as any speculation about the impact of his womanizing and health problems on his post-1963 presidency are possible dealings with Cuba and Vietnam and additional nuclear arms talks with Russia.

The failed invasion at the Bay of Pigs, the subsequent unproductive efforts to topple Castro organized around Operation Mongoose, and the Cuban Missile Crisis had made Kennedy receptive in the last three months of his term to a possible accommodation with Havana. In the aftermath of the missile crisis, Castro seemed ready for a rapprochement as well. He privately announced himself interested in an agreement with the United States, but his conditions for an accommodation—an end to Washington's economic embargo, subversion, exile raids, U-2 overflights, and U.S. departure from the Guantanamo naval base— were more than any American government could accept, especially if it hoped to avoid a firestorm of criticism from Cuban exiles and their American allies.

Nevertheless, Kennedy remained open to the possibility of improved relations. In the spring of 1963, James B. Donovan, a New York lawyer who had negotiated the release of nearly 1,200 exiled Cubans captured at the Bay of Pigs, became an intermediary between Havana and Washington. During discussions about releasing twenty-two imprisoned Americans accused of being CIA agents, Castro asked for suggestions on "how relationships could be established with the United States." He pressed Donovan to say how Havana and Washington could achieve better political relations and raised the possibility that Donovan be given some official status that would allow him to continue these discussions. Unhappy with Moscow's treatment of Cuba, Castro saw official relations with the United States as a "necessity." Donovan's report to JFK on the conversation greatly interested him. The National Security Council's acknowledgment that all of the existing courses of action proposed for toppling Castro "were singularly unpromising," coupled with national security adviser McGeorge Bundy's assertion that the anti-Castro measures being considered "will not result in his overthrow," made Kennedy more receptive to resolving differences with Havana.

He relied on William Attwood—a former *Look* editor who had interviewed Castro; a former ambassador to Guinea, where he had helped improve relations with the United States; and now a U.S. adviser to the U.N. mission—to explore possibilities of a rapprochement. If it included the removal of all Soviet forces from Cuba, an end to Castro's hemisphere subversion, and Havana's commitment to nonalignment in the Cold War, Kennedy believed he could sell it to the American public.

No one knows what the future of Cuban-American relations would have been after November 22 or during a second Kennedy term when he would not need to answer to American voters again, especially in Florida, where Cuban exiles could turn an election against a presidential candidate favoring accommodation with Castro. The great likelihood that Castro was going to outlast U.S. plotting against him made it almost certain that Kennedy would have had to deal with him during the next five years. And given the growing interest in moving beyond the recent stale conflict, who can doubt that a Cuban-American rapprochement might have been an achievement of Kennedy's second four years? Whatever the uncertainties in November 1963 about future Castro-Kennedy dealings, it is clear that they had signaled a mutual interest in finding a way through their antagonisms, which were doing neither of them any good.

No question of what Kennedy would have done in the five years after 1963 has generated more discussion than Vietnam. Would he have added to the 16,800 military advisers he had put into Vietnam during his thousand days in the White House? Would he have begun the bombing campaign, Rolling Thunder, Johnson launched in March 1965 in response to Viet Cong/North Vietnamese aggression destabilizing the Saigon government? And would he have put in 100,000 combat troops in the summer of 1965 to fight a ground war when the aerial attacks did not halt the Communists? Or would Kennedy have concluded that fighting a land war in Southeast Asia with an unreliable ally was a poor idea and have found some way to extricate U.S. military forces?

There is evidence on both sides of the argument. Lyndon Johnson certainly believed that he was following Kennedy's design when he escalated U.S. involvement. He pointed to JFK's introduction of all those advisers and his words about blunting aggression in Vietnam, as well as a declaration in February 1962 by the president's brother, Attorney General Robert Kennedy: "We are going to win in Vietnam. We will remain there until we do win." Moreover, Johnson believed that in 1963 when Kennedy signed off on a Vietnamese generals' plot to overthrow Ngo Dinh Diem's government, which had lost popular support and seemed certain to lose the civil war, JFK was committing the United States to a long-term part in preserving South Vietnam's autonomy.

At the same time, however, there are striking indications that Kennedy wanted to avoid significant additional commitments to Saigon, which could Americanize the war. He feared that growing U.S. involvement could produce irresistible pressure to do more and more. "The troops will march in; the bands will play; the crowds will cheer," he told Arthur Schlesinger Jr., "and in four days everyone will have forgotten. Then we will be told we have to send in more troops. It's like taking a drink. The effect wears off, and you have to take another."

Throughout his thousand days in the White House, Kennedy consistently resisted proposals to have U.S. forces take over the war. In November 1961, for example, Maxwell Taylor, Kennedy's handpicked successor to General Lyman Lemnitzer as chairman of the Joint Chiefs of Staff, recorded that Kennedy "is instinctively against introduction of U.S. forces." At an NSC meeting that same month, Kennedy "expressed the fear of becoming involved simultaneously on two fronts on opposite sides of the world. He questioned the wisdom of involvement in Vietnam since the basis thereof is not completely clear." Comparing the war in Korea with the conflict in Vietnam, he saw the first as a case of clear aggression and the latter as "more obscure and less flagrant." He believed that any unilateral commitment on our part would produce "sharp domestic partisan criticism as well as strong objections from other nations." Between the summer of 1962 and the fall of 1963, Kennedy directed Secretary of Defense Robert McNamara to chart plans for a systematic withdrawal from Vietnam.

Nothing openly signaled Kennedy's intentions toward Vietnam more clearly than his dealings with the U.S. press corps in Saigon. Journalists there were highly critical of U.S. policy. They decried administration efforts to hide the extent of U.S. involvement in the fighting and White House ineffectiveness in discouraging Diem from the repression of Buddhist dissenters and compelling him to fight the Communists more aggressively.

Kennedy believed that newspaper stories from Saigon criticizing the combined Vietnamese-American war effort made it difficult for him to follow a cautious policy of limited involvement. If people thought that we were halfheartedly fighting a losing cause, it seemed likely to create additional pressure to expand U.S. commitments. Kennedy's political strategy was to keep the war off the front pages of America's newspapers. Press accounts arousing controversy drew more attention to Vietnam than he wanted, and an inflamed public debate would make it difficult to hold down commitments and maintain his freedom to withdraw when he saw fit.

If Kennedy was going to limit U.S. involvement in the conflict, it made eminent good sense to mute public discussion. Indeed, if he believed it more essential to stop a Communist advance in Vietnam than restrict America's part in the fighting, he would have been more open about administration efforts to preserve Saigon's autonomy. As a student of American involvement in World Wars I and II and Korea, he knew that fighting a costly foreign war depended on steady public commitments, which could only follow a national discussion educating Americans about the country's vital stake in the conflict. (Lyndon Johnson's failure to encourage a debate that could lead to a consensus provoked domestic opposition and drove him from office.) By trying to obscure America's role in Vietnam, Kennedy was making it more, rather than less, difficult to escalate U.S. involvement. But that is just what he intended; he rejected a large U.S. part in fighting Saigon's war as contrary to the national well-being.

In an undated, unsigned memo in the president's office files from the late summer or fall of 1963 (possibly even after November 1), an administration official provided "Observations on Vietnam and Cuba." Since the Soviets seemed to feel trapped in Cuba and we in Vietnam, might it not make sense to invite de Gaulle to propose a swap with the Soviets of neutralization for both countries? this official asked. Whether Kennedy ever saw this memo or what reaction he might have had to it is unknown. Nonetheless, it is clear that by November 1963, Kennedy welcomed suggestions for an alternative to a Vietnam policy that had had such limited success. On November 21, as he was leaving for Texas, Kennedy told Mike Forrestal, a senior staff member on the National Security Council and an assistant to the president on Far Eastern affairs, that at the start of 1964 he wanted him "to organize an in-depth study of every possible option we've got in Vietnam, including how to get out of there. We have to review this whole thing from the bottom to the top," Kennedy said.

It is imaginable that a review of alternatives in Vietnam would have led to a decision to leave the fighting to Saigon after 1964. With only about a third of the U.S. public paying any attention to Vietnam in the spring of that year, Kennedy had the flexibility to reduce U.S. involvement in the struggle without serious domestic political repercussions. As a president who had succeeded in resolving the Cuban Missile Crisis and persuaded Moscow to sign a limited test ban treaty, Kennedy's credentials as a foreign policy leader were impressively strong. His standing gave him the wherewithal to lead the country away from a war in Vietnam by arguing that such a struggle would be as costly as Korea, where the United States had lost almost thirty thousand lives. Moreover, he could have asserted that a Communist victory in South Vietnam would have limited repercussions: the Vietnamese Communists were at odds with the Chinese, who were their traditional enemies, and Moscow was less interested in exploiting a Communist takeover in Saigon than in better relations with the United States and a reduction of Cold War tensions.

A key to reduced involvement in Vietnam was through another arms control agreement with the USSR—specifically, a transformation of the limited test ban into a comprehensive agreement. Kennedy would have had no higher priority in a second term. Nuclear proliferation was a central concern of his thousand days in the White House. Nothing seemed more important to him than reining in possibilities of a nuclear war, which he described as the ultimate failure. According to Deputy Secretary of Defense Roswell Gilpatric, Kennedy was "horrified" by "how little positive control" he initially had over America's nuclear arsenal. He successfully ensured that responsibility for using a nuclear weapon would rest with him and not his military chiefs. During the test ban negotiations in Moscow in the summer of 1963, Kennedy systematically excluded the chiefs, who were opposed to a treaty, from a role in the talks. He included no military officer in the American delegation and ensured that cables coming from Moscow not go to the Defense Department.

Like Kennedy, Khrushchev, who needed to focus attention on improving his domestic economy to preserve his hold on power, had been happy to reduce Cold War tensions by signing the limited test ban treaty. It is easy to imagine that he would have seen fit to reach a more comprehensive agreement, which would have further improved Soviet-American relations and produced the likelihood of a détente in the Cold War.

The passage of Kennedy's principal domestic reforms, coupled with an easing of Soviet-American antagonism and the danger of mutually assured destruction, put JFK in a position to handpick his White House successor. A fight to succeed Kennedy would have erupted between Bobby and LBJ. And though Johnson's age—sixty years old in 1968— and experience made him a potentially more competent chief executive than the forty-three-year-old Bobby, whose public service included eight years as attorney general but no elective office, JFK's hold on the Democratic party and popularity assured his brother's nomination. The election campaign against Richard Nixon rivaled the 1960 contest in intensity and resulted in a victory for Bobby by a narrow margin, reflecting doubts about a dynastic successor. Nevertheless, JFK's generally successful eight-year term gave Bobby sufficient appeal to ensure that Nixon never reached the White House, where many feared he might act without sufficient regard for legal and institutional traditions. The victory of RFK meant a history without Watergate and some of the cynicism about American politics that has reduced voter participation and regard for government over the last thirty-five years.

LAWRENCE MALKIN AND JOHN F. STACKS

WHAT IF WATERGATE WERE STILL
JUST AN UPSCALE ADDRESS?

The very improbability of the events surrounding Watergate has a novelistic quality in its stretching of what we normally think of as the truth. The entire story, as narratives sometimes do, dangles on the slimmest of threads, or, in this case, a strip of tape. Suppose that, one late spring night in 1972, a security guard named Frank Wills, working the graveyard shift at the Watergate hotel–office complex in Washington, D.C., had not noticed something covering a door latch. That door opened on a stairwell leading up six flights to the Democratic National Committee headquarters and two years of national nightmare, which only ended with the resignation of the thirty-seventh president of the United States, Richard M. Nixon.

While we're at it, what if the White House, in the persons of the president's men, had not condoned covert operations by the Special Unit of the Committee to Re-Elect the President (the plumbers, as they were originally called when they worked out of the White House itself, because their mission was to plug leaks)? What if Nixon, always with an eye on the verdict of posterity, had not maintained a secret taping system, which would catch him in a clear obstruction of justice? He instructed the FBI not to pry into the Watergate break-in because, he claimed, it was a "national security" operation. His words were recorded. When the tapes were subpoenaed, he told a White

House staffer that he wanted them stored under his bed. The order was never carried out: it would have meant raising the ceiling of the presidential bedroom by some twenty feet.

Had it not been for Watergate, how might the history of America have played out in the last quarter of the twentieth century? That is the question that Lawrence Malkin and John F. Stacks address here.

In a counterfactual world, we would think of a better ending for the life of the late Frank Wills, the security guard who set Watergate in motion. After his brief moment in the limelight, he had trouble finding work: potential employers were afraid that they might draw down the wrath of the government. Eventually he returned home, penniless. He was arrested and convicted of shoplifting a pair of sneakers. He took care of his sick mother, the two of them living off her $450 monthly Social Security check until she died. He couldn't afford to bury her, so he donated her body to science. No publisher ever offered him hundreds of thousands of dollars for his tell-all account. But then, doing right is not always that interesting.

LAWRENCE MALKIN was the national economics correspondent in the Washington bureau of *Time* during the Nixon administration. He is the author of *The National Debt* and collaborated with Paul Volcker on his memoirs. He now lives in New York City. John F. Stacks was the news editor of the Washington bureau of *Time* during the Watergate years. He is the author of *Scotty: James B. Reston and the Rise and Fall of American Journalism* and collaborated with Judge John Sirica on his memoirs.

Eᴀʀʟʏ ɪɴ ᴛʜᴇ ᴍᴏʀɴɪɴɢ of June 17, 1972, five men led by James McCord, the security director of Richard Nixon's reelection campaign, were arrested in the Watergate office building in Washington, D.C. They were attempting to eavesdrop on the headquarters of the Democratic National Committee for the second time in three weeks, their first telephone taps having failed. They carefully taped open the basement garage doors, which the night watchman, Frank Wills, spotted and peeled away as he made his rounds, believing it might have been left there by a maintenance worker. When the watchman next came by and found the doors taped open again, he called his superiors, then the police.

Three plainclothes officers quickly responded to the burglary call. They were in a nearby bar having a drink after work, and unlike uniformed police, they traveled in an unmarked car. Thus they were able to surprise the burglars because no approaching siren warned them to scatter. But G. Gordon Liddy and E. Howard Hunt, who had planned the operation and were supervising it from the Howard Johnson Hotel across the street, fled in disarray. Although the burglars were wearing Playtex surgical rubber gloves, and McCord, Liddy, and Hunt had all previously been agents of the CIA or the FBI (in McCord's case, both), they left a trail of evidence that would shame even an amateur second-story man. Police found pen-sized tear gas guns, packets of consecutively numbered $100 bills, and address books with Hunt's name and a White House telephone number.

At first the police and even *The Washington Post*, in the memorable phrase of Nixon's own spokesman, regarded the break-in as something

The tale of the tape: Frank Wills, right, the security guard who discovered the Watergate break-in, is interviewed by the media. But for his sharp eyes, the greatest political scandal of the twentieth century might have remained in the shadows. © Owen Franken/CORBIS

close to "a third-rate burglary." The *Post*'s regular reporter at police headquarters funneled information to the newsroom. The raw details were passed to two ambitious young reporters on weekend duty, Bob Woodward and Carl Bernstein. Woodward took it on himself to attend the arraignment of the burglars. To the judge's routine question about their occupations, one proudly answered, "Anti-Communists." The bemused magistrate persisted until he elicited a whispered admission from McCord that he had recently retired from the CIA. Woodward felt a reportorial rush of adrenaline. Even so, managing editor Howard Simons, a deliberative individual of great intelligence, refused to let the story lead the paper because, he warned, it could be the work of "crazy Cubans." In fact, except for McCord, he was right: the other burglars were anti-Castro exiles.

It was Nixon himself who later provided the most damning evidence by secretly taping conversations with his most intimate advisers. The tapes confirm his own attempt to obstruct the investigation into the break-in. They record him personally approving hush money to the burglars and pressing the CIA to derail the FBI's investigation. This was the essence of the crimes that led to his forced resignation, but the very existence of these incriminating tapes tumbled out almost by accident during the ensuing congressional investigation.

If Watergate was Nixon's Waterloo, the emergence of the scandal that destroyed his presidency was, in the words of the Duke of Wellington, "a damned near-run thing, the damndest near-run thing you ever saw." This tenuous chain of evidence could have snapped at any point. What if it had? What if the thirty-seventh president had been reelected by the greatest landslide in modern American history (as he was), but without this worst stain on his long-speckled reputation?

The post-Kennedy years would probably not be seen as a cynical age of failed presidencies extending from Lyndon Johnson and the Vietnam War to Jimmy Carter and the American hostages in Iran. There would have been no call for a permanent mechanism to appoint a special prosecutor, and probably few other attempts to make government more ethical. Perhaps most surprising of all, the United States would have some form of national health insurance. That is perhaps as good a place as any to start this bizarre story of what might have been.

From Nixon's first days as president, his house intellectual, Daniel Patrick Moynihan, persuaded him he could not lead the American imperium if it was based on a divided nation. Moynihan made Nixon a reader of the British historian Robert Blake's definitive biography of Benjamin Disraeli. Like Nixon, Disraeli was an outsider who turned his party into an incomparable vote-getting machine by playing an imperial game for the ruling classes and a reformist one for the workers at home. Nixon wanted to be "the architect of his times," according to Elliot Richardson, the Boston Brahmin in the cabinet of this California grocer's son.

Nixon first locked up Middle America through its patriotic support for the war in Vietnam and vitriolic attacks on its liberal opponents. He dared not squander it by producing anything less than "peace with honor." That was why the war dragged on until it finally ended in defeat after he was gone, and on terms he could have obtained during his first weeks in office. This helped him organize what his political acolytes called the Emerging Republican Majority of blue-collar Northerners, not-so-secret segregationists in the South, antibusing suburbanites, and Western libertarians who mistakenly took Nixon as antigovernment because he had made his name fighting Communists at home.

By 1970, Moynihan was drafting a bill mandating private health insurance with three-quarters of the premium to be paid by employers and government-paid insurance for those with very low or no incomes. There would have been maternity care for mothers and preventive care for children as well as catastrophic coverage; Nixon never forgot the cost of caring for his tubercular older brother. It was not perfect, but once a program so intimately connected with people's lives had been established, it would have taken root.

Health care was part of Nixon's 1971 State of the Union message, which was gearing up for his reelection campaign the next year. On the eve of that election, with the Democratic party self-destructing under the leadership of George McGovern, the president told the political writer Theodore White that although he had come into office with no domestic mandate, "now we've got an opportunity we couldn't even dream of four years ago." He never mentioned Watergate.

Was Nixon really serious, or was such domestic reform just another of his eponymous political tricks? The most scrupulous chronicler of his administration, the author and journalist Richard Reeves, believes that Nixon's "New Federalism" was essentially a sham because as president he was consumed by international affairs. But how could it have been otherwise? There was a war on—both hot and cold. Virtually every to-do list that this inveterate memo writer composed on yellow pads in his hideaway office touted his domestic programs with genuine pride.

He just didn't want to be bothered with them, although some of the important parts were enacted: sharing federal revenue with states and cities to relieve middle-class property taxpayers; environmental laws to clean up the mess left by heavy industry in the countryside used by hunters, fishermen, and family vacationers. Finally but most tragically, there was health-care reform.

Trying to deliver—too late—on his promises in February of 1974, he advanced an even more comprehensive health-insurance program as "an idea whose time has come." Congressional cynics muttered that he was trying to divert attention from Watergate, but even the enhanced health plan was still not good enough for the leaders of the big industrial unions, whose members already had open-ended health insurance with no co-payments. Nor did it satisfy liberals who refused to compromise; they bet on obtaining a much more comprehensive bill from the veto-proof Congress that they expected out of a midterm Democratic sweep in November. But the health-insurance coalition was quickly dynamited apart by the usual suspects—small business on the right, I'm-all-right-Jack unions in the center, and liberal utopians on the left. A crippled president was unable to hold these normally feuding elements together, and after a constitutional crisis, his unelected successor, Gerald Ford, was preoccupied with healing the country rather than its individual citizens. In the end they all got nothing.

Health insurance could have been Nixon's crowning domestic accomplishment to match his historic achievement in foreign policy, America's belated opening to communist China. Winding down the Vietnam War and ending the draft had dampened dissent, or at least helped drive public alienation into a private world through controlled substances. Nixon's political mastery might also have softened the effects of the first OPEC oil shock, but as Watergate deepened, he could barely attend to such things. The 1973 Arab oil embargo was imposed on the same day as the Saturday Night Massacre; Solicitor General Robert Bork fired Special Prosecutor Archibald Cox on Nixon's orders after

Richardson and his deputy refused to dump his Harvard law professor and resigned.

And finally, had Nixon completed his second term unstained by Watergate, he might have handed on the solid Republican majority that he had set out to build. At the 1976 convention, Ronald Reagan, the darling of the Republican conservatives, would not have faced Ford as a sitting president and almost certainly would have won the nomination. Nixon would have engineered the vice presidential nomination of his favorite, the turncoat Democrat John Connally. He had entered politics as Lyndon Johnson's Texas sidekick and returned to Washington as Nixon's secretary of the treasury. But would Reagan have won an election as closely fought as Ford vs. Carter?

The message of the nationally unknown Georgia governor Jimmy Who—"I'll never lie to you"—was powerful stuff after two seasons of LBJ and Tricky Dick. He also ran as a Washington "outsider," a campaign that might have been less resonant if Nixon had been seen as a successful president. But if Nixon had served out his full term, he would have been in office when Saigon fell, perhaps after yet another spasm of fruitless B-52 raids on North Vietnam. The outgoing president and probably his party could have been blamed for wasting thousands of lives to achieve precisely nothing. But Connally would have snatched at least some of the South from Carter, and Reagan also would have campaigned against Washington. He would have presented his irrepressible optimism and a Hollywood actor's appearance of strength. This contrasting temperament would have promised relief from war and stagflation, upstaged an honorable scold such as Carter, and helped to eclipse Reagan's fearsome reputation as a Cold War Warrior and right-wing partisan.

It is simply impossible to know the outcome. But since Carter's four years were essentially an interregnum, it is intellectually intriguing to consider the possibilities of continued Republican governance. We already know that Carter's indecisive presidency contributed to the fear that the country was ungovernable. Under Reagan, the Nixon coalition would have mutated much sooner into voters who were dubbed Reagan Democrats.

Although Reagan would have governed in difficult times, he would have railed against Arabs even as they raised oil prices, making Americans feel he was at least fighting back. He would have peddled the same supply-side economic nostrums of huge tax cuts. This vulgarized Keynesianism would probably have been better medicine than the zigzag economic management of both Ford and Carter. It would have been supported at the Federal Reserve by the sound-money policies of Paul Volcker. Although a Stevensonian Democrat, Volcker had served Nixon well as Connally's deputy by working out their strategy of devaluing the dollar and freezing prices and wages.

Entrusting Volcker with the Fed two years earlier than he actually got the job in 1979 would have been a great improvement over Carter's choice, the hapless businessman G. William Miller. When Reagan and Volcker finally did serve together, the president never got in the Fed chairman's way when he tightened money mercilessly to bring down double-digit inflation. Under a Reagan administration starting in 1977 instead of 1981, the Fed would have put the economy through the wringer sooner rather than later. Reagan's defense would have been to claim blithely but incorrectly that a million more people were at work and simply shrug it off when "some fellow out in South Succotash or somewhere gets laid off." These were his exact words in 1982 when unemployment rose to postwar highs.

Reagan's greatest challenge to a second term would have been posed by Iranian student radicals (assuming that like Carter he would have been conned by David Rockefeller into accepting the Shah of Iran in the United States for medical treatment, which was by no means certain). Reagan would have supported America's imprisoned diplomats in Tehran in the same way that Commander in Chief Teflon did after 241 Marines were killed by a suicide bomber in Lebanon in 1982. Instead of agonizing publicly over the hostages like Carter, Reagan and his image machine would have praised them as patriots for doing the duty for which they had volunteered, never flinching and never bowing their heads, just as our pilots did in Vietnam until we brought them home, as we surely will from that den of evil in Tehran, etc.

By the time the economic revival came around in 1984, another Republican would have coasted into the White House (as Reagan did) on the theme of "Morning in America." It could have been Connally, who had a Texan's ability to leverage political eminence for financial gain and thus would have been spared his eventual fate as a footnote in American history: the only treasury secretary to die bankrupt. If Connally's aggressive nature turned off the voters, the indefatigably loyal and opportunistic Republican George Bush was always waiting in the wings, ready "to do whatever it takes" to win with the help of the Republican hit man Lee Atwater and the Bush family consigliere, James Baker.

Whatever Republican it was, the most lasting result of the Republican ascendancy would have been a Supreme Court tilted even more to the right, and smarter. Nixon would have had the opportunity to appoint a conservative clone of William Rehnquist, his last appointment in 1972, instead of the pragmatic jurist John Paul Stevens. He was Ford's only appointment, made in 1975 on the advice of Stevens's fellow Chicagoan, Attorney General Edward Levi, who had been brought in to clean up the Justice Department.

During Reagan's presidency, the radical conservative Robert Bork, unblemished by his role in Watergate, would have joined his ideological soul mate Antonin Scalia on the bench instead of causing an uproar that killed his nomination in the Senate. Reagan's successor would then have felt free to appoint yet another conservative instead of the low-profile David Souter, who made no waves in Congress but later drifted toward the Court's liberal wing.

The only imponderable is whether a two-term Republican, unable to run again in 1992, would have made such a naked grab for the black vote by nominating Clarence Thomas. Instead, he might have made a more subtle bid for Jewish campaign money by filling the Jewish vacancy on the court with an intelligent moderate such as Leonard Garment. Alan Greenspan's political mentor and Nixon's former chief counsel, Garment also would have been unstained by the undiscovered Watergate.

But here our speculations must end, because a generation later it is impossible to separate the ripples of scandal from the stream of events. Any business-oriented Republican—and that was the only kind the party would tolerate—would have failed to confront the rise of globalization and the restructuring of American industry during the early 1990s (George Bush majored in economics at Yale and was still clueless). Saddam Hussein would still have grabbed Kuwait and forced America into the Gulf War, and the overwhelming American military victory would still have scared off most Democratic contenders except the dogged and indomitable Bill Clinton.

But a Nixon without Watergate would have permitted Clinton to take office without a health-care crisis. Clinton also would have been relieved of the pursuit by an institutionalized special prosecutor into his financial and sexual affairs. These two factors alone would have made his presidency different, although in what way it is only possible to say very narrowly.

History (although perhaps not the private life of Hillary Clinton) would have been spared the moonfaced Monica Lewinsky and her paramour's self-righteous nemesis, the special prosecutor Kenneth Starr. The travails of far more distinguished public servants would not have continued to stoke public suspicion of government. Victims ranged from Clinton's idealistic interior secretary Bruce Babbitt, who was caught in a political crossfire between rival Indian casino operators, to Reagan's Republican secretary of labor, Ray Donovan, who ruefully asked after being cleared of corruption, "Where do I go to get my reputation back?"

Well-intentioned post-Watergate laws to regulate campaign finance, avoid financial conflicts of interest, and punish misbehavior by politicians in office would not have been enacted, or at least not with such reformist zeal as to encourage the exploitation of loopholes generating much public cynicism. The attack-dog Washington press, bred in the secret recesses of Credibility Gap during the Vietnam War, would have lacked some of the legitimacy it still claims from exposing the Watergate scandal.

The press exaggerated its own role in Watergate, even more in the movie version of *All the President's Men*. But reporters had to find something to make up for the public trust they had already lost by allowing themselves to be manipulated by Lyndon Johnson and Henry Kissinger. Despite triumphant claims, news about Watergate had little political impact until the official investigations began. More than half of Americans polled had never even heard of Watergate by election day, because very little of the worst "Watergate horrors" (the term coined by Nixon's attorney general, who later went to prison) had reached the public outside Washington.

Woodward and Bernstein had spent most of their time tracking secret Republican campaign funds; after most political and corporate crimes it is easier to establish a money trail, as prosecutors have known since Al Capone was jailed for income tax violations instead of murder. What the *Post* later claimed as its most glorious moment, it did not claim even on the day of Nixon's second inauguration. On January 20, 1973, its review of his first term did not mention Watergate. The case was cracked wide open shortly afterward by Judge "Maximum John" Sirica, a Republican former prosecutor with a streetwise Washington upbringing who threatened the Watergate burglars with decades of prison time unless they came clean. That led to the grand jury investigation that put the president's men in jail. Sirica forced the release of the White House tapes, and Senate hearings exposed the Watergate cover-up. What the media did then was simply report the official activity in full.

The identity of the *Post*'s Deep Throat, the most famous anonymous source in the history of journalism, may never be disclosed. Before the case came before Judge Sirica, *Time* magazine matched Woodstein nearly story for story (the *Post*, of course, publishes every day, and with more prominent headlines). *Time's* sources lay in the career officials of the Justice Department, who had previously directed the magazine's investigative reporter, Sandy Smith, to stories about labor union and allied corruption. *The New York Times*, to the newspaper's undying chagrin, misread the story and virtually ignored it until after Nixon's reelection. Twenty years later, when a piddling real estate scandal fortuitously known as Whitewater was dredged up from Clinton's past, the *Times* led the pack.

On the thirtieth anniversary of the burglary, the *Post's* great editor, Ben Bradlee, remarked that it was Watergate that "put us on the map." Otherwise the paper would probably be a prosperous provincial daily with must-read coverage of its dominant local industry, which happens to be the government of the United States. The *Post's* Bob Woodward would probably also be only part of what he is now, a reporter with superb connections but not the nationally known Louella Parsons to the capital's chattering classes. In fact, government at all levels might have a little less celebrity and a little more honor, although that would be a near-run thing given the influence of television, the Internet, and the coarsening of public life that accompanied the dumbing down of American culture.

It was only a week before the Watergate burglary that George McGovern won the Democratic primary in California. His nomination was thus as assured as his defeat in the general election was certain, and the Watergate tapes show that a jubilant Nixon knew it. There is no evidence that Nixon knew any details of the Watergate burglary beforehand. If he had quickly denounced it and thrown McCord, Hunt, Liddy, and some of their superiors to the wolves, he would almost certainly have distanced himself from the scandal, and the air would have gone out of it. But it was in Nixon's nature to manipulate interest groups and nations, whether friends or enemies, and divide them all—not least his enemies in the Democratic party, who could not unite behind a credible national candidate. This devious and manipulative man could not turn off the vindictive political machine of his own creation. Studious and even intellectual to the point of introversion—"This would be an easy job if you didn't have to deal with people," he once said—Nixon was to ordinary politics what antimatter is to the physical universe.

But even if Watergate had been overlooked, is it possible that this brilliant paranoid would have lasted another full term without some other politically fatal activity coming to light? Watergate was part of a pattern that may have been unstoppable—raiding the office of the psychiatrist of Daniel Ellsberg, who leaked the Pentagon Papers; ordering a break-in at the liberal Brookings Institution; trying to underwrite the Southern segregationist George Wallace so his candidacy would split the Democratic vote. He obviously believed to the bitter end that he had done nothing wrong, for as he told the television interviewer David Frost in 1977, "When the President does it, that means it is not illegal." If not Watergate, something like it was waiting to happen. History would then not have been that different after all, and we would still be kicking Dick Nixon around anyway.

If this is so—and who can ever know?—what we gain by the valuable intellectual exercise of turning history on its head can also be lost by ignoring another rule of the historian's and indeed the dramatist's art: that fate is character. This is a truth known to anyone familiar with Hamlet, the ur-character of our culture. Richard Nixon as Richard III, Lyndon Johnson as King Lear, or even Ronald Reagan as the wastrel Prince Hal metamorphosing into the peacemaking conqueror Henry V, are pictures that not only reflect real life but lodge so deeply in our imaginations as to help guide them. But then, few characters have been as influential as Richard Nixon in diverting the course of events into unpredictable channels, for good or ill.

ROBERT COWLEY is the founding editor of MHQ: *The Quarterly Journal of Military History*, which has been nominated for a National Magazine Award for General Excellence. He is the editor of *What If?*™, volumes 1 and 2; *With My Face to the Enemy: Perspectives on the Civil War; The Great War: Perspectives on World War I*; and *No End Save Victory: Perspectives on World War II*. Cowley, who has held several senior positions in book and magazine publishing, lives in Connecticut.